BAJA CAMPING

The Complete Guide

✺ ✺ ✺ ✺

by Fred and Gloria Jones

ISBN 0-935701-11-7

51295

Foghorn Press
BOOKS BUILDING COMMUNITY™

D1409853

Foghorn Press
555 DeHaro Street #220
San Francisco, CA 94107
415-241-9550

Foghorn Press titles are distributed to the book trade by
Publishers Group West, Emeryville, California. To contact
your local sales representative, call 1-800-788-3123.

To order individual books, please call Foghorn Press at
1-800-FOGHORN (364-4676).

Printed in the United States of America.

BAJA CAMPING

The Complete Guide

by Fred and Gloria Jones

Foghorn Press

BOOKS BUILDING COMMUNITY™

Credits

Managing Editor—*Ann-Marie Brown*
Editors—*Howard Rabinowitz & Samantha Trautman*
Maps—*Michele Thomas & Samantha Trautman*
Cover Photo—*Gloria Jones*

Dedication

This book is dedicated to the Vagabundos del Mar Boat and Travel Club. Our involvement in the management of club affairs has given us access to the experiences of thousands of Baja aficionados who fan out over the entire Baja Peninsula every year. The club, with its sense of camaraderie and esprit de corps, has afforded all of us the opportunity to form lifelong and enriching relationships with great people who have a special common bond. The body of knowledge from this group, previously untapped, plus our own extensive Baja travels, has made this book possible. We also wish to recognize the continuing assistance given by one particular Vagabundo—Richard Seleine. Richard contacts every campground in Baja every year. His frequent communiques on changes are invaluable.

Disclaimer

Due to continuing instability in the Mexican economy, prices are in a constant state of flux. We list them as we found them.

The Color of Commitment

Foghorn Press has always been committed to printing on recycled paper, but up to now, we hadn't taken the final plunge to use 100 percent recycled paper because we were unconvinced of its quality. And until now, those concerns were valid. But the good news is that quality recycled paper is now available. We are thrilled to announce that Foghorn Press books are printed with Soya-based inks on 100 percent recycled paper, which has a 50 percent post-consumer waste content. The only way you'd know we made this change is by looking at the hue of the paper—a small price to pay for environmental integrity. You may even like the color better. We do. And we know the earth does, too.

Contents

How To Use This Book

You can refer to your ideal camping spot in two ways:

1) If you know the name of the campsite you'd like to visit, or the name of the corresponding geographical area (town name, beach name, *bahía*, *punta* or river name, etc.), use the index beginning on page 265 to locate it and turn to the corresponding page. If you are looking for a particular campsite name, you'll find that all campsites are listed in the index in capital letters.

2) If you'd like to camp in a particular part of Baja and want to find out what camps are available there, use the Baja map on page 10. Find the area you'd like to camp in (such as Map A for the Tijuana area or Map J for the La Paz area), then turn to the corresponding pages in the book.

Baja California consists of two states. The northern state is officially known as Baja California, but since that name is easily confused with the name for the entire peninsula, it is commonly referred to by visitors and locals alike as Baja Norte. The southern state is officially Baja California Sur, but is shortened to Baja Sur by one and all.

For greater detail, we have conveniently divided Baja into five regions; each region has two maps, except the Central Peninsula area, which has three maps.

The five regions that constitute chapters in this book are:

Northwest Baja Norte, Pages 76-125 (maps A & B)
Northeast Baja Norte, Pages 126-159 (maps C & D)
Central Peninsula, Pages 160-185 (maps E, F & G)
North Baja Sur, Pages 186-219 (maps H & I)
South Baja Sur, Pages 220-263 (maps J & K)

Within each of these regions, you will find further area divisions that constitute natural clusters of campgrounds. At the beginning of each chapter, you will find a general description of the area and the outdoor activities and points of historic and cultural interest that can be enjoyed there.

10 Best Beaches

At the end of each chapter, we have highlighted the 10 best beaches in the region. While these sometimes overlap with the general campground listings, each beach is marked with a sunburst symbol (☀) to avoid confusion. On the maps, beaches are marked as numbers with a "B" in front of them, such as "B1," and campgrounds are marked as numbers only.

Mileposts

Often we identify campground locations as Kilometer such-and-such, referring to numbered posts you will see along most stretches of highway. Some are white, round concrete posts, while others are narrow metal signs. All have black numbers painted vertically, most with "Km." written at the top. While some are missing or hard to see, you will spot another before long. These kilometer posts run sequentially between certain cities—from north to south in Baja Norte and from south to north in Baja Sur. Just keep track of whether the numbers are increasing or decreasing as you move along, so you can tell whether your destination is coming up or whether you have passed it.

Ejidos

Some campground names will be followed by the word "ejido" in parentheses. These were built by the federal government many years ago to accommodate tourists on the recently paved Highway 1. They were all built on the same plan and were turned over to the local *ejido* to operate and maintain as income-producing facilities. *Ejidos* are government-supported agricultural cooperatives. However, since nearly all of these parks are in remote areas, the people were unable to keep the electrical, water and sewer systems in dependable operating condition. Several are open for camping, but they often lack services and facilities.

Refer to the section on Information Sources in the Appendix for addresses and telephone numbers of agencies and organizations mentioned elsewhere.

Introduction

During our many years of traveling up and down the Baja California Peninsula, living in tents and campers, we have paid particular attention to places to camp, as well as other aspects of road travel. Writing assignments from various magazines and our responsibilities in helping manage the Vagabundos del Mar Boat and Travel Club—particularly preparing the Club's monthly newsletter, *Chubasco,* since 1988—have required it. We have had a continuing obligation to keep the thousands of members of Baja's oldest and largest travel club, and the multitude of readers of the several magazines for which we have written, informed of everything to do with Baja travel.

We have found the unbroken flow of written and verbal communications from individual Vagabundos, popularly known as Vags, to be an extremely rich source of information. This, coupled with our personal inspection of campgrounds and beaches and experience on the road, constitutes the source of material for this book. We wish to share the knowledge we have gained ourselves, and distilled from such a huge number of other Baja campers, with the wide audience this book will reach.

Camping on beaches is one of the great attractions for Baja travelers. The fascination of surf washing onto mile after mile of lovely white sand, the calls of sea birds and the splashing of pelicans, the spicy salt-tinged ocean air, cool breezes, seclusion and many other special attributes draw people from all over the world to Baja's beaches. Many beaches are accessible only by four-wheel-drive vehicles and others only by boat. Reaching some constitutes high adventure. We have included details on those that are popular for camping and normally accessible by highway vehicles, including midsize motor homes and trailers. We have also listed the 10 best beaches in each of the five regions that constitute chapters, including some that are only accessible by off-road vehicles, boats or hikers. Information is also given on backpacking and horseback pack trips into the mountains.

Campgrounds for recreational vehicles in Baja come in all shapes and sizes. Some are dedicated solely to annual lessees (commonly referred to as permanents) who have installed trailers or constructed other housing. Others have some permanents, but cater to overnight travelers as well. Still others have no permanents and cater entirely to transient travelers. We have only included those campgrounds which are willing and able to accommodate transient travelers in some way.

These campgrounds are in a continuing state of flux—new ones pop up and existing ones disappear as they are taken over for other types of development. Sometimes, the owners fill their transient spaces with permanents or simply close the park altogether. Since tourist travel is primarily in the winter months, park owners are motivated to generate the dependable income that annual leases provide.

Keep in mind that road conditions in Baja change frequently. Heavy rainfall may temporarily or permanently wipe out a road. Never go off the beaten path without checking locally for suitability for your particular vehicle at that particular time. Nothing is more miserable than getting stuck or breaking down in a remote spot.

Be sure your maps and source materials are reliable. We have helped many weary, stuck travelers out of a jam, some due to bad maps. The most frazzled was a Canadian couple with their motor home wheels buried and its rear end hung up on the bank of an arroyo on the rough coast road between San José del Cabo and Los Frailes. The map they had brought from Canada showed that road as paved, which it possibly may be some day.

Helping anyone in trouble in Baja has always been an unwritten code among locals and tourists alike. We have benefited from others' helping hands several times. We hope in some way this book helps to keep the process going.

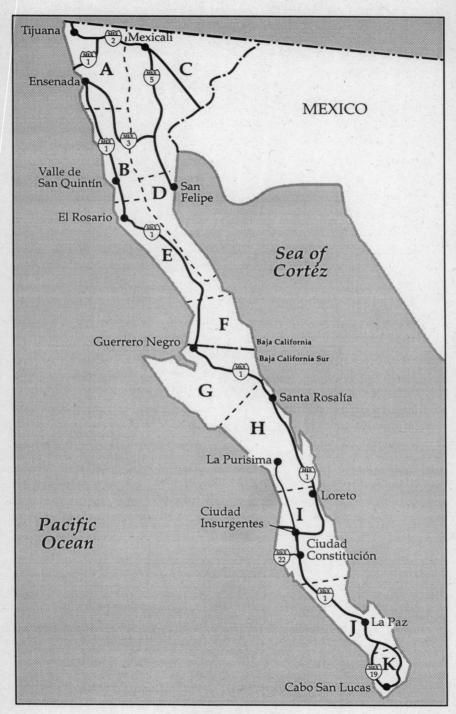

Baja History

✸ ❁ ❁ ✸

Baja History

The border between San Ysidro, California and Tijuana, Baja California Norte is the world's most heavily used border crossing—more than 100 million people cross it per year. It seems so much like an extension of California and the United States that visitors may not at first realize they have arrived in a foreign country. And at one time it was all one country, México.

The Name

In a popular Spanish novel published in 1500, "California" was the name of an island of women warriors armed with gold weapons. The Baja Peninsula was originally thought to be an island full of gold and the name California appears to have been applied from the novel in a spasm of wishful thinking.

The Indians

Huge multicolored murals of Indians and animals exist in shallow caves in and above the deep and rugged canyons of Central Baja California. Their beauty, artistry and mystery excite the imagination. The greatest concentration of cave murals is in the Sierra de San Francisco, north of San Ignacio. They also occur south through the Sierra San Pedro and in other small, jumbled mountain ranges to the southern end of Bahía Concepción—a total spread of about 125 airline miles.

The earliest eyewitness report of these magnificent paintings comes from a missionary who was at San Ignacio from 1759 to 1768. The oldest Indians there and at the Missions of Guadalupe and Santa Rosalía preserved an oral tradition about the Painters (a name coined by Harry Crosby in his definitive work, *The Cave Paintings of Baja California*), which had been passed on from generations of fathers to sons. According to the story, in very ancient times a group of men and women of extraordinary stature (possibly an assumption based on giant figures painted high on cave walls) had come from the north fleeing from one another. Some of them died at each other's hands and some were killed by the ancestors of the tellers, who would not tolerate such strange residents in their land. Obviously, the Painters had plenty of time to create their murals over a large area. Expert Harry Crosby estimates the Painters created their murals over about 1,000 years, from roughly 500 A.D. to 1500 A.D.

An interesting report, *Shamanistic Elements in Sierra de San Francisco Rock Art* by Bernard M. Jones, Jr., published in *Rock Art Papers, Volume 7* by the San Diego Museum of Man in 1990, hints at a clue to the possible origin of the Painters. Mr. Jones comments on the striking resemblance of a group of three huge human figures in Cueva Pintada in the Sierra de San Francisco to a trio of dancers used in the Hopi snake dance ceremony and describes what he terms "fascinating parallels." He stops short, however, of hypothesizing a Hopi origin for the Painters. (Personally, we are very intrigued by the possibility that these hitherto "mystery" people might be linked to the Hopis in origin.)

We have Erle Stanley Gardner, the prolific mystery writer, to thank for bringing these great art works into the public consciousness in the 1960s. In 1962, *Life* magazine ran a story of his, "A Legendary Treasure Left by a Long Lost Tribe," and he also published a book, *The Hidden Heart of Baja*, later that year. In 1967, he published another book, *Off the Beaten Track in Baja.* Having made several expeditions into the heart of the cave painting country by Jeep and helicopter, Gardner passed on his entrancement with what he saw to a legion of avid readers. His graphic descriptions alone fired the public's imagination.

At the time the Spaniards arrived in Baja in 1534, the Peninsula was populated by several groups of Indians. The Pericús occupied the Cape Region, the Guaycuras north to about Loreto, the Cochimís north to about San Felipe and the Yumanos, with several sub-groups, on north to the border.

The Spaniards estimated there were perhaps 50,000 Indians in Baja when they arrived. Successive estimates we have seen

in the Anthropological Museum in La Paz show a steady
decline:

1697:	41,500
1728:	30,500
1742:	25,000
1762:	10,000
1768:	7,149
1772:	5,094
1775:	3,972
1777:	5,424

The 1790 census estimated 4,076 Indians, six Europeans, 235
Spaniards, 183 mulattos and 418 Indian *mestizos.*

The report *Lower California and Its Natural Resources* by
Edward W. Nelson, published by the National Academy of Sciences in 1922, shows 104 Indians in Baja California in 1857.
Various reports show there are still a few hundred in Baja Norte
today. European diseases and casualties in various uprisings
essentially wiped out the Indians.

The Discovery

It all began with Hernán Cortéz, an adventurous plunderer
who took México by storm beginning in 1519. His men worked
their way to La Paz in Baja California in 1534 for a short-lived
stay, ending when all but one were killed by Indians. Cortéz
came a year later, but the country and the Indians were too
tough for even the tough Spaniards and they lasted a mere two
years. Others explored the coasts and futilely tried to found
colonies in order to exploit the pearl oysters that have since all
but disappeared.

The Pirates

Spain was also spreading its influence across the Pacific
Ocean, conquering the Philippines in 1565. It then began annual
voyages of galleons across the North Pacific from Manila to
Acapulco, then on to Spain. These galleons carried the riches of
the Far East—spices, silks and gold coins and artifacts. It was

necessary for them to follow the coast of North America south along the Baja Peninsula. After their long voyage from Manila, many needed to stop in Cabo San Lucas or La Paz for water and other provisions.

The valuable cargoes being transported to Spain attracted Dutch and English pirates who had been raiding Spanish settlements on both sides of the Pacific Ocean. At Cabo San Lucas, it was possible to place a lookout with a spyglass on a high point of land to scan the horizon until sails were sighted, then intercept the galleon with cannon fire. The galleons that anchored in Bahía de La Paz were vulnerable to attack when the regular daytime winds blew from the north into the bay. The pirate vessels would sail in on the wind, while the galleons could not escape against it. The reverse of these winds comes from the south from the Pacific Ocean over low hills in the evening and night. These are called Coromuels and constitute natural air-conditioning for La Paz during the hot summers. Coromuels also allowed the pirates to return to their hiding spots.

Many galleons were plundered and much wealth was confiscated over a period of about 150 years until Spanish *padres* colonized the area in the 1700s and Spain finally gained control over Baja waters.

The Padres

It was not until the Jesuits came along that settlements took hold. The most cherished mission in all the Californias was founded in Loreto in 1697—163 years after the first landing. Being the first, the Loreto mission is properly titled "The Mother of Missions of California," and so says the inscription over the front door. The Jesuits worked their way north founding mission after mission for 70 years, until they fell out of favor with the King of Spain and were replaced by Franciscans.

Franciscan missionary Junipero Serra, a prominent figure in California's history, established only one mission in Baja, then moved on to San Diego to fulfill his destiny, creating California's mission system.

The Dominicans were handed Baja California in 1773 and set about establishing and operating more missions in Baja Norte for the next 73 years. At that point, in 1846, the reign of Spain in México came to an end and the last of the Spaniards, including the *padres,* were expelled.

The Mexican-American War

In 1845, contentious relations between the United States and México fulminated into full-scale war. Displays in the La Paz Anthropological Museum document that the United States Navy blockaded Mulegé, Loreto, La Paz and San José del Cabo. In 1847, the year the war ended, troops landed at La Paz and marched to San Antonio, Todos Santos, Santiago and San José del Cabo, opposed by guerrillas all the way.

The United States was given Baja California, along with a good part of México, but handed it back as not being worth much. And it is a good thing we did, or else all the beaches would have been long since blocked by concrete and asphalt and the Baja we love to escape to wouldn't exist.

The Modern Era

Known in México as *La Frontera* (The Frontier), the Baja Peninsula was considered a remote outpost until recent years. Mexico made Baja Norte a state only in 1952 and Baja Sur in 1974. Currently, the country is devoting great attention nationally to developing tourism in both states. Modern transportation and communications are bringing Baja into the fold.

With the completion of the Transpeninsular Highway from Tijuana to Cabo San Lucas in 1973, Baja initiated in earnest a new era of tourism.

It is difficult to determine who has conquered whom in the past 150 years. The United States has impacted the Baja economy with tourists' spending and Baja has captivated Americans with its beauty, charm and hospitality. We have created a marvelous symbiotic relationship—we need each other. And the U.S.-Mexico border has become like Swiss cheese—

we have assimilated each other. *Gringos* (Americans) live in Rosarito and commute to San Diego jobs. San Ysidro has become a Mexican city to all appearances. Mexicans have repopulated California and tourists outnumber locals in many areas of Baja.

Even the language is succumbing. In many instances, it is easier to accommodate tourists than struggle with them. Mail is an example. Tourists receiving mail in Baja automatically use the familiar "P.O. Box" terminology, as at home. The term in México is *Apartado Postal,* abbreviated to "Apdo." or "A.P." The mail goes through either way in Baja. Each year "P.O. Box" becomes more common in advertisements by Mexican businesses.

Whither next?

Coyote Bay on Bahía Concepción has many lovely beaches (see pages 200 to 205 for nearby campgrounds).

Camping Tips

When to Go

Every camper with Baja in his or her sights has to decide when to go. The answer swings on several considerations—why you are heading south, what you plan to do and where you hope to do it.

Many frequent visitors to Baja are "snowbirds," northerners who head south annually for the winter season. The hint of frost in their nostrils and the promise of bone-cracking, subzero temperatures and multiple feet of snow falling in any given night simplifies the planning—get out of town before it's too late. The old timers return year after year to their favorite havens and lead the way for new migrants.

With nothing snapping at our heels, the rest of us campers have the luxury of examining all the pros and cons of sea coast versus mountain, Pacific coast versus Sea of Cortéz, northern Baja versus southern Baja, and beach camping versus full hookups.

The most common notion is that winter is the time to go, but we are convinced this has its limitations if you have a choice. We have bundled up in heavy jackets, knit caps and gloves in Cabo San Lucas while singing Christmas carols around Baja Christmas trees (dried flowering stalks of century plants called "chiotes"—pronounced key-*oh*-tays) decorated with handmade wicker ornaments.

We have hunkered down indoors for days on end in January, watching our trailer boat bounce around at anchor under strong East Cape winds, which kept us from the marlin frolicking around out there. We watched the tour promos for great East Cape winter fishing change to tour promos for winter windsurfing, as the travel industry realized that the winter winds had always been there, just waiting for the clientele needing them.

After reading scads of charts showing when each game fish is most common in each area, a common denominator became apparent: Game fish follow warm water, and that means sum-

mer. There are exceptions, many of them. The most important
one is that striped marlin are off the tip of Baja all year, making
it the greatest big game fishing spot anywhere, at whatever time
of the year you are there. But if you want marlin, sailfish,
dorado, yellowfin tuna or roosterfish up in the Sea of Cortéz,
the warmer the better.

So, if fishing is your thing—and it is the single most popular
activity in Baja—summer is the time to go. "Wait a minute,"
you say. "It's *hot* down there then!" Unfortunately, that's true.
However, hot is relative and everyone has different tolerances.
Also, everywhere does not have the same kind of hot.

San Felipe, in the northern Sea of Cortéz, is in the hottest and
driest zone since it's behind the big windbreak of the Sierra San
Pedro Mártir, which keeps cool, wet Pacific air away. La Paz,
on the other hand, is east of a low dip in the central mountain
chain and enjoys daily air-conditioning from the Pacific called
the Coromuel wind. One July, we had Sonoran thunderstorms
and high humidity in San Lucas Cove just south of Santa
Rosalía and sweltered all night—but the lightning over the Sea
of Cortéz was spectacular.

The Pacific coast is the place to be in summer if you like it
cool and want to be on the water. San Quintín in the north and
Bahía Magdalena in the south offer great fishing, fog and ocean
breezes.

If you prefer to find cooler weather in the mountains and
have a small vehicle, try the Sierra de Juárez between the border and Highway 3. Laguna Hanson in the pine forest of Constitution of 1857 National Park is a pleasant spot on a dirt road, or
try Sierra San Pedro Mártir National Park with the highest elevation in Baja California—El Picacho del Diablo at 10,154
feet. Nearby is Baja's only observatory, accessible by a rather
steep dirt road. Tired of camping? There are accommodations
below at the historic Meling Ranch (see page 120 for more on
the park). Places to go in the mountains are limited and are suitable only for smaller vehicles, but the pine forests and trout
streams make the trip worthwhile.

Another inland destination for small vehicles is Guadalupe Canyon Hot Springs and Campground, 27 miles south of Highway 2 at the bottom of the Rumorosa Grade. (For details, see the listing on page 133.)

Southern Baja can experience big winds *(chubascos)* in summer. From June to October, sometimes even from May to November, is hurricane season. A late hurricane in December of 1982 tossed several large cruising boats onto the beach at Cabo San Lucas. But hurricanes are not all that common in any particular spot and usually do no more than bring gales and deluges of rain along the coast. The threat of one should not be enough to keep campers away if summer is when they want to travel to Baja.

Winter storms bring rain to northern Baja and summer thunderstorms bring it to the south. The winter storms also blow all along the Sea of Cortéz, making windsurfers happy, but giving fishermen fits.

So what's left? You guessed it—spring and fall. The nice thing about spring is that the weather is warming up and by Easter the winter crowds have left. Incidentally, Easter week is a great time *not* to be on the road in Baja. Everyone is out having fun and boosting sales of *cerveza* (beer). Police conduct safe driving campaigns and erect impressive arrays of wrecked vehicles along Highway 1 to make everyone think. Be even more alert if you drive during Easter week.

What is not so nice about spring is that the Sea of Cortéz is still in the grip of winter chill. Swimming, snorkeling and scuba diving are uncomfortable without a wet suit. Also, most migratory game fish have not yet arrived.

This leaves fall. The water is still warm from heating up all summer, the temperature has cooled off, *chubasco* season is winding down, game fish are still likely to be around and winter tourists have not yet arrived. Take your pick.

Water

The question most commonly asked about Baja is "Can you drink the water?" The simplest answer is "Yes, if you stick to the purified water *(agua purificada)* available in plastic jugs in all grocery stores." Beyond that, it's a maybe. It isn't that the water is necessarily contaminated, it's just that your body may not be adjusted to the local flora and fauna. Mexicans may experience distress when visiting our side of the border and sometimes we require an adjustment when returning home after camping in México for several months. Should you get caught, Pepto Bismol is helpful, as is Lomatil. You can buy Kaopectate ("kah-oh-peck-*tah*-tay" in Spanish) in pharmacies *(farmacias)* if you write it out or pronounce it right; otherwise, they won't know what you are talking about.

Upon arriving at Pamul RV Park on the Yucatán Peninsula of México's mainland, we inquired about the water and were told that the locals had no problem with it, but it might not be good for us. The water source was a *cenote* (open pool in the limestone bedrock) into which everything could fall. Interestingly enough, a jaguar also drank there. So, what do you do to resolve the maybe?

The old standard for purifying water is to boil it for at least 30 minutes at sea level, or longer at higher altitude. For good measure, throw a quarter ounce or so of bleach in the dish rinse water.

A compact, lightweight, inexpensive water filter that we have used in Baja is Coghlan's Water Filter. It filters out *Giardia lamblia,* a microscopic parasite, and other organisms and particles of similar size. It can be used as a pump to take water out of a source or as a straw to drink directly out of a container. We paid $20 for one.

If you're in a motor home, there are all sorts of filters that can be installed in your water system. However, to be certain you are screening out bacteria, the filtering element must be extremely fine. Some RVers chlorinate their water tank at the rate of 8 to 16 drops of liquid bleach per gallon, then use a filter to take out the taste. Campers using jugs allow 10 drops of bleach per quart of water, then let the solution sit for at least 30 minutes so the bleach can do its work and allow the chlorine taste to dissipate.

We like Microdyn, a non-toxic product available in the produce section of Mexican supermarkets like Gigante and in pharmacies. It destroys bacteria in water and disinfects fruits and vegetables. One drop treats two liters of water and 10 drops treats 18 liters. A 30-milliliter squeeze bottle sold for about $2.50 on our last trip. Yodo is another similar product.

As a practical matter, we ask people staying in a campground if they drink the water there without further treatment. If we find several who do and appear to be reasonably healthy, then we will, too. If we're uneasy about taking a chance, we simply keep several jugs of purified water available for drinking and cooking and use the park water for washing up. When we're confident that the water is all right, we'll top off our water tank. We prefer the purified water for making coffee and iced tea and for brushing teeth, in any event—it just tastes better.

There are different schools of thought on purifying produce. Many people just rinse fruits and vegetables in plain water, but our Mexican friends advise purifying. If you don't have Microdyne or Yodo, use a bleach solution for 30 minutes. For items like tomatoes, soak them for 20 minutes in one position, then turn them over for another 20 minutes. If you have room to pack a salad spinner, lettuce will last much longer. Another way to dry lettuce is to wrap it in layers of paper towels or in dish towels.

When living on the boat or camping on a beach, we wash dishes in salt water. Rinse the dishes lightly in fresh water and soak any metal utensils to avoid rust. Melamine or plastic dishes hold up well with this treatment.

We also take saltwater baths. Joy liquid soap for dishes lathers very nicely and does not produce a salt feeling on your skin, but leaves it soft. It is, joyfully, biodegradable. Another product for saltwater bathing is Sea Savon, a light green liquid which is also biodegradable. It is found in scuba shops in the United States. Coconut bar soap found in México also lathers in salt water.

Ice

Hielo (pronounced *yea*-low) or ice is sold in cube form *(cubitos)* and small blocks at most grocery stores, liquor stores, beer agencies and some RV parks. Cubes and small blocks bagged up by companies like Diamonte are made from purified water. The plastic bag will usually say *purificada*, but if it doesn't, ask. If the cubes or blocks are made in the store where they are being sold, which often is the case in out-of-the-way places, the water used is very likely not purified.

Block ice from an ice plant *(planta de fabrica de hielo)* is not made from purified water either and it gets dirty from being dragged around on the floor and loading platform. A good practice is to only use these big blocks for keeping food cold (without direct contact with the food) and the bagged ice for all other purposes.

Place your food in double Ziplock freezer bags to keep it from getting wet. Change the outer bag occasionally as it will leak after repeated use. We put a little bleach in the water as the block ice melts. If you are on a boat or in a remote area where fresh water is scarce, save the water off the ice for rinsing or bathing out of a Sun Shower.

In remote areas where ice is scarce, keep it longer by wrapping the ice chest, or at least place a silver-colored quilted windshield dash saver on top of it. This reflects the heat and provides a little insulation. On a boat trip out of La Paz, we placed a big block of ice in an extra ice chest, taped the gap between the lid and the chest, wrapped it and didn't open it for three or four days. When it was needed, there was still a sizeable chunk left.

Conserving What You Have

After crossing the border, the special necessities you bring with you become more precious. In the cities of Baja, you can find almost anything if you have the time to shop for it, but asking and searching can be time consuming. We find it easier to bring items that are hard to find, then save and conserve them by using them with greater care than we might at home. Would that we could bring this frame of mind back with us.

It's not so much the money involved when supplies of special necessities are depleted or a piece of equipment breaks or is lost—it's the deprivation of not having it while you are there and the time and energy it takes to replace it that is more important. Space is limited, so choose the items you bring with care, keeping in mind where your travels will take you. When packing our 20-foot Born Free camper, which has two large storage pods on the roof, an inventory list of what was packed in each pod and in other nooks and crannies saves nerves and time later on. After being on the road for a few days, everything seems to shake down and is easier to find.

Sustenance

The Baja travel club we belong to and help to manage, Vagabundos del Mar Boat and Travel Club, sprang from the desire of travelers to meet Baja and the Sea of Cortéz on their own terms. To us, it made much more sense to bring our friends along from a purely practical standpoint—we'd have more spare parts and more mechanical know-how and ingenuity, not to mention much more fun in sharing experiences.

On our first trip with a Vagabundo group many years ago, we carried enough provisions to supply a unit of the National Guard. It just seemed that this strange and wondrous remote land of mountains, deserts and beaches wouldn't have enough food to sustain us for a whole month. The camper was so packed with canned goods, including canned bacon and butter, that it was difficult to determine what we had and where to find it since everything was packed so tight. Much of it came home with us. Now, though, if there is extra, it's left with a longtime or new Mexican friend from a smaller village.

Although canned goods are necessary sometimes, especially if you are planning to be in a remote area for a period of time, they are inherently full of salt and not the healthiest for you. A trick to reduce the salt is to run the item (particularly meats like corned beef and bacon) under hot running water. Another method is to place the meat in cheesecloth to keep it from coming apart and boil it in hot water for 10 minutes or so. This greatly cuts the salt taste and makes the food more palatable.

For backpacking and horseback pack trips where weight is a factor, dehydrated food found in grocery stores and most sporting goods stores comes in handy. A brand we like and have used extensively is Mountain Home. Be sure you have ample purified water to rehydrate these foods.

Half the fun of traveling in México is learning to exist on the food in the local markets. Of course, if you like fish, you're liable to supplement your diet with all kinds of fresh seafood that you can catch or gather. Even if you don't fish, there is a bounty of fresh and frozen seafood available. You don't want to miss the fresh fruits and vegetables, either, both familiar and exotic. Agriculture is big business in Baja and the United States imports much of Baja's produce—tomatoes, melons and much more. The Saladette tomatoes with the best tomato flavor you can find in winter come from México.

Be prudent in your provisioning and be assured that you will be able to find most of what you need in the local market. There are also many good restaurants, if you need a change from shopping and cooking.

There are supermarkets, many that carry much more than just food items, in all the major cities of Baja, and *tiendas* (small food stores) in most villages. When shopping at the *tiendas,* try to have small bills and change with you. Also take a shopping bag. The Mexican bags made of plastic mesh come in a variety of sizes and are most helpful for shopping and for many other uses, like carrying wet bathing suits or storing garlic and onions.

Another rewarding and colorful experience is shopping at the municipal markets in the larger cities like La Paz and San José del Cabo. These markets have everything, but practice your Spanish a little and learn about their metric weights and measures. (For a conversion chart, see the Appendix, page 284.)

The fish displays will offer a full array of choices for fresh seafood and give you an idea of what fish are being caught at the time. If you are lucky, you might even see a big behemoth being dragged in whole before it is cut up. You can bargain with the vendors. Take a first walk through and check prices in different stalls for a particular item. The second walk through is the time to buy. Be careful when buying shellfish—your nose is the best indicator of freshness. Seafood in the markets comes from all over Baja and is usually very fresh, but you should always be careful buying shellfish, no matter where you are.

If shrimp is your fancy, keep a sharp eye for vendors. On a street corner in Rosarito, a young girl with a covered basket was selling delectable shrimp. She wouldn't come down on her price, but we bought some anyway. As it turned out, her price was close to the going rate elsewhere.

In larger campgrounds, usually once a week or so, a produce truck will come through with fresh vegetables and fruits and sometimes shrimp. Don't be surprised if the shrimp market is the trunk of a car or the bed of a pickup. Just make certain the catch is fresh and negotiate a price.

For regular supplies, a good stop is a Gigante grocery store. These are found in shopping centers with plenty of parking and easy access. Gigante is a "superstore"—it has a pharmacy and carries clothes, sundries, prepared food for takeout and baked goods (at its *panadería* or bakery). Stock up on fresh produce, lettuce, eggs, milk and meat. Don't pass up the *bolillos,* a delicious bread roll that comes in large loaves or smaller rolls, and *orejas,* a flaky pastry from the *panadería.*

In these superstores that sell prepared foods, and in certain shops and restaurants in larger towns, a quick and easy meal is roast chicken *(pollo rostizado)*. The chicken is slowly cooked on a rotisserie over charcoal. This is a very good meal in the present, or pop it in the ice chest for lunch or dinner later.

Prices for United States' goods are higher throughout Baja. You can find most anything in the larger supermarkets, but some of the specialty items like low-fat, low-calorie foods will be quite a bit more. One item we priced, Lipton's decaffeinated iced tea mix with artificial sweetener, was 25 percent more. It was a pleasant surprise to find it available at the big Centro Comercial Californiano (CCC) supermarkets in La Paz—one at Isabel La Católica and Bravo, the other at Abasolo and Colima. If your taste buds have been longing for something familiar, CCC is the place where you most likely will find it. There is a large freezer section where pizza and frozen cakes can be found, as well as most anything else you would find in a freezer section north of the border. Our major provisioning is done here. If you need liquor, prices in the grocery stores are generally less than in the liquor stores.

Aramburo's at Madero and Hidalgo in La Paz also stocks United States' items and has great meat, but their prices are higher than at CCC. The Aramburo's in Cabo San Lucas is a larger store with a greater selection. On each successive trip, we find a wider variety of foods available in CCC and Aramburo's.

It's best to pack items that are difficult to find everywhere—special diet items like Nutrasweet, light or low-cholesterol mayonnaise and margarine and favorite salad dressings and salad dressing mixes. Diet sodas and other diet drinks are available, but not everywhere. We even found non-alcoholic beer—a big surprise in beer-drinking México.

Another item that is invaluable is the dry Mexican sauce packet with spices and herbs made by French's, Lawry and Schilling for tacos, taco salad, burritos, fajitas, enchiladas, Spanish rice and more. Just cook the ground beef, meat strips or whatever you like and add the sauce packet, mix and stir and you have it. Dried spices which add flavor and take up little room are helpful in giving a varied taste change—you might bring dillseed, thyme, minced onion, parsley, garlic powder or paprika, among others.

Ziplock freezer bags are very handy for storing or freezing fish and other foods, but are not readily available. Bring them with you.

Small fruit and vegetable stores *(fruiterias)* have fresh fruits and vegetables, usually a small supply of canned goods and juices and sometimes flour tortillas. Pick up corn tortillas at special shops *(tortillerias)* where they are cranked out by the thousands and sold by the kilo for next to nothing.

Don't be afraid to try new and different fruits. *Guayabas* (small round yellow guavas, pronounced guay-*yah*-bahs) are very sweet. *Chayote* (pronounced kay-*oh*-tay), a hard, light-green vegetable which becomes tender and opaque when cooked, is delicious. *Jícama* (pronounced *he*-cah-mah) is a round, hard, brown root with a firm white interior that is sweet and crunchy. The small round *limones* (limes, pronounced lee-*mo*-naise) are found everywhere. They are great for *ceviche* (pickled fish, pronounced say-*vee*-chay), salsa and iced drinks like margaritas, or just sprinkled over seafood. Limes are said to have medicinal properties and taken along with garlic ward off many intestinal problems before they begin. Mexicans use limes in many more ways and they are found on the table with the salsa in many restaurants.

Fresh cuts of meat are found in supermarkets, municipal markets and meat shops *(carnicerías)*. The beef is leaner than that found in the United States because cattle are allowed to roam on open range and are rarely put in feed lots for fattening. The meat is also not aged in the same way. Mexican beef is tasty and, being leaner, is better for you. Just learn the different cuts and weights so it will be easy to prepare. With ground beef, use the sauce packets for tacos, burritos, fajitas and enchiladas for an easy meal. Adolph's Meat Tenderizer or your favorite marinade helps with the steak cuts.

Meat Market Talk

We have Jack Poole to thank for this lexicon, most of which doesn't show up in dictionaries. He submitted it a few years ago for use in the Vagabundos del Mar Boat and Travel Club monthly newsletter, *Chubasco.*

- *Res de Sonora:* Sonora beef—the best.
- *Carne molida:* ground meat—*hamburguesa* when in a bun.
- *Pulpa:* round. To get it ground, ask *"Lo muele, por favor."*
- *Pulpa steak* (pronounced more like "stek"): full round.
- *Pulpa cuete:* eye of round.
- *Pulpa negra:* top round.
- *Pulpa bola:* tip roast.
- *Pulpa larga:* rolled roast—you roll it yourself. (Note: *Pulpo* is octopus, so watch your tongue.)
- *Schuck steak:* chuck (seven-bone) steak and blade steak.
- *Asado de paleta:* arm roast, also chuck.
- *Chuleta costado:* club or top loin steak.
- *T-bone:* Porterhouse or T-bone steak.
- *Chamorro:* shank crosscuts.
- *Costillas:* short ribs.
- *Pecho:* brisket.
- *Flank steak:* flank steak.
- *Chuleta entera:* rib roast.
- *Filete de res:* filet mignon.

For pork, try these:
- *Chuletas ahumadas:* smoked pork chops.
- *Tocino:* bacon.
- *Pierna ahumada:* smoked ham, either sliced *(rebanada)* or whole *(entero).*
- *Costillos de puerco:* spare ribs—you may have to help by showing where to cut.
- *Chuleta de puerco entero:* pork loin.
- *Chuletas de puerco:* pork chops—specify thickness.
- *Rebanadas de paleta:* shoulder steaks.

For variety, try these:
* *Conejo:* rabbit.
* *Cabra:* goat, or *cabrito* (kid). Cook like lamb.
* *Higado:* liver—beef *(de res)* or pork *(de puerco)*.
* *Rinon:* kidney.
* *Chorizo:* sausage.

Primitive Camping

Camping Outside of Established Campgrounds

Baja is a desert bordering on the tropics. The sun is intense and both air and ground temperatures can be hot. The air is usually very dry, but it can also be very wet when storms set in. The Pacific coast is subject to periodic fog and frequent dew.

A basic rule for desert camping is to be wary of camping in *arroyos* (streambeds). Infrequently a cloudburst occurs in the mountains, out of sight and hearing. A good night's sleep can be ruined by a wall of water rolling big boulders down the arroyo to scour out your campsite and you along with it. Keep in mind that these are the very forces that carved out the arroyo in the first place and they do occur periodically.

Beach Camping

When you set up camp on a beach in Baja, whether it's in a tent or RV, be prepared for primitive camping. You may find yourself on one of the few beaches with improvements or in one of the handful of RV parks situated on a beach. Elsewhere, you won't find picnic tables, restrooms, parking areas, trails, signs or water spigots. You may find trash barrels.

What you will certainly find is privacy and beauty—mile after mile of pristine sand beaches, white enough to blind you, where you can walk and walk until you drop and never see another soul. What looks to be a mile away will prove to be four miles. When you go off beach walking, it does pay to bring something to drink and only to go so far that you won't be too tired to return to camp.

It also pays to plan ahead on what to do with your trash and human waste. A firm commitment to carrying out what you carried in will keep camping spots attractive and safe for all. It's worth the effort. Burn paper, cardboard and toilet tissue. Crush the rest, bag it up and take it to the next town dump *(basurera)*.

Bring a shovel—the small folding ones take little space. Emulate the cat by burying your personal deposits well back from the high tide line. If you settle in with an RV, drive it away when you have to dump your holding tanks. Don't put paper in the sewage tank and use discretion in selecting a spot in which to dump it, preferably the sewer system of the nearest RV park. Offer to pay for the privilege.

People who settle into a beach spot for the winter in an RV are accustomed to digging a hole, covering it with a piece of plywood and running their sewer hose into it. Some popular spots with a high density of such campers have become noxious and badly polluted, adversely affecting adjacent beaches.

Accordingly, some beaches have been fenced off to prevent vehicular access and overnight camping. Usually a pedestrian walkway is provided for day use. All of the former camping beaches between Cabo San Lucas and San José del Cabo have been restricted in this way. Hotels and condominiums now dominate that coast and more are coming.

The right of public access to beaches in México has its limitations. There is a federal zone *(Zona Federale)* extending 20 meters back from the mean high tide line around the entire coastline of the country which is open to public access. However, adjoining landowners can be held responsible for the cleanliness of the beach in front of their property. Abuse leads to fences.

The federal ministry currently in charge of the *Zona Federale,* SEDESOL, has erected small signs along the paved highways identifying access to many of the better beaches for either camping or day use. These signs are in a standard format, saying "SEDESOL" on the top line, "Acceso a Playa" on the middle line and the name of the beach on the bottom line.

We have done considerable camping in both tents and campers on Baja's beaches over the years and have found a few security precautions to be well advised. There is nothing so effective as camping with other people to establish a comforting peace of mind. That way, there can always be someone in camp to deter those who may consider appropriating your equipment and belongings. Do everyone a favor and don't create temptation.

We lost a clam fork many years ago from alongside our tent, which undoubtedly better served a local youngster. However, we weren't through chasing clams and missed it. Other campers have mentioned ice chests and other easily portable items walking off, including small boats and motors. The worst offenders are other campers, particularly those who have established semi-permanent quarters on a shoestring and can use just about anything that comes their way. Your unattended campsite will look like an open bazaar to someone seeking acquisitions.

The local fishermen and ranchers are hospitable folk who work for what they have and respect the property of others, but kids will be kids—like the little shavers who peeled a magnetic sign off one of our truck doors while we were sitting inside the camper having lunch. They apparently told their mother we gave it to them. We should have caught on when she came over and politely asked if she could have the other one.

A sound practice is to avoid sharing alcohol with strangers completely. What starts out as jovial conviviality can quickly turn unpleasant and unmanageable—the more remote and isolated the area, the less inhibition there is.

Stuck in the Sand

One of the little chores you learn how to do when getting off the beaten path in Baja is how to get unstuck. Years ago we used to tent camp on Playa Santa María south of San Quintín behind the dunes, just about where the La Pinta Hotel now sits. We had a standard two-wheel-drive station wagon and loved to drive the beach in it. The drill was to reduce tire pressure to about 15 pounds, determine a path through the dunes, then make a mad dash to the beach. Once there, we drove on the hard sand below the high tide line and had about eight miles of beach to play on.

One day, full of confidence, we tried coming off the beach in a new spot and dug in. Most of the afternoon was spent jacking up the rear wheels, packing brush, driftwood and whatever else we could find under the wheels, then surging ahead a few feet to repeat the process. It was definitely not fun.

More recently, our one-ton Ford truck (the worst vehicle to get stuck we've ever had)—with nothing behind or on it, just the naked truck—buried itself in the middle of the Villa Vitta RV Park at Bahía de Los Angeles.

In another instance, while towing our 5,000-pound, 21-foot boat behind our 20-foot Born Free camper, we turned off Highway 1 near Puerto Escondido onto what looked to be hard-sand wheel tracks. They weren't. Everything got totally buried. We had to unhook the trailer, tow the truck and camper out, then pull the boat and trailer out with a long cable. That qualified as one of the dumbest moves of all time, for which we earned the label of "Sand Crabs" from a sneaky Vagabundo who happened by and ratted on us.

Some people carry two long pieces of canvas or carpet to put under the drive wheels. Others find wetting the sand makes the difference.

Nylon tow straps can apparently be used to slingshot the stuck vehicle out of its hole by a second vehicle. Have that vehicle run out to the limit of stretch (about another one-fifth the length of the strap), then slam on the brakes. As the brake lights come on, pour the gas to the stuck vehicle. We haven't seen this done but we've been told of the technique. It presents a pleasant mental image of the stuck vehicle simply shooting forward like a rocket. When you're stuck, you'll try anything, right? We'll just keep on with the old jack-it-up-and-stuff-it method.

One more stuck story. Once, during the year we spent in Iran, we ventured out on a dry lake bed in our standard station wagon, decided we had gone far enough as the bushes were petering out, stopped and tried to back up. We dug in. We jacked up the rear wheels, stuffed thorn brush under them, went back a couple of feet, got stuck and repeated the process numerous times. A sheep herder headed his flock over our way to see what these goofy foreigners were up to, gave us an enormous toothless grin, put one finger on the top of his six-foot-long staff and gently pushed it all the way down. When he pulled it out, wet muck was clinging to it. Goggle-eyed, we realized the station wagon was resting on a very thin crust over mushy goop. With renewed vigor and a sense of the whole *shebang* slowly sinking out of sight, we jacked and stuffed in a frenzy to the limit of our endurance. Once we had traction, the pedal went to the floor, the wagon shot up and over a six-foot tall thorn bush in reverse and finally reached solid ground.

Moral: Getting stuck isn't such a big deal; it's what you do next that counts.

Backpacking

Unless you have a great deal of experience backpacking in the desert, we do not recommend backpacking in Baja. If you get too far away from the car, even in the mountains, you can encounter a water problem. It is easy to forget that this is an arid peninsula that has very limited water sources and finding them may take local knowledge. It is also dry and can be numbingly hot.

Read *Into a Desert Place* by Graham MacIntosh before you think about backpacking in Baja. He walked the entire coastline on both sides of the peninsula, carried all the water he could, including a gallon plastic jug in each hand, and tried several types of water distillation devices. He still had some close calls. It is an unforgiving, harsh environment, not to be approached lightly.

Having said that, the mountains do offer some challenging backpacking opportunities. The Sierra San Pedro Mártir in Baja

Norte is a massive mountain range with a high forested plateau some 40 miles long and 10 miles wide between roughly 6,000 and 8,000 feet in elevation. Jeffrey pine is the dominant forest tree, alongside some sugar pine and incense cedar. At higher elevations, you will find lodgepole pine and white fir. There are huge meadows on which cattle graze.

Off to the east is the highest peak in Baja—El Picacho del Diablo at 10,154 feet. Climbing it is a major event and is usually done from the eastern base of the steep escarpment of the Sierra San Pedro Mártir because of the 3,000-foot-deep Cañon del Diablo separating the plateau of the main range from El Picacho. This canyon is a rather weird geological quirk—as if extra effort was expended to isolate El Picacho from mankind.

Trails were established long ago by Indians and have been further delineated by *vaqueros*. Unlike what we are accustomed to in the United States, there are no signs, no trail markers and no good maps. Trails peter out. You can get lost. You can fail to find water.

Before setting out, drive to the Meling Ranch and talk to the people there about where to go, how to find your way and other lifesaving advice you can't leave without. Hire a guide if you feel the slightest bit doubtful about your outdoors expertise. We packed out of there on horseback many years ago with a guide and packer and had a great experience. You can, too, on foot or horseback, if you go about it right.

If you're an angler, you can enjoy trout fishing for Nelson rainbow, native to Arroyo San Antonio and later introduced into Arroyos San Rafael and La Zanja. They are not big—up to a foot long—but they are fun to catch in such an unlikely place. There is also a scenic waterfall in Arroyo San Antonio.

To get to the Meling Ranch, drive about 6.5 miles south of Colonet or about eight miles north of Camalu on Highway 1. Turn east to San Telmo and beyond it to the ranch—a total distance of about 31 miles. The road is dusty and has some fairly steep grades, which were all we wanted to handle with our big camper.

At the other end of the peninsula, the Sierra de La Laguna rises high in the sky above the desert. Surrounded by the tourist centers of La Paz, Los Cabos and the East Cape, its isolated lushness is unsuspected by visitors in the popular resorts fronting the ocean. The heart of the sierra can be reached only by arduous effort over rugged, steep, centuries-old trails that are unsigned and difficult to find. They are beaten two to three feet into the rock by thousands of hooves and feet over the past 200 years or more.

The sierra's rugged peaks can be seen from the surrounding circle of Highways 1 and 19. An especially striking vista is from Highway 1 between Buena Vista and San José del Cabo, from which jagged peaks loom to nearly 7,000 feet.

The area's most startling feature is the dense forest of 60-foot pine and oak trees with trunks up to three feet in diameter, a scattering of huge red-trunked *madronos* with large, glossy, bright-green leaves and the bizarre *sotol* with clusters of long, slender yucca-like leaves atop tall thin trunks.

The pines are Mexican *pinyon,* others of which are found far away in northern México and adjoining Arizona and Texas. The massive black oaks and *madronos* are species unique to the Sierra de La Laguna. The *sotol* occurs elsewhere only in a few widely-scattered groups farther north in Baja. In a moister, cooler climate in the far distant past, the progenitors of all these species found their way out of northern México and down the Baja Peninsula. When the climate became drier and warmer, they became isolated in the higher, moister reaches of the Sierra de La Laguna. As time went on, most were supplanted by new species.

Up in the sierra, level land is hard to find. The one sizeable meadow, about one mile by a half mile, is known as La Laguna. Local lore has it that originally there was a lake there, which broke out of its confines 100 years or so ago.

The shortest route to it is from Rancho La Burrera at a 1,600-foot elevation out of Todos Santos. Some maps show this as San Juan del Asserradero. Start at the microwave dish on the south side of Todos Santos on Highway 19. Drive 1.3 miles south just past Kilometer 54 and turn left on a sandy road across a cattle guard at the top of a hill. Starting from zero on the odometer, ignore a road to the left at 2.2 miles. Continue straight ahead toward the fire-watch tower. At 4.0 miles, take the left fork. Cross a cattle guard at 5.4 miles, pass a dam on the left at 6.4 miles and cross another cattle guard at 7.2 miles. At 8.8 miles, continue straight past a signed road on the left to San Martín, then pass another road to the right. At 12.3 miles, the road makes a steep descent down the north bank of an arroyo to the ranch at 13.3 miles. You must build momentum to traverse the drifted humps of sandy soil on the return out of the arroyo. Our conventional one-ton pickup, which has a propensity for digging in, handled it easily. Motor homes and trailers should not make the drive, however.

The trail heads easterly from La Burrera up the big wash coming out of the mountains, then climbs up the north slope. The 4,000-foot climb of seven miles to La Laguna took us about four hours on horseback. A shaded water source about midway affords refreshment.

At La Laguna, a two-room *casita* (house) in the trees at the meadow's edge is used by "forest guards" who keep an eye on things and gauge rainfall in the meadow. Another little two-room *casita* in the open can be used for shelter and cooking. Cattle and pigs forage over the land, watering in the stream that runs east into Cañon San Dionisio. The trail continues down that canyon to a ranch of the same name.

Backpackers have used two other trans-sierra routes with hard-to-find ancient trails. South of Rancho La Burrera, the next trail goes from Rancho Santo Domingo on the west to Rancho Boca de La Sierra on the east. Another trail farther south goes from Rancho El Guerigo on the west to Rancho El Salto on the east. Farther south yet, the iffy Naranjas Road crosses from its junction with Highway 19 at a sign to El Saltito de Los Garcia to Highway 1 at a point 9.5 miles south of the turnoff to Miraflores.

Things to Bring

Horseback pack trips

Here is what we bring on horseback pack trips (we've been into the Sierra San Pedro Mártir, Sierra de San Francisco and Sierra de La Laguna):

- Eureka two-man mountain tent with an anteroom that can be closed and a sun fly
- Nylon or plastic ground cloth to go both under the tent and serve as an apron for wiping your feet before entering the tent
- Rubber air mattresses with box sides and built-in pillows
- Sleeping bags that zip together so we can snuggle
- Small folding table
- Coleman propane three-burner stove and folding aluminum stand
- Several disposable propane bottles
- Coleman two-lamp fluorescent lantern with a new battery
- Cooking kit with pots, frying pan, plates, cups and utensils
- Small plastic squeeze bottle of Joy dish soap
- Dish rag, scrub brush and dish towel
- Food, including Mountain Home dehydrated meals, canned chicken and shredded beef for tacos, etc., eggs in a plastic egg carrier, powdered iced tea mix with sweetener and lemon, cheese, salami, crackers, cookies, tortillas and other goodies our taste buds require (several planned meals, including for the guide, plus a little extra)
- Clothes, including jeans, hiking boots, lightweight tennis shoes and sandals for around camp, hats, light jackets, lightweight long-sleeved cotton shirts, T-shirts, underwear, socks, swim suits, plastic ponchos (good for groundcloths and rain, too) and shorts
- Swiss army knife, ever-present on the belt
- Pair of binoculars
- Cameras and ample slide and print film
- Notebook (we're writers)

- First-aid kit in an easy-to-pack container off the shelf, prepared for the usual cuts, punctures and abrasions
- Bug spray and squeeze bottle
- Sunglasses
- Medications and personal hygiene items
- Chapstick
- Sunscreen
- Flashlights with spare bulbs and batteries
- Nylon cord
- Small water filter and collapsible five-gallon plastic water jug with a spigot
- Quart canteens
- Ziplock bags for trail snacks and other unforeseen uses
- Plastic garbage bags—what goes in, goes out

Backpacking equipment
We would pare down our horseback pack-trip list and substitute more lightweight items:
- Sleeping pads instead of rubber air mattresses
- No table
- Small single-burner stove
- No lantern
- No canned goods
- Fewer clothes

Camping out of a vehicle
In addition to what we'd bring on a horseback pack-trip, we add:
- Water in two five-gallon collapsible plastic containers
- Ice chest
- Small propane grill
- Small folding shovel
- Tow cable
- Sun Shower
- Rope
- Bungee cords—a bag full

- Duct tape—a great fixer-upper
- Field guides for birds, plants and fish
- Fishing tackle essentials—filet knife, spinning rods and reels, hooks, swivels, swivel snaps, sinkers and several lures of the Rapala, Scampi, tuna feather and jig types (if we charter a boat, we take marlin rods and Penn International 50W reels; the rods and reels take the most room, while the rest fits in a small ladies cosmetic case)

Boat camping

Camping either in the boat or in a tent on shore has a great deal of potential in several sections of the Sea of Cortéz. The many islands around Bahía de Los Angeles, Puerto Escondido and La Paz have attractive coves and beaches. Since stretches of open ocean must be crossed, small open boats like inflatables and car-top aluminum models are not suitable. Strong winds can whip up on short notice, churning the ocean into a maelstrom. Trailer boats of 20 feet or so can handle rough seas, although the open-cockpit, center-console models can get awfully wet. Cuddy cabins give protection and are adequate for sleeping. Camper canvas to the stern makes a cozy home for living on board.

We have lived aboard our old 21-footer for several weeks at a time, though our present 27-footer is far more comfortable with its aft-cabin layout. We have lived in it for four months while on the road to and from Florida and cruising in the Bahamas as comfortably as in our big camper. We have spread mosquito netting across the deck and slept comfortably under the stars in a double sleeping bag.

We once set up a tent camp on the beach on Isla Partida north of La Paz for a week with some dive buddies who had a small compressor. We had a great time exploring the underwater world there.

Boats require special equipment. It is much tougher to get help having broken down on the water than having broken down on the highway. You must be more self-sufficient with tools and parts. Having a buddy boat may mean the difference between getting back to shore or being stranded. There are times when being towed is unavoidable. Necessary items in addition to those listed for vehicles and for primitive camping are:

- Towing bridle
- Propeller
- Water pump impeller
- Hoses
- Belts
- Marine alternator
- Distributor parts
- Spare gas

Critters to Fend Off

Two kinds of insects can make your life miserable and sooner or later you will run into both of them. When you do, have plenty of bug spray. Then there are a few other creatures to be wary of:

Mosquitoes

These ubiquitous pests can be controlled with any of the commercial compounds with Deet (N, N-diethyl-metatoluamide), the one chemical that can be counted on to do the job. We have a squirt bottle of United States Army-type with 71-percent Deet—and it works. A popular spray brand, Off, contains 14.5 percent—it works, too, but does not last as long. Get both squirt bottles and spray cans. Keep covered up and spray or rub the repellent on exposed skin. Also spray clothing. There is one thing about Deet—it melts certain kinds of plastic, like watch bands and eyeglass frames, so be careful with it. We know that a lot of people don't like using strong doses of Deet on their skin because it is so potent, but when the bugs are biting, it works.

Gnats

The most vicious biting bug in Baja is the *jejene* (pronounced hay-*hay*-nay). It is a teeny-weeny gnat which everyone likes to call a no-see-um, but you can-see-um—barely. They walk right through mosquito net. The first thing you'll notice is that something is biting you and you are beginning to sting and itch all over. Soon you'll have scads of little welts that itch even more. A photo of one our friends looks like a bad case of measles. He was one unhappy camper.

In our experience, Deet repellents aren't as effective on *jejenes* as on mosquitoes, but if you keep slathering it on it helps a lot. People are usually happier when they depart the *jejene* encampment. If you can find a breezy spot, it should blow them away. Fortunately, they are not troublesome in many places, but when you are among them they will drive you crazy.

Many people swear by Avon Skin-So-Soft as a bug repellent. We haven't found that to be so, but it may be just the right combination for you. Avon won't say what is in it and doesn't sell it to chase away bugs, but your friendly Avon lady may be happy to sell you some with no questions asked.

Sting rays

They can whack you if you carelessly wade around in salt water. Sting rays are common and should be kept in mind, for their barb can inflict a painful wound. The best thing to do is shuffle your feet or keep thrashing a stick ahead of you. They bury themselves in the sand and can't be seen, but as they don't relish being stepped on they will swim away if alerted. Be particularly cautious when stepping down off a surfboard or sailboard or out of a boat.

If you are unlucky enough to get hit, standard advice is to cleanse the wound with cold salt water and extract all pieces of the barb or its sheath. Soak the injury in hot water at as high a temperature as can be tolerated for 30 to 90 minutes. Disinfect and bandage it as you would any other puncture.

Sea urchins

Some with long slender spines are present in both the Pacific Ocean and the Sea of Cortéz. These types of spines penetrate booties, sneakers or bare skin like needles and are difficult to remove since they are barbed. It is important to try to extract all pieces of broken spines. Local remedies may involve frequent dousings with citrus juice to help eliminate unremovable bits of spines. Disinfect the punctures and keep them clean.

Jellyfish

We have encountered tiny stinging jellyfish now and then, which encourage you to leave the water. Rub in meat tenderizer—Adolph's is considered good. If there are tentacles, they can be covered with dry sand, then scraped off after a few minutes.

Cactus

It was an exciting moment. Fred was assisting biologists in Arizona on a desert bighorn sheep project. While hiking up an arroyo, he spotted a big ram climbing out on one side. He plunked down to a restful sitting position for a steady look with the binoculars and nailed his Levis to his butt by landing on a jumping cholla cactus ball. The ram was forgotten and total attention was devoted to getting unstuck. A wadded up handkerchief held around the spiny ball gave sufficient leverage to pry it loose without impaling his fingers. These little devils are barbed and resist being pulled out.

On a similar expedition in Baja, Gloria brushed too close to a cactus alongside a steep rough trail and collected a cactus spine in her leg. One of the Mexican biologists whipped a pair of tweezers out of his shirt pocket and had that rascal out of there in an instant.

If you walk around where cacti live, it is best to be fully clothed, pay them serious respect and carry a pair of tweezers. Carelessness can be painful.

Cactus spines are also disrespectful of automobile tires. We have had flats in big truck tires after four-wheeling on desert roads and have had to endure the big grin of the tire guy (the shop is a *llantera,* pronounced yawn-*tear*-uh) as he holds up a little spine in his pliers and says, "Espina!" We now watch out for chunks of cactus branches across the road and get out and remove them. That takes less time than changing a tire.

Problems with Sun, Heat and Cold

Sunburn

People are a lot wiser today than they used to be about taking it easy in the sun. If you want to avoid getting burned when you hit Baja, give yourself only a half hour of exposure the first day, then a half hour more for each of the four or five days it takes to start tanning. Use sunscreen or sunblock ointments all the time. Sunscreen protection factors (SPFs) range from two to fifteen or higher, meaning you can stay out in the sun two to fifteen times longer than without any. An SPF of 15 or higher will block most of the sun's harmful rays. Put it on about one-half hour before exposing yourself and reapply if it gets washed off.

Exposure may get away from you anyway and you may develop some bright red spots. For instance, switching to a smaller swimsuit can expose white skin that needs to be protected. Light-skinned people burn very quickly and are better off completely covered. At the other end of the spectrum are those who tan readily but will burn if they push it too fast. Everyone should determine how they react and protect themselves accordingly.

If you get burned, get out of the sun, cover yourself up and apply a soothing ointment such as Solarcaine or Noxema. Suffer as silently as possible and be wiser the next time.

Heat exhaustion

We were having a great time fishing in a friend's *panga* off of Isla San José north of La Paz. It was hot, but Fred was comfortable in a swimsuit and cap. After several hours, we headed back to San Evaristo, where he became a little nauseous and couldn't eat the delicious *tacitos* our friend's wife had prepared. During the long drive back to La Paz, Fred became more uncomfortable and climbed right into bed, feeling disoriented and woozy.

Some years before, while hiking strenuously on a July desert bighorn sheep survey in Death Valley National Monument, Fred became overheated from the exertion. His legs ceased to function and drinking copious quantities of water and pouring it over his head had no effect. He was able to move to a nearby spring by lifting each leg by hand from behind the knee, swinging the leg forward, then doing the same thing with the other leg. Finally at the spring, he fell headlong into a pool. The rising steam blotted out the sun and he was soon able to stagger to the car.

Both of these events were cases of heat exhaustion, which is caused by loss of fluids and salt. Hot, dry desert air sucks moisture out of the body at a high rate. One may experience muscle cramps and headaches, pale and clammy skin, and dizziness and fainting.

Here's what the *American Medical Association Family Medical Guide* says to do: Lay the person down in a cool, quiet place with feet raised a little. Loosen any tight clothing and give them water to drink, adding a teaspoonful of salt to each quart.

In order to avoid heat exhaustion, it is important to maintain adequate moisture in your body and also to limit your activity level. We have learned from United States Army studies (made when General Patton's tank corps was undergoing training in the California desert) that strenuous activity in the desert requires at least two gallons of liquid a day to offset losses. It was also demonstrated that water by itself is not sufficiently palatable to consume in such quantities. You can guzzle it every time you have the slightest desire and still not take in enough. It is necessary to improve it by adding flavoring—citrus juice, chocolate, powdered tea, whatever you can do to make it more interesting. We have adopted the attitude that it is foolish to carry water around with you when you could be drinking it. It only has value in your stomach, not in a canteen. Just be sure you have enough.

Fred took two college students into the Santa Rosa Mountains of California one July to make bighorn counts at waterholes. When it's hot, desert bighorn stay close to water, so it's a good time to count them. Prospectors they talked to said they couldn't survive in those hot, hot canyons at that time of year. However, armed with the findings of Patton's troops, they guzzled water like it was going out of style and had no problems. The prospectors were right about one thing: Those canyons were like ovens, with rocks so hot they blistered the skin.

Heatstroke (sunstroke)

Heat exhaustion can lead to heatstroke under prolonged exposure to very hot conditions. Body temperature can become very high, the skin can become flushed, hot and dry and the pulse can be strong and rapid. The *AMA Family Medical Guide* says to remove clothing and wrap the sufferer in a cold, wet sheet or sponge them with cold or lukewarm water. Fan them by hand or with a fan until the body temperature comes down, then turn them face down in a comfortable sleeping position with upper arms and one leg at right angles to the body, bent at the elbows and knee. Cover the person with a dry sheet and continue to fan. If their body temperature starts to rise, repeat the cooling process.

Hypothermia

Baja really does have everything. If you work it right, you can freeze and fry in the same place on the same day.

After a hypnotic night sleeping to the rhythmic slosh of waves on the beach at San Pedrito RV Park south of Todos Santos, Fred decided the surf must be full of a great many fish. At dawn, he donned his swimsuit, firmly grasped his surf-casting rod and plunged in waist deep for a couple hours of fruitless casting. Deciding it was time for breakfast, he gave it up to return to the camper.

Funny thing! He was shaking so badly he could barely navigate up the slope of the beach. Inside the camper, he went into a frenzy of shivering and shuddering and felt like an ice cube through and through. Gloria whipped up hot chocolate, wrapped him in a blanket and sweetly told him what a horse's patootie he was. There was nothing he could say, as it was true.

For such cold Pacific Ocean water all the way south to Cabo San Lucas, you can blame the Japanese current which sweeps north past Japan, across the frigid North Pacific, then south along the North American coast without warming up a whole lot.

Even in the Sea of Cortéz the water can be too cold for long immersion, except in the shallows where it warms up nicely. When we dive in the Cortéz, we always wear a wet suit or jeans and a long-sleeved cotton shirt, depending on the water temperature. It's true that we have never won any awards for sartorial elegance among the diving crowd, but it's also true that we enjoy our dives. One thing about wet clothes is to get them off when back in the boat. Nothing robs heat from the body faster than wet Levis.

On an early spring raft trip on the Yampa River in Utah, Fred nearly did it again with the hypothermia by wearing wet Levis. A few rapids soused his trousers, clouds blocked the sun and he went into that deep shivering mode. Gloria forcibly pulled his pants off, to the delight of our Vagabundo friends, and with dry legs he warmed right up. We had wondered why all the oarsmen wore nothing but shorts and sandals—they got wet all the time, but dried off quickly.

When prolonged exposure to cold drops the body temperature more than four-degrees below normal, hypothermia has hit. Our source, the *AMA Family Medical Guide,* says to get the person into warm, dry clothes and give warm drinks. Hey, that's just what Gloria did at San Pedrito! Hypothermia can become very serious if it's allowed to progress, so catch it at the first shiver.

Medical Care

Gloria developed an infected finger while in La Paz, so we asked our Mexican friends where to go. There are several hospitals to choose from. We went to the closest one, displayed the finger and were ushered right into a doctor's office. He specified an antibiotic (no prescription needed) which we obtained at a pharmacy.

Clinics are available in small communities and can handle minor scrapes and cuts. The cities have hospitals where treatment for more serious ailments can be obtained. Prices are minimal compared to what we are accustomed to.

Major problems may require transport back home, which can be very expensive if a special medical airplane must be flown in with a doctor and nurse. But if it is a life-threatening situation, that is what must be done. Elderly people, particularly, may secure peace of mind by subscribing to one of several air evacuation programs ahead of time for a fee.

Viewing Wildlife

Whales

By far the stars of the wild animal scene, gray whales fascinate nearly everyone. Endangered after decades of unrestricted slaughter, they have been restored recently to healthy population status, thanks to the laws that protect them. The dedication of the Mexican government in protecting the whales' all-important breeding and calving grounds has been critical in their recovery, as has the cessation of hunting. Scammon's Lagoon (Laguna Ojo de Liebre), Laguna San Ignacio and Bahía Magdalena have become prime whale-watching spots in the winter months, from January through March. Arrange for guided *panga* trips in Guerrero Negro, San Ignacio or Puerto López Mateos for a wildlife experience of a lifetime. If you are moderately lucky, a "friendly" will come alongside and you may be able to touch it. Beach campers can expect to see gray whales broaching and spouting close to shore as they swim south from the Arctic in the fall and north in the spring.

In the midriff area of the Sea of Cortéz, you can see resident fin whales—second in size only to the monstrous blue whale. With luck, any number of different kinds of whales can be seen in Baja's waters—blues, sperms, minkes, killers, Brydes, humpbacks and perhaps others.

During a Vagabundo fishing tournament at Bahía de Los Angeles, a whale leaped out of the water and crashed onto the bow of a fast-moving boat. The bow rail was broken and the captain broke a finger as he was bashed about. The whale went on its way. We surmised that either the boat had come between a mother and her calf or else the whale had been on *loco* weed.

Dolphins

Several species of dolphins are commonly seen in Baja—common, bottlenosed, long-snouted and spotted—some playing in the surf and others in huge schools in the open ocean (often with yellowfin tuna). They enjoy playing around the bow waves of boats. They are always uplifting to see because of their grace, speed and beauty.

Big fish

The largest fish of all, the whale shark, is sometimes seen in Baja waters. We have not been lucky enough to see one, but people we have traveled with have.

The huge 20-foot manta rays have become quite scarce. Most of them, and the smaller ones as well, have wound up as dried, shredded manta raya *machaca*. What a shame.

Billfish (marlin and sailfish) sometimes will be seen jumping or snoozing on the surface. It's always a thrill to see one of these well-crafted swimming machines come clear out of the water, often in a long series of leaps.

Sharks are not seen as often as they once were, due to heavy fishing for fins shipped to Asia to become soup. It is exciting to see one of those distinctive fins cleaving the water, however.

While cruising from Bahía de Los Angeles to Bahía Kino with a group of Vagabundos, we suddenly saw a fin sticking three feet out of the water just off our starboard bow and heading across our path. There was no time even to pull the throttle back and slow down. We were sure we were going to hit the shark's back, but we didn't. We passed over it without a bump. It had to be a whopper with a very tall dorsal fin, for our sterndrive extended three feet below the surface. We wished we could have seen the entire creature.

A real oddball that we have seen just once is the sunfish or *mola-mola*. These goofy fish get up to 1,000 pounds or so and flop around weakly on their sides, creatures of the currents with little or no movement control.

Birds

By far the most engaging wild camping companions are birds. Brown pelicans give endless entertainment, their lumbering flight instantly transformed into precise dive bombing attacks on schools of baitfish. Underwater photography discloses that they hit the water with their beaks open, ballooning out their pouches to unbelievable dimensions—which also stops them dead in their tracks. They close their beaks and squeeze the water out, swallowing the fish. They have a very solemn look when they perch with their long beaks tucked down against their breasts. Their coloration is very handsome.

In the southern part of the Peninsula, frigate, or man-o'-war, birds circle endlessly on long wings, adroitly riding thermals. When they begin to gather over a spot in the ocean, that is the signal for fishermen to put the boat on plane and head over there, for game fish are working bait. They are great thieves, outmaneuvering gulls and boobies in the air to force them to drop fish they have picked up, then gracefully snatching their booty as it falls.

On the beach, sandpipers and other shorebirds put on a constant show of feeding activity as they race to follow a receding wave, then reverse to keep just ahead of the next one. With a bird identification book in hand, you can readily identify all the varied species you'll encounter. Once in awhile, you find a stray from somewhere far away which doesn't belong in Baja. It's like looking for a pearl in every oyster, for the thrill is in the seeking.

The gulls, of course, are always entertaining with their boldness, well-groomed coiffures and constant mewing. They are fun to identify, too, as are the terns.

In the southern part of Baja, you might spy a very handsome hawk with white chest, pale patches on dark wings, black crest and red face sitting on *cardóns*. This eye-catching fellow of the south is the *caracara* or Mexican eagle.

Ospreys, or fish hawks, are common and are often seen carrying a fish with the head pointed forward as it is tightly gripped by both talons. A pair has nested on a pole near the steel eagle monument at the state line north of Guerrero Negro for years. They have created a huge pile of sticks, adding to it each year.

Exotic animals

A remnant population of 100 or so pronghorn antelope hang on in the Vizcaíno Desert south of Guerrero Negro. It is a vast area and they are seldom seen except by biologists making aerial surveys. Once populating Baja's flatlands north into California and over to Sonora and Arizona, now they are nearly gone from Baja. There are severe penalties for killing a pronghorn antelope, which are well known among the local population, and there is hope for their survival. The antelope drink no free water, getting what they need from nightly condensation on plants and from the plants themselves, which is most unusual for an animal of their size.

Desert bighorn sheep inhabit the rougher, more remote mountains from the border south to about 40 miles north of La Paz. It has always been impossible to police the hunting of them and the population is way down from what it originally was. There have been no legal hunting seasons for desert bighorn for several years for there has been insufficient knowledge on which to base the number of permits to be sold. Tourists will not encounter bighorn sheep unless they go out of their way to arrange for a guide. This might be done in San Felipe, Bahía de Los Angeles, Santa Rosalía or Loreto.

Travel Tips

✳ ✳ ✳ ✳

México has a different legal system, different customs, a different culture and is—well, different. That is why we all go there—to get away from it all and have fun. Here are the most important things to do and become accustomed to.

Licenses and Permits

Permits and documents are essential for traveling in Baja California—even more so when going to the mainland of México from Baja.

Tourist cards

The first thing to think about is a tourist card. Most tourists call it a visa or visitor permit. The formal identification is Form FMT. It is a two-piece, 5.5-by-7.5-inch form with a carbon insert. Legally, everyone needs one if going to Ensenada or Mexicali for more than three days or farther south for any length of time. If you can't obtain one from a Mexican Consulate or Mexican Tourism Office, phone our Vagabundos del Mar Boat and Travel Club at (800) 474-2252. (We always have a supply and they are free, even to non-members.)

Some officials in Baja insist the form is not necessary unless you are going to the mainland by ferry. However, others say it is required by Mexican law. We prefer to have all papers in order in case of a situation involving the police or if someone should need to fly out of the country. Airport officials may refuse to let you on the plane without your visitor permit. If you plan to take a ferry from Baja to the Mexican mainland, you will need a visitor permit.

Once you have the form filled out, it must be endorsed in México at an Immigration *(Migración)* Office. The easiest to locate is in Ensenada on the waterfront on the north side of town, just south of the shipyards (where all the big speed bumps are) and just before the arterial stop sign, where you turn right onto the four-lane divided street along the bay in the main shopping district. A *Servicios Migratorios* sign identifies it. Parking is limited, so you may have to park nearby and walk back. Bring a passport or copy of your birth certificate for identification and your vehicle registration slip just in case they want it. See "Ensenada area" in Northwest Baja Norte (page 84) for further details.

Vehicle permits

If you are going to the mainland by ferry from Santa Rosalía (to Guaymas) or La Paz (to Topolobampo or Mazatlán), a Temporary Vehicle Importation Permit is necessary. Do not count on obtaining one in Santa Rosalía. Either procure it at a Customs *(Aduana)* Office at the border, in La Paz at the Customs Office in the Treasury *(Hacienda)* building across from the city dock *(Muelle Fiscal)* in the center of town, or at the vehicle control booth at the Customs Office at the Pichilingue Port where the ferry dock is located.

To obtain the permit, you need: four photocopies of your driver's license; a tourist card; vehicle registration; a leasing contract (if the car is leased or rented) in the name of the individual importing the car; if it's a company car, a document certifying you work for the company; and an international credit card (American Express, Diner's Club, MasterCard or Visa) in the name of the owner or driver of each vehicle. (Each person may bring in only one vehicle, so if you are towing a second one it must be in the name of another person with you.)

You must pay an $11 fee, by credit card only, for three items: 1) a six-month Temporary Vehicle Importation Permit; 2) a form on which you promise to take the vehicle back out of the country; and 3) a windshield sticker. Cash is not accepted. If you don't have a credit card, you must go to the nearby Mexican bonding agency, which is the Bank of the Army *(Banjér-cito)*. The bond will cost between one and two percent of the Blue Book value of the vehicle, plus tax and processing costs.

When you leave the Mexican mainland with the vehicle, you must return the permit, form and sticker to Customs, unless you are positive the vehicle will be driven back into the Mexican mainland within the permit period. If you have any doubt at all, turn everything in. It is much simpler to pay the small fee again rather than let the permit expire while you are at home. Customs will have no way to determine that you did not illegally leave the vehicle in México. You may be fined or confronted with other bureaucratic problems. For the current official word on all this, call a Mexican Department of Tourism *(Turismo)* office. If you are going only to Baja and will not be on the Mexican mainland, you will not need the vehicle permit.

Fishing licenses and boat permits

These are much simpler permits to deal with. Regulations state, "In order to operate a boat in Mexican waters, it is necessary to hold a boat permit and personal fishing licenses for everybody aboard the boat, regardless of age and whether fishing or not." We are informed that boat permits and fishing licenses are needed only if there is fishing tackle on board (a single hook or a spear gun is enough). These can be obtained from the Mexican Department of Fisheries *(Pesca)*. They can be obtained in México, but it can be a chore to locate a Pesca office. Contact the U.S. office at 2550 Fifth Avenue, Suite 101, San Diego, CA 92103; phone (619) 233-4324. For faster service, phone our Vagabundos del Mar Boat and Travel Club at (800) 474-2252.

Pets

If you have a pet, obtain an International Health Certificate from your veterinarian as close to departure as you can and bring it with you. We have never been checked in México for this when we bring our cat, but we have been asked for it when crossing back into the United States.

Insurance

Liability

Mexican law is considerably different than that in the United States. In the event of an accident, both parties are held until it is determined who is responsible for what, including damage to the highway, and how the debt is to be paid. Liability coverage with a Mexican company takes care of your end of it. Liability coverage with foreign companies is not recognized, regardless of what your insurance agent may tell you. Without the Mexican coverage, you may wind up in jail.

Mexican vehicle liability policies include coverage for anything towed, including boats and trailers. For an additional fee, liability coverage while on the water can be purchased for boats. While the risk of an accident is less than for vehicles, the same consequences can follow if there is no insurance coverage. Liability-only coverage for vehicles costs only $53 for a full year for any vehicle.

Physical damage

Coverage for damage to your vehicle and boat can also be purchased from a Mexican company. Sample rates from our Vagabundos del Mar Boat and Travel Club range from $88 per year for a vehicle valued up to $5,000 to $144 up to $20,000, $200 up to $40,000 and $302 up to $80,000. Some United States companies extend coverage for a short distance into México, up to about 75 miles south of the border, which doesn't take you very far.

Vehicle preparation

México is full of good mechanics and they are very inventive in getting things fixed with what they have to work with. However, they are not into on-board computers, turbochargers or other high-tech innovations. The simpler the workings of your vehicle, the better your chances of getting it fixed. The government also provides a safety net for travelers in need in the form of Green Angels.

These green utility trucks are manned by English-speaking mechanics and cover each section of most paved highways in Baja California. They have spare gasoline, for which you pay, and a few tools. Most importantly, they have short-wave radios linked in a network by numerous microwave towers. If they can't get you going, they can call a tow truck and get you to a shop. Tips are appreciated, but seldom offered by tourists. Feel free to help them out in return.

Have your vehicle serviced and thoroughly checked over before leaving home and stock some basic spare parts that might be needed if you break down in a remote area. The following items are suggested:

Pre-travel service:
- Tune-up
- Oil and filter change
- Air filter change
- Gas filter change
- Lubrication
- Check and/or pack wheel bearings
- Inspect all hoses under the hood and replace if unduly soft or brittle
- Inspect all belts and replace if frayed
- Check wiper blades and replace if necessary
- Check shock absorbers and replace if necessary
- Check and clean battery terminals (fluid level and general condition)
- Check front end alignment
- Check tires for condition and pressure, including spares
- Check turn signals
- Check wheel lug nuts for tightness (periodically recheck in Baja, too)

Spare parts:
• Belts, one spare for each one under the hood
• Air filter, one
• Points and plugs, one set each
• Tire, one mounted on a wheel
• Tire tubes, one (if you have tube-type tires)
• Hitch ball, one (if you are pulling a trailer)
• Hoses, one for each under the hood
• Keys, one spare set
• Oil, enough for a change plus extra for an emergency (like when we poured in a quart of transmission fluid by mistake and decided to drain the oil right then and there—it was time anyway)
• Oil filters, two
• Gas filters, two (if you have a gasoline-burning vehicle)
• Diesel filters, two (if you have a diesel-burning vehicle)
• Octane booster, if premium gas is required (you may have to use some low octane Nova gasoline)

Obtaining spare parts for vehicles and boats from the U.S. has become very difficult. Currently it is necessary to carry them by hand instead of having them shipped. Carriers are not willing to hassle with required customs duty.

Tool box:
We carry a simple metal tool box measuring 19 inches long, 7 inches wide and 7.5 inches high. It has no trays—just one big compartment into which everything is layered. Over the years, we have tossed in one item after another. Here's what it holds:
• 22-piece socket set with $1/4$" and $3/8$" drives in a carrying case, including 6" and 12" extensions
• $3/4$" socket set
• 8" and 12" crescent wrenches
• Four-piece SAE flare-nut wrench set
• Nine-piece combination wrench set
• Distributor wrenches
• Monkey wrench

- Pipe wrench
- Oil filter and gas filter wrenches
- Regular pliers
- Vise-grip pliers
- Channel-lock pliers
- Lineman's pliers
- Needle-nose pliers
- Wire cutters
- 18-piece hex key set
- Claw hammer
- Hacksaw
- Keyhole saw
- Battery terminal cleaning tool
- Tape measure
- Half-round file
- Round file
- Half-round wood rasp
- Pry bar
- Two putty knife scrapers
- Wire stripping/crimping tool
- Spark plug tool
- Five blade and four Phillips head screwdrivers from
  small to large sizes
- Brake adjusting tool
- Drive pins
- Assorted taps
- Cold chisel
- Scissors
- 12-volt test light
- Alligator-clip test leads
- Steel wool
- Spool of fine copper wire
- Duct tape
- Plastic ties

Additional essential items that won't fit in the tool box:
• Jack, one heavy enough for your vehicle
• Lug wrench
• Flashlights, two, plus extra batteries
• Jumper cables
• Small shovel
• Small axe
• Volt meter
• 110-volt tire-inflating compressor

Customs

México

Each tourist may bring into México duty-free:
• Items for personal use, such as clothes, shoes and toiletries
• One video camera with battery packs, two cameras, 12 rolls of film or video cassettes and one pair of binoculars
• Magazines and books
• Camping and sporting equipment
• Twenty packs of cigarettes, 50 cigars, 150 grams of loose tobacco and three liters of alcoholic beverages (must be over 18 years of age)
• Medicines and prescription drugs with a doctor's prescription
• One portable television, one radio, one tape recorder, one video cassette player and 20 cassettes
• One typewriter
• One musical instrument that can be carried by hand
• One boat, one jet ski, one ATV (all-terrain vehicle) and one sailboard
• One bicycle

The first $50 worth of dutiable items is free. Campers may have their vehicles searched, but unless a tourist is carrying commercial quantities of marketable goods, furniture or household appliances, there should be no problem. If asked what you have, the simple answer "things to camp with" will usually suffice.

You may be searched for fruits and vegetables at Guerrero Negro going either way across the Baja Norte-Baja Sur stateline, or you may simply be asked what you have. Sometimes they will take things; other times they won't. The station is located a few hundred yards south of the big steel eagle at the stateline.

United States

Clearing customs is not a particularly pleasant experience upon returning home from an idyllic sojourn in Baja, but informed travelers can ease the strain. Customs officials state that in order to get across the border quickly you must take an active role. It is your responsibility to be prepared, to be cooperative, not to be offended by the questions and to have whatever documents you need ready to be presented.

Your attitude has a lot to do with how quickly or slowly you get across. If you cooperate with the inspector, it speeds things up. Answer questions fully. Don't come with all your purchases wrapped up. Have them in the cab with you as you arrive at the gate. Have a list of everything you have purchased in México with the value of each item. If you will be bringing dutiable items (cameras, lenses, binoculars, radios, etc.) into México, avoid possibly having to pay duty on them when returning to the United States by taking them to a Customs Office beforehand. There they will record serial numbers for each item and prepare a "Certificate of Registration For Personal Effects Taken Abroad." Keep these documents with you.

It helps to understand how customs inspectors perceive the people they are dealing with. Protecting national sovereignty is their main concern. What we normally consider our constitutional rights were deliberately excluded by the framers of the Constitution for citizens crossing back into the United States. We can be detained legally, strip searched without probable cause, or examined without the usual need for prior information. The only right we have is to be treated courteously. If we approach customs with the attitude that we have rights, we are on the wrong foot.

It helps to accept that the burden is on us and to realize that the questions are not meant to be personal, demeaning or degrading. Rather, they are designed to help us get across the border by sorting out what the inspectors need to know.

A lot of people react very negatively to the questions. Beyond certain questions that must be asked, each inspector must determine what to ask you personally to try to get a sense of you to speed up the process. Sometimes the best way to do this is to ask a question deliberately intended to get a reaction, like "What are you smuggling?" A lot of people smile and laugh. Other peoples' knuckles go white or other parts of the body respond involuntarily. For instance, the carotid artery jumps under stress. We were told of one fellow who opened the trunk and showed the inspector what he was smuggling.

Consider the process from the viewpoint of the inspectors, who work under very difficult circumstances. An eight-hour shift may run 16 hours. At the San Ysidro-Tijuana port of entry, they average about 100 cars per hour with three people per car, so they talk to 300 people per hour. Of these, the usual 10 percent are on the fringes of sanity. Rain, heat, cold and noxious fumes take their toll. Inspectors move from lane to lane at the primary gates and to the secondary gates or the pedestrian area, but are on their feet for most of the day.

Immigration and Naturalization Service (INS) and Customs Service inspectors each staff half of the primary gates. Their purpose is to sort out at primary which arrivals need more scrutiny at secondary, but also to keep the primary lines moving. We were told there is about 20 percent more traffic each year and that they handle upward of 100 million crossings annually at San Ysidro-Tijuana—more people than all but a few nations have.

Customs and INS inspectors all receive cross training and do their jobs at the primary gates the same way. The people at the secondary gates do specialized work—Customs, INS or Agriculture.

Despite years of study, the problem of long customs lines has not yet (and may never be) solved. The weather has more to do with it then anything else. If it is pleasant in San Diego, everyone heads for Tijuana. In spite of how long the line seems, the usual crossing is done in 45 minutes.

Intercepting smuggling is the major purpose of our border people. Smugglers watch the border constantly to see if inspectors are easing off near the ends of their shifts. They even have nicknames for each inspector.

Smugglers have become very sophisticated, building compartments in drive shafts and otherwise manufacturing cars with invisible joints so inspectors can't tell where things are hidden. They hire and use grandpa-and-grandma types or 30-year-old clean-cut couples with a child. Since smugglers go to great lengths to blend in, the customs game is to keep a few moves ahead and intercept as many of them as possible. Those of us who make up the 90 percent who are plain old tourists can contribute to the effort by submitting gracefully to the necessary inconveniences.

You can expect to be sent to the secondary gates if you have been in México any length of time. Permitted fruits available in México are: bananas, cactus fruits, dates, grapes, melons, papayas, pineapples and strawberries. All other fruits are prohibited and will be confiscated.

Most vegetables are permitted, except sweet potatoes, yams, uncooked potatoes and avocados with seeds.

Also prohibited are pork, including sausages, cold cuts, skins and pork tacos, and raw poultry. Be aware that when crossing into the United States at Mexicali, inspectors make periodic checks of white fish filets to assure that they are not protected *totuava* fish. Unless the meat can be identified by patches of skin, it may be taken for laboratory identification. If it's *totuava*, you will be hearing from them; if not, you have lost your fish.

Each individual is allowed $400 of dutiable items. Be sure to include all fruits, vegetables and alcoholic beverages (one-liter limit in California) on your list, whether purchased in México or brought down with you. At this point the inspector can only assume it all came from México. Before leaving home, obtain the booklet, *Know Before You Go*, from a United States Customs Office.

Aside from the 24-hour San Ysidro-Tijuana port of entry on United States' Interstate 5 and Baja's Highway 1, there are four other Baja ports of entry:

• Otay Mesa on the east side of Tijuana near the airport is usually faster than the San Ysidro-Tijuana port, but it requires too much driving in heavy traffic through Tijuana to suit us. We had to change a traffic-side boat trailer tire on an overpass in Tijuana after sunset (with no place to get off the road) and have had no further desire to use Otay Mesa. It is open from 6 a.m. to 10 p.m.
• Tecate off United States Highway 94 and on Baja 2 and 3 is very quick to get through. It is open from 6 a.m. to midnight.
• Mexicali on United States Highway 111 and Baja 5 is open 24 hours.
• Algodones, about 47 miles east of Calexico on United States Interstate 8 and three miles south on Highway 186, and about 19 miles east of Mexicali on Baja 8, is open from 6 a.m. to 8 p.m.

Driving Safely

Keep firmly in mind that Highway 1 from Tijuana to Cabo San Lucas and all the other paved roads in Baja were built for trucks and buses that keep the necessities of life flowing. The highways were not designed for tourists accustomed to zipping around on freeways.

Something to consider is what you will do if your vehicle stops moving down the highway (for one of innumerable unpredictable reasons) and you have to go for help. Who goes and who stays with the vehicle? This amounts to a major decision fraught with conflicting imperatives.

Aside from the companionship, there is much to be said for traveling with others. On one of our trips with a boat and trailer behind our camper, the tongue broke and the boat and trailer had to be left alongside the highway while one of us drove off for a tow truck. Assuming that the boat would attract the curiosity of passersby and generate a desire to see what it contained, we were convinced that someone had to stay with it. Gloria volunteered, feeling a sense of security because of a group of field workers just across the highway. If they had not been there, we could not have left her alone.

It would have been much simpler if we were traveling with another couple who could have parked alongside the boat while we went off to get help.

Something else to keep in mind is that turn signals are used differently in México. A driver ahead of you will use his turn signal to notify you to come ahead and pass. You have to decide if it is safe to do so, but don't count on him turning left. However, if an intersection is coming up, it is wise to wait to see if he does. Keep this in mind when you use your left turn signal in the usual fashion—or else you may turn into someone who misread you.

If you want to become an old Baja hand, adhere diligently to two simple lifesaving rules:

Rule #1: *Don't drive over 50 miles per hour.*

Baja's roads are narrower than we're used to and they don't have shoulders. Trucks and buses drive fast. You are certain to meet one just where the highway is the narrowest—where concrete abutments for culverts pinch in on the pavement on each side. This is when you must have precise control of where your right wheels are, even more so if you are towing something. Slowing quickly from 50 miles per hour allows precisely controlled evasive action—safely.

Take it for granted that sooner or later you will enter a curve to meet an oncoming truck or bus taking part of your lane, but you won't be able to pull to the right because of a row of boulders in your way. Instead of flares or reflective markers, the locals use boulders to steer you away from their stalled vehicles—then often leave them in place when they move on. You must be able to stop or slow down enough to let the truck or bus go by.

Rule #2: *Don't drive at night.*

The dangerous situations that are mentioned in Rule #1 become impossible to deal with safely at night—plus black cows that roam on open range which cannot be seen until you are right on them. They love to feed on the side of the highway where the vegetation grows the most lush from rainfall sliding off the pavement and, of course, they usually stand right in the middle of the highway to contemplate their next move.

If you are thinking of driving to Cabo in two days from the border, have your affairs in order—it's suicidal.

One of Parkinson's laws of management is that work expands to fill the time available in which to do it. The corollary is that grand vacations are compressed into the limited time available in which to do them. If your Scrooge of a boss will give you only a week off and you have been dying to spend it in Cabo, forget driving—fly, that's what airplanes are for. If you must drive, forget Cabo. Settle for some place you can reach comfortably without violating these rules, like San Felipe, San Quintín or Bahía de Los Angeles.

After a day of driving, take a cooling, refreshing shower, then kick back. Get into the Baja mindset and have a stress-free, relaxed stay in mañana land.

Fuel

Gasoline and diesel fuel are readily available on the Transpeninsular Highway and in all cities from the Pemex service stations at prices roughly equal to, or slightly higher than, the highest you might encounter on the United States

Interstate System. Gasoline comes in two grades: leaded Nova rated at 80 octane (blue pumps), and unleaded Magna Sin rated at 92 octane (green pumps). Some people feel that these ratings are a few points higher than the rating system to which we are accustomed. Diesel comes in red pumps.

The vehicles that we use run on unleaded regular gasoline in the United States and run just fine on Magna Sin, while Nova creates pinging. Vehicles that need premium gas in the United States should not be taken into Baja.

One of the precautions we exercise in Baja is to drive off the top one-quarter of our two tanks (full on one, half-full on the other). As soon as you pass a Pemex station with less than three-quarters of a tank left, you can count on finding the next two temporarily out of gas. We have had to take gas out of our boat to get optimists on their way after having waited a day or two for a gas truck to arrive. This is where a realistic understanding of the word "mañana" comes in handy—it really means "not today."

Several games are played at gas stations to extract more money from you than you owe. It pays to have locking gas caps so that no one can start pumping until you are standing there. Otherwise, the pump may not be reset to zero. You also have to watch to see that the attendant does not suddenly reset the pump, then restart it without you knowing what you had on it. At least know the maximum number of liters your tank will hold and you can refuse to pay for more than that. Have your own calculator, since many pumps have inoperable total price indicators. We pay in pesos because it avoids varying dollar exchange rates.

Losing a little at these low-stakes games once in a while keeps us attentive for new variations. Look at them as contests that enliven the tedium of steady driving. On the other side of the coin, we have had some amazing experiences with attendants returning substantial overpayments when both of us later realized what happened. One fellow had written the calculations on the palm of his hand and referred right to it when we came back for a recount. Fortunately, he had not needed to wash his hands in the interim.

Some vehicles run on propane *(gas butano),* which is sparsely available. On the Transpeninsular Highway, there are plants only in Ensenada, Colonia Vicente Guerrero, Guerrero Negro, Santa Rosalía, Ciudad Constitución, La Paz and San José del Cabo. Propane is provided for household use rather than vehicles. While it can be obtained for vehicles, it is difficult to do so.

Money

Dollars are universally accepted, but we like to have sufficient pesos for gas stations and other businesses with prices in pesos to avoid losing on the exchange. We stop on the United States side of the border to pick up a few hundred dollars worth, then rely on buying more at banks with American Express traveler's checks. Debit cards and regular credit cards work at some banks for obtaining cash, but we haven't used them because banks in the smaller communities don't always do everything the larger ones do and we hate chasing around for cash. It takes too much time away from having fun.

For some time to come, there will be three sets of peso bills and two sets of coins—until the older versions wear out. When inflation grew to where it took 3,000 pesos to buy one United States dollar, the Mexican government dropped the three zeros. So, a whole new set of bills (and recently a second new set) and coins came out that way and all sets are still in use. Accordingly, you have to examine carefully how much you are handing over to someone and the change you get back. Since tourists are notoriously careless about keeping track of such things, vendors count on taking advantage. Don't confuse three new pesos (N\$3) or 3,000 old pesos with \$3US. Here's the simple equation: 3,000 old pesos = N\$3 = \$1US.

Telephone

There are several ways to make long distance phone calls from Baja, either to another country or within México. The time-honored, cheapest method is to find a long distance service and let them do the work for a small fee. Look for a *Larga Distancia* sign with a telephone icon. You will find them in drugstores *(farmacias),* grocery stores or all by themselves— just keep your eyes peeled for the sign, or ask. You can pay there, but will have to wait for time and charges and it's more expensive, or call collect *(por cobrar)* and avoid a 50-percent tax. After filling out a slip with the phone number and your name, you will wait until the operator signals you into a booth to pick up the phone.

You can pick up any pay phone on the street, insert a small coin and dial 09 for the English-speaking operator. (Most pay phones have a sign illustrating the different coins that can be used, but if in doubt, hold out a handful to someone nearby and let him/her pluck out an appropriate one.) Give the phone number and your name, then say it's collect. Charging to an international calling card will avoid a large tax, but since we have heard stories of tourists using a card in a *larga distancia* and later having other international calls charged to it, this may be too risky.

There are some new wrinkles. You can dial 95-800-462-4240 from any public telephone marked *Ladatel* to get AT&T in Houston, Texas. Give the number you are calling and your calling card number, just like at home. Some RV parks, hotels and sidewalk stations have direct phones—you simply pick them up and dial the operator to place your call. The charge is higher, as you might expect, since the establishment gets a big cut from the private company providing the service. Also, you can sign up for Mexican cellular service and use your cellular phone— but this is the most expensive way to go.

Stick with the cheaper methods, unless your constitution is strong enough to stand enormous phone bills when you get home. You may get all tensed up again and have to go back to Baja to relax.

Firearms and Drugs

Save yourself inestimable grief by leaving these seriously illegal items home. Pistols are an absolute no-no. Don't bring boxes of .22 shells for trading stock either. If they are found, it will be assumed that a gun to use them is close at hand and your vehicle may be demolished in the search. If you are expecting to hunt, be sure you have all firearm permits, as well as hunting licenses and permits, beforehand.

Have prescriptions for all medications that may be suspect and no street drugs or funny cigarettes. Mexican jails are not pleasant places to spend your vacation. Once you break the law, you cease to be a tourist and any assistance tourists are entitled to disappears.

Ferries

There is ferry service between Santa Rosalía and Guaymas, La Paz and Topolobampo (Los Mochis) and La Paz and Mazatlán. Fares and departure times are subject to change without notice. Arrival times depend upon the weather.

Departures from Santa Rosalía are 8 a.m. Sundays and Wednesdays, arriving in Guaymas about seven hours later. Departures from Guaymas are 8 a.m. Tuesdays and Fridays. The Santa Rosalía terminal is on the pier in the middle of town on Highway 1.

The ferry office in La Paz is at Cinco de Mayo and Guillermo Prieto. The departure and arrival terminal is north of town at Pichilingue. Departures for Topolobampo are 8 p.m. daily except Tuesdays, arriving about 10 hours later. Departures from Topolobampo are 9 a.m. daily except Sundays.

Departures for Mazatlán are 3 p.m. daily during vacation periods and daily except Saturdays at other times, arriving about

18 hours later. The reverse trip is on the same time schedule. Fares increase periodically. The latest in dollars were:

Class	Guaymas	Topolobampo	Mazatlán
Salon	$13	$13	$20
Tourist	$26	—	$40
Cabin	—	—	$60
Special cabin	—	—	$80
Autos to 5 meters	$102	$89	$146
Autos to 6.5 meters	$133	$115	$190
Auto/trailer to 9 meters	$184	$160	$263
Auto/trailer to 17 meters	$348	$302	$496
Buses/motor homes	$175	$152	$248
Motorcycle	$15	$11	$19
Motorcycle/sidecar	$25	$23	$32

A "salon" has numbered seats. "Tourist" fare is for a stateroom with two to four berths, with a washstand inside and bathrooms and toilets outside. "Cabin" fare is for a stateroom with two berths with complete bathroom facilities inside. A "special cabin" is a suite with a living room, a complete bathroom, bedrooms and a closet.

Information and reservations can be obtained at a central source in Mazatlán by calling SEMATUR at their toll-free number, 91-800-6-9696, from inside México, or at these departure points:

- Muelle Fiscal, Apartado Postal 72, Santa Rosalía, Baja California Sur, México; 011-52-115-2-0013 or 0014.
- Guillermo Prieto y Cinco de Mayo, La Paz, Baja California Sur, México; 011-52-112-5-3833 or 5-4666; Pichilingue Terminal 011-52-112-2-9485; fax 011-52-112-5-6588.
- Muelle Fiscal, Guaymas, Sonora, México; 011-52-622-2-3390; fax 011-52-622-2-3393.
- Muelle Fiscal, Topolobampo, Sinaloa, México; 011-52-686-2-0141; fax 011-52-686-2-0035.
- Terminal Transbordadores, Mazatlán, Sinaloa, México; 011-52-69-81-7020 or 1-7021, fax 011-52-698-1-7023.

•Paseo de La Reforma 509 - 4o. Piso, México, D.F.; 011-52-5-286-1267; fax 011-52-5-533-7935.

On-board services include: information and passenger assistance office; a cafeteria; a kiosk with magazines, film, pharmacy items and gifts; free medical service (medications must be paid for); projection of video films; a cellular telephone; toilets; a restaurant-bar and disco with live music on the ferries *Azteca, Coromuel* and *Puerto Vallarta;* and lockers.

Time Zones

Like California, Baja Norte is on Pacific Standard Time during the winter and Pacific Daylight Time in summer. Baja Sur, on the other hand, is on Mountain Standard Time all year and doesn't observe daylight savings time. Accordingly, in the summer Baja Sur is on the same time as Baja Norte, while in the winter Baja Sur is one hour later than Baja Norte.

Tourists have been known to miss a whale-watching reservation in Guerrero Negro by failing to remember to set their clocks ahead an hour when crossing the stateline.

MAP A

BAJA MAP (general) .... see page 10
adjoining maps
NORTH .... California
EAST (map C) .... see page 126
SOUTH (map B) .... see page 77
WEST .... Pacific Ocean

32 CAMPGROUNDS
7 BEACHES
PAGES 76-125

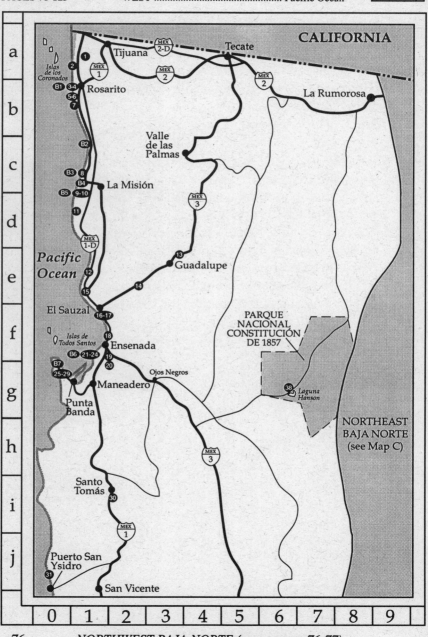

CALIFORNIA

Tijuana

MEX 2-D

Tecate

MEX 1

MEX 2

MEX 2

La Rumorosa

Islas de los Coronados

B1

Rosarito

Valle de las Palmas

B2

B3

La Misión

B4

B5

MEX 3

MEX 1-D

Guadalupe

Pacific Ocean

El Sauzal

PARQUE NACIONAL CONSTITUCIÓN DE 1857

Islas de Todos Santos

B6

Ensenada

B7

Ojos Negros

Maneadero

Punta Banda

Laguna Hanson

NORTHEAST BAJA NORTE (see Map C)

MEX 3

Santo Tomás

MEX 1

Puerto San Ysidro

San Vicente

0 1 2 3 4 5 6 7 8 9

a b c d e f g h i j

MAP B

7 CAMPGROUNDS
3 BEACHES
PAGES 76-125

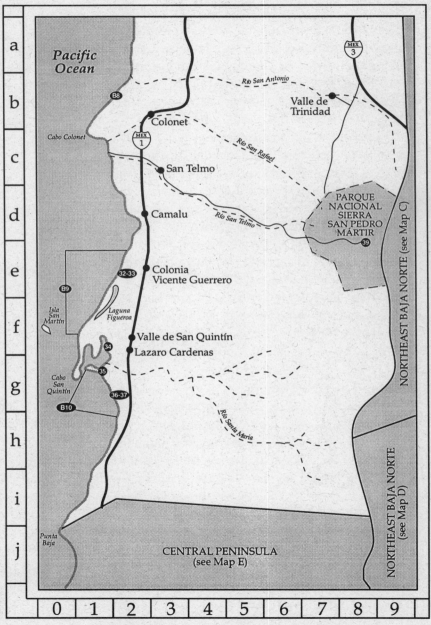

NORTHWEST BAJA NORTE

❃ ❃ ❃ ❃

The Pacific coast from the border to where Highway 1 turns inland toward El Rosario is very popular with tourists because of its proximity to the United States. It is very easy to throw some things in the rig on the spur of the moment and head south for a few days of relaxation and decompression from the hustle and bustle of life in Southern California.

People suffering from summer heat in inland areas can hole up on a cool southern beach and dunk themselves in the nippy Pacific Ocean, still carrying overtones of the frigid Arctic via the Japanese current. Accordingly, summer is the high season.

Fishing can be very good in the surf and even better offshore. Pismo clams lurk beneath the sand at low tide and the waters draw surfers and scuba divers. Forays can be made inland by agile vehicles to hot springs, mountain national parks, an observatory and other hideaways.

Those who prefer the urban scene can knock about in glitzy Tijuana and somewhat more sedate Ensenada. There is great opportunity for golfers. In short, there is something for everyone in Northwest Baja California Norte.

Getting Through Tijuana

The first thing you have to do is wend your way through Tijuana without getting off course. As you approach the border from the north you will see an overhead sign identifying the proper lane for pickups, trailers, vans and motor homes. Once through the border gate into México, stay in the right-hand lane going up the overpass ahead. You should be beneath the sign saying "Río Tijuana, Río Zone, Rosarito, Ensenada." The next signs over that lane say "Highway 1D Rosarito-Ensenada" as it swings left in a circle to deposit you along the south side of the border fence.

Drive carefully and don't let the local speeders rush you

along. Stay to the right as you climb a big hill so you can exit to the right after the road swings left and drops down into an arroyo. You will come onto a wider thoroughfare heading west up a steep grade. If you are towing anything behind you, maintain your momentum. Keep following signs to Rosarito-Ensenada. A left turn over the last hill puts you onto the *cuota* (toll) road. Current tolls are:

	Pesos	Dollars
Two-axle passenger cars, pickups and motorcycles	N$ 7	$ 2.35
Two-axle buses and trucks	N$14	$ 4.65
Three-axle buses and trucks	N$21	$ 7.00
Four-axle trucks	N$28	$ 9.35
Five-axle trucks	N$35	$11.65
Six-axle trucks	N$42	$14.00
Extra axles for passenger cars	N$ 4	$ 1.35
Extra axles for buses and trucks	N$ 7	$ 2.35

(dual rear wheels count as an extra axle)

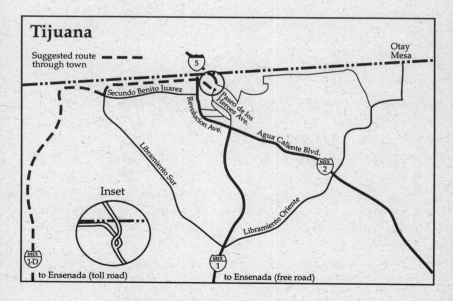

Rosarito-La Misión area
(campgrounds 1-11, pages 92-99)

This area is almost a suburb of Tijuana, but not quite, with less than 10 miles between them. For tourists it offers the first beach-town environment south of the border and is very popular.

Developers are building up this coast with hotels and condominiums. Still, you'll find quite a cluster of RV parks in and around Rosarito. Several in town have been around for many years and are mostly full of permanently dug-in trailers showing the debilitating effects of sitting for years in a salt-air environment. If you favor this area, look over your options before settling into one to be sure you have found the spot that suits you best. The high season here is summer.

Golf

Two highly regarded golf courses are nearby and a third is about 47 miles south at Bajamar.

The Tijuana Golf and Country Club is on Agua Caliente Boulevard, past the twin towers of the Grand Hotel Tijuana. Its 18-hole course is open from 7 a.m. to 8 p.m. seven days a week. Green fees on weekdays are $22 per person and on weekends $27. Phone 011-52-66-81-7855.

The Real del Mar Golf Club in San Antonio has 18 holes and green fees are $39 per person. Follow signs on the toll road, Highway 1D. Call 011-52-661-3-3406 for reservations. Tee times are taken 30 days in advance and a deposit is required. Starting times begin at 10 a.m. seven days a week.

The Bajamar Oceanfront Golf Resort about five miles south on Highway 1 has 18 holes and green fees are $40 per person Monday through Thursday and $60 Friday through Sunday. Phone 011-52-615-5-0151.

Shopping

In Tijuana, shopping can be both exciting and rewarding as a major event. Tijuana is no place to shop for day-to-day necessities, though. Do that in Rosarito.

The center of activity in Tijuana for buying traditional Mexican things is Avenida Revolución from Calle 1 to Calle 9, plus all the side streets and alleys. There are many, many shops offering everything you can imagine. The storekeepers are fairly aggressive about herding you into their places of business. That's fine—go on in and look around. Ask prices for those things that appeal to you. Feel the storekeeper out on what price he might accept, then go on your way and start comparing prices. You'll find identical items all along the street and will gradually get a good feel for what is a fair price for both of you. Don't be afraid to haggle. It's part of the enjoyment for everyone, seller and buyer alike. Keep a smile on your face and talk softly. Develop a rapport. Admire workmanship and quality. Politely make your offer. If you go too low, you may be considered insulting. Developing a feel for the "real" price is important.

Tijuana is a manufacturing center for leather and onyx items, wood work, metal fabrication and many other goods. Accordingly, you can buy these things cheaper than in other cities because there are no freight costs. We once bought some little onyx carvings near El Mármol, nearly 300 miles south of Tijuana. Since the onyx came from there, we thought it was the place to purchase the manufactured items. Then the lady told us they shipped the uncarved blocks to Tijuana and had the finished items shipped back. We'd have done better on Avenida Revolución.

Be careful of leather goods made from unfamiliar animal skins. If United States Customs officers suspect they are from endangered species, they may relieve you of the items for closer inspection and you may not see them again.

A more modern shopping area is Plaza Río Tijuana. Here you will find the large department stores and upscale shops. We have made several pre-Christmas forays here with shopping lists for everyone in the family and have come away feeling we saved a bundle. Many groups of people come across the border from the United States for a fun day here.

Be careful of the flea markets you encounter around Tijuana. Customs officials have found that many things sold in them, particularly electronic items like stereos and TVs, were heisted in the United States. Get receipts to show you did not purchase items at one of the flea markets that is "hot" at the moment.

Rosarito has some nice shops, particularly in the arcade at the Rosarito Beach Hotel. The free road south of Rosarito is lined with pottery shops and a few small pottery factories. Check out the prices in the factories—they're generally lower, as this is where the shops buy their products. We often stop on the way home from a Baja trip to add to our collection of Mexican pottery.

Sporting events

Bull fighting is a traditional Mexican performance. Every summer Sunday from May to September, there is a *corrida* in one or the other of Tijuana's two bull rings—the old Plaza de Toros downtown on Agua Caliente Boulevard or the newer ring by the beach against the border. Tickets can be obtained at the ring or the ticket office downtown from $15 to $46, depending on whether you want to sit in the afternoon sun *(sol)* or shade *(sombra)* and how far away from ringside you are. *Sombra* is definitely more comfortable. Reserve tickets by calling 011-52-66-85-2210.

Jai alai is never dull. The action can be riveting as the hard little ball flies around almost faster than the eye can see. The skill and agility of the players is astounding. You can bet on each match and the program tells you all about each player. In the evening, when you're tired of shopping on Avenida Revolución, simply walk up the street to Calle 7, go in the palatial building, sit down and watch the guys with the long basket on one hand do their work.

Horse and dog racing can be found at the Agua Caliente Racetrack—it's been around forever. Go east of downtown on Agua Caliente Boulevard; every map shows it as a landmark. Greyhounds race around during the week and horses on weekends.

Dining

If you have ever enjoyed a Caesar's salad, you might want to stop in at Caesar's Hotel on Avenida Revolución and Calle 4 for one. This is where it was invented, supposedly.

There are lots and lots of restaurants in Tijuana. We won't even try to sort them out. However, there is one we have considered special for decades that we highly recommend—the Coronet on Calle 7, off of Avenida Revolución. The quail entrée has brought us back again and again.

The village of Puerto Nuevo, south of Rosarito, specializes in lobster. If you're there for lunch or dinner, try one of the smaller restaurants where the atmosphere is more homey and the prices a bit lower. We like Nachos on Chinchorro, the second street on the left as you enter town.

At La Misión, we particularly enjoy dining at La Fonda on the outside patio overlooking the surf.

Sightseeing

The Tijuana Cultural Center in the Zona Río at Paseo de Los Heroes and Avenida Independencia has a museum and various shows in an Omnimax theater with a 180-degree wraparound screen on which special films are shown and a performing arts theater which offers changing performances. There is also a shopping arcade. Admission to Omnimax is $4.25. Admission to the theater depends on the performance. The Cultural Center is open from Monday to Friday from 11 a.m. to 7 p.m. and on weekends from 11 a.m. to 8 p.m. The phone number is 011-52-66-84-1111. If you get a chance to see "Los Voladores de Papantla," don't miss them. These men climb a tall pole, attach themselves to long ropes, then swing down to the ground in a breathtaking spiral.

Mexitlan on Calle 2 and Avenida Ocampo in Tijuana covers a city block with more than 150 scale models of México's pyramids, colonial churches and modern buildings. There are also shows featuring music and dances from different regions of México. After dark, there is exceptional illumination. Mexitlan is open daily, except Tuesday, from 10 a.m. to 8 p.m. and in summer from 10 a.m. to 10 p.m. There are extended hours on holidays and weekends.

Nightlife

There are several discos and nightclubs. Some that are well known are: Mike's Bar, on Revolución and Calle 6; Disco Regine and Disco Cosmos, together in the same building on Revolución and Calle 6; and 2001 Disco Club, at 3401-4 Agua Caliente Boulevard.

Ensenada area
(campgrounds 12-31, pages 99-113)

Ensenada is not quite a border town, but since it's only 68 miles south via the fast toll road, many people from Southern California flock to this area for weekends. Another popular route is from Tecate on Highway 3, which is only four miles farther from Tijuana than Ensenada is. Though it takes a half hour longer, this is a very pretty drive through mountains and valleys lush with vineyards, orchards and other agriculture. An exceptional benefit of re-entering the United States through Tecate instead of Tijuana is much lighter traffic and the ease of clearing customs. Be sure to arrive before midnight, as it closes down until 6 a.m.

Ensenada is the most convenient place to validate your Visitor Card (visa). On the way into town, you will go along the shipyards with huge *topes* (speed bumps) in the street. At the end of these, there is an arterial stop sign and a Pemex across the intersection. Just before the stop sign, look for a white

building on the right with a sign, "Secretaria de Gobierno—
Direccion General de Servicios Migratorios Delegacion."
Pickups can pull in to park, but longer rigs must find another
spot and walk back. Go on around the waterfront to the right
and find a parking place. Bring your visa, identification and
vehicle documents. The office is open from 8 a.m. to 8 p.m.
on weekdays and off and on during weekends between times
when the officer on duty has to go out to cruise ships. Phone
011-52-617-4-0164.

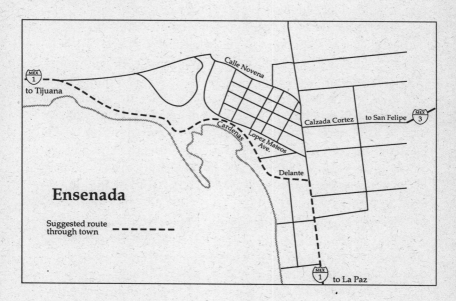

Fishing

Fishing can be good out of Ensenada off Islas de Todos
Santos and Punta Banda for albacore, barracuda, bonita, mackerel, kelp bass, lingcod and other rockfish. Ensenada has several
fleets that operate out of the sportfishing dock just east of the
fish market. Access and parking is very tight, as you have to
thread your way around and between buildings. Once past the
big speed bumps in front of the shipyards coming into
Ensenada, turn right at the arterial stop sign (a big Pemex gas
station is across the intersection). Go through the first light and

take the first possible street to the right (the Hotel Santo Tomás is across the street). Go a very short block toward the fish market and take the first possible left turn, which is in front of the fish market. Continue and take the first right turn, then head left to the sportfishing fleet offices on the waterfront. Passenger cars and pickups do much better than motor homes on this route. Look it over before committing yourself. It may be better to take a cab from wherever you are staying. If you are going to the fish market, after going the very short block toward it, take the first possible right turn and find a parking place.

Gordo's Sportfishing has five boats ranging from 36 feet (which can seat 12 people) to 70 feet (which can seat 35 people). They will go with seven to 10 people at the minimum. They provide life jackets and tackle if needed. Many fishermen bring their own gear. The boats leave the dock at 7 a.m. and return at 2:30 p.m. The cost is $35 per adult and half price for children. There is always live bait. It is best to purchase tickets at the office, for you can be cheated on the street. You must receive a printed ticket with a copy of the fishing license on the back. Contact them at Apartado Postal 35, Ensenada, Baja California, México; phone 011-52-617-8-2377 or 3515; fax 011-52-617-4-0481.

Ensenada Clipper Fleet has four boats from 46 feet to 85 feet. The price is $35 per person, which includes a life jacket, a license, a rod, a reel, hooks and sinkers for top fishing. Daily trips leave at 7 a.m. and return at 3 p.m. Contact them at 2630 East Beyer Boulevard, Suite 678, San Ysidro, CA 92143; phone 011-52-617-8-2185 in México.

Ensenada Sportfishing Charters can be contacted at 8030 La Mesa Boulevard, No. 136, La Mesa, CA 91941; phone 011-52-617-8-2185 in México.

Smaller boats can be engaged at the docks or at Punta Banda from independent sportfishing operators or *panga* fishermen who sometimes rent their boats and services as guides. Punta Banda is about 25 miles from Ensenada and takes about one hour driving time.

Golf

The entrance road to the Baja Country Club is two miles south on Highway 1 from the Estero Beach Hotel turnoff. On the left, there is a sign and two large pillars. Drive three miles east to the entrance, then around the golf course to the left to the clubhouse. Green fees are $25 per person, plus $19 for a cart for two people. Phone 011-52-617-3-0303.

Shopping

Ensenada is one of Baja's best places to shop and Avenida Lopez Mateos is the center of it. Just strolling down Lopez Mateos and window shopping is a delight. Bargaining is enjoyed by both shoppers and shopkeepers, provided it is kept light with a tinge of humor and respect for both the merchandise and the vendor. Don't be shy about bargaining—you can be certain there is no way you will purchase an article for less than its bottom price.

The Ensenada fish market is an interesting place to shop, dine or just look. The displays of fish are colorful and attractive. The food stalls have wonderful fish products. We particularly enjoy the deep-fried *vieja*. Follow directions to the sportfishing dock listed above.

Sightseeing

There is much to see and do in Ensenada. Pick up a complimentary copy of the *Baja Sun* newspaper and its special publication "Baja Visitor—Ensenada and the San Quintín Valley." It tells you what to do, where to shop, where to go, how to get there, where to eat and where to stay.

Try a winery tour at Bodegas Santo Tomas, México's oldest winery at 666 Avenida Miramar between Calle 6 and Calle 7 in Ensenada. Wine tasting and a tour costs $2. Tours are given at 11 a.m., 1 p.m. and 3 p.m. every day.

Be sure to drive out to Punta Banda and see La Bufadora, the Blowhole, spout its geyser of seawater up the cliff face.

Dining

One of our favorite restaurants is El Rey Sol at 1000 Avenida Lopez Mateos, a famous French restaurant since 1947. It is open from 10 a.m. to 10 p.m. and can be phoned at 011-52-617-8-1733.

Another good restaurant is KAIA on Avenida Moctezuma between Fourth and Fifth; phone 011-52-617-8-2238. It specializes in Basque cuisine and paella at its finest.

San Quintín area
(campgrounds 32-37, pages 113-118)

This portion of Northwest Baja Norte's Pacific Coast, while a bit farther south, is still in easy reach of Southern Californians. It is popular for long weekends and longer vacations. Many people have established residences here for temporary use. It is also a convenient overnight stop for those traveling down the peninsula or returning from there, since Ensenada is often a shopping stop when traveling in either direction.

Fishing

This is the pre-eminent activity that draws tourists to the area. Isla San Martín, Roca Ben and other high spots in the ocean off the mouth of Bahía San Quintín offer good enough fishing to draw the long-range boats from San Diego, even though it is a long and expensive boat ride. Now that fishermen can get out there easily with their own boats from the launch ramp at the Old Mill (Campground #36), or on an Old Mill boat, they can enjoy the same great fishing at a fraction of the cost, plus they can have the satisfaction of doing it on their own.

Offshore there are yellowtail, tuna and bonita and, on the high spots, ample lingcod and rockcod. Inshore behind the surf there are sand bass, corvina, halibut, perch and others which can also be taken in the surf from shore. In the bay, there are white sea bass, halibut and others. Bahía San Quintín also has large blue crabs, the same critter that is considered so delectable on the East Coast of the United States. Large Pismo clams inhabit the beaches.

The Old Mill takes up to four people on each of their boats and charges $160 a day for a *panga* ($192 for two fishing) to $280 a day for 25-foot fishing boats ($336 for two fishing). A guide and safety equipment are provided. Phone (800) 479-7962 or (619) 428-2779 in California; fax (619) 428-6269.

Boating

The Old Mill management will use their truck to launch and retrieve your boat if your tow vehicle will not handle the sandy access road and slick mud of the launch area. The "ramp" is slated to be paved with concrete soon and that will be a major improvement.

Keeping in the channel to the mouth of the bay requires local knowledge. Guides move or remove markers so as to protect their income. Inexperienced boaters have been known to spend the weekend stuck on the mud flats. It's cheap insurance to hire a guide to take you out if you cannot contrive to follow one of the Old Mill boats in the morning.

Hunting

Waterfowl hunters find brant goose hunting to be very good in the marshes at the north end of Bahía San Quintín in winter. Quail hunting on surrounding ranches can also be very good.

Surfing

Surfers favor the beaches on the Pacific Ocean to the west, south to the mouth of Bahía San Quintín and along Bahía Santa María.

Off-roading

Off-roaders find great enjoyment following wheel tracks on the peninsula between Bahía San Quintín and the Pacific Ocean. The volcanic cones that spread their lava and ash across this rugged land are prominent landmarks. There is much to see and many flat tires to fix when exploring here. Pristine campsites can be found on the remote Pacific shores for tent campers, vans or small truck campers.

Birdwatching

Bahía San Quintín is one of Baja's great estuaries for wintering migratory waterfowl. A growing group of dedicated birdwatchers, led by Pro Esteros, a Mexican conservation organization, is focusing their attention here to assure the future health of the estuarine system. Fish populations require it for breeding, as do many birds, plus others that must have it for winter grounds.

Sightseeing

A sidetrip can be taken to the ruins of Misión Santo Domingo de la Frontera, which was established by the Dominicans in 1775 at a site two miles downstream from where the ruins are now. It was moved in 1798 to obtain a more constant water supply. Aside from the usual cultivation of fruits, beans and grains, it obtained additional income from the sale of salt from San Quintín and sea otter pelts to Russian and United States traders. Epidemics that struck the Indians caused the mission to be abandoned in 1839.

Partial adobe brick walls of about five buildings are all that remains today. The drive in involves crossing the trickle of the Río Santo Domingo several times, which adds an adventurous note to the trip.

Drive on Highway 1 about 1.5 miles north of Colonia Vicente Guerrero. Take the signed turnoff 2.5 miles east to the Mission.

A longer junket can be taken to the Meling Ranch about 31 miles east of Highway 1 through San Telmo.

The Meling Ranch is an historic, operating cattle ranch, originally known as Rancho San José, that has developed facilities for tourists, including a pool. Pack trips by horse and mule can be arranged into the vastness of the Sierra San Pedro Mártir—a trip we have made. It was founded in 1910 by Harry and Ella Johnson, was destroyed in 1911 during the Mexican Revolution and then rebuilt. Gold from placer deposits at Socorro was an important source of income. One of the Johnson daughters, Alberta, married Salve Meling and they acquired the ranch in 1919.

The dusty dirt road turns off Highway 1 about 6.5 miles south of Colonet, or eight miles north of Camalu. Heavy vehicles should not be taken, as there are steep grades. We drove up once with our 20-foot Born Free camper, which has its own axle behind the truck to support its rear end. One of the ladies at the Meling Ranch looked at it in wonder and asked, "You drove that up here?" We didn't know how to respond. Another 25 miles over steeper grades gets you to the observatory high in the pine forest of the Sierra San Pedro Mártir National Park. We wisely decided not to tackle that with our heavy rig. The ranch can put you up for the night in a room. They serve great meals.

Mountain national parks area (campgrounds 38-39, pages 119-120)

Baja has two mountain national parks in which camping is allowed at undeveloped sites, both in Baja Norte. The northernmost, Parque Nacional Constitución de 1857, covers 28,000 acres in the Sierra de Juárez. Its main features are conifer forest and a lake, Laguna Hanson. The other is Parque Nacional Sierra San Pedro Mártir, covering 160,000 acres. Its main features are conifer forests, trout streams, the highest peak in Baja—El Picacho del Diablo at 10,154 feet in elevation—and the National Observatory.

1. ROSARITO KOA

Reference: **In San Antonio; map A, grid a1.**

Campsites, facilities: There are 40 campsites with water and electricity, but no sewer hookups. There are flush toilets, hot showers, laundry, a dump station and a small store. Don't drink the well water, which is mineralized. The park is secured with a night watchman from 9 p.m. to 6 a.m. Tent campers are welcome. Obtain limited supplies here and go to Rosarito for the rest.

Reservations, fees: Reservations are accepted. Fees are high— $17 per night. Long-term rates are $80 per week and $185 per month.

Who to contact: Rosarito KOA, Apartado Postal 2082, Tijuana, Baja California, México; 011-52-66-13-3305 at park or 011-52-66-84-4814 for answering service. U.S. address: P.O. Box 430513, San Ysidro, CA 92143.

Location: Take the San Antonio exit off the toll road about 7.5 miles south of the Tijuana toll gate. Cross over the toll road to the east and drive up a cobblestone driveway to the hillside site.

Comments: You might have guessed that the first campground you will encounter is a KOA. Though it is not up to their usual standards, it is comfortable and attractive. There are lots of small trees and the site slopes to the west so that each space has a distant ocean view. When asked what people do there, the manager said the permanents come to do nothing and most overnighters come in late evening to stay over before crossing the border the next day. There are many things to do, however, for those inclined to be active. Unfortunately, Tijuana is difficult to drive around, due to hectic traffic, unless you know where you are going. If you are towing anything, it isn't worth the aggravation. If you're RV-ing it, the best way to do Tijuana is from one of the parks in California's San Ysidro or Chula Vista. You can get to the border by taxi or the Tijuana Trolley, which runs frequently from San Diego. Walk across the border, then catch a cab.

Summer is the time to visit, as winter is chilly. For things to do in Tijuana and the surrounding area, please see page 80.

---

2. OASIS HOTEL AND RV RESORT

Reference: **North of Rosarito; map A, grid a1.**

Campsites, facilities: There are 55 pull-through campsites with full hookups, concrete pads and barbecues. There are flush toilets, hot showers, laundry, two pools, restaurants, a store, horses, a live-music bar, billiards, ping-pong, two Jacuzzis, mini-golf, a volleyball court, a gym, a sauna and a playground. Don't drink the water. The resort is secured with a guard gate. Obtain supplies in Rosarito.

Reservations, fees: Reservations are accepted. Fees are very high—$25 per night during the week in winter, $30 on weekdays in summer, $30 on weekends and holidays in winter, $33 on weekends and holidays in summer. Long-term rates are $157 per week, $540 per month and $1,350 for six months.

Who to contact: Oasis Hotel and RV Resort, P.O. Box 158, Imperial Beach, CA 91933; phone 011-52-661-3-3250, 3253 or 3255 in Rosarito or (800) 462-7472 in the United States; fax 011-52-661-3-3252.

Location: Drive about 10 miles south of the Tijuana toll gate. It is on the beach at Kilometer 25, off the toll road.

Comments: This is a first-class resort with everything you could want to do. They also offer transportation to Tijuana, Rosarito and Ensenada. If luxury is your camping style, you will be comfortable here. Summer is the time to visit, as winter is chilly. For things to do in Tijuana and the surrounding area, please see page 80.

---

3. COCO LOCO TRAILER PARK

Reference: **In Rosarito; map A, grid a1.**

Campsites, facilities: There are nine campsites with full hookups and concrete pads. There are no facilities, not even toilets or showers. The park is secured with a gated wall. The manager lives on the premises. Don't drink the water. Obtain supplies in Rosarito.

Reservations, fees: All sites are first come, first served. The fee is very high—$25 per night.

Who to contact: Phone the park at 011-52-661-2-2238. There is no available mailing address.

Location: Turn west off the main street of Rosarito at Quinta Plaza to the beach. This is one-quarter mile north of the big orange building. A prominent sign at the corner says "Restaurant Bar La Hacienda de Villa." Look for the trailer park sign one block toward the beach.

Comments: The location, right on Playa Rosarito, is choice and the park is clean. The price is high, however, given the lack of facilities. Summer is the time to visit, as winter is chilly. For things to do in the Rosarito area, please see page 80.

---

4. CHUY'S TRAILER PARK

Reference: **In Rosarito; map A, grid a1.**

Campsites, facilities: There are 26 campsites with full hookups and concrete pads. There are flush toilets, hot showers and a restaurant. Don't drink the water. The park is secured with a night guard. Obtain supplies in Rosarito.

Reservations, fees: Reservations are accepted. The fee is high—about $20 per night. Fees vary with the season.

Who to contact: Chuy's Trailer Park, Costa Ázul 75, Rosarito, Baja California, México; phone 011-52-661-2-1608.

Location: Turn west off the main street of Rosarito to the beach at Thrifty's, 100 yards north of the big orange building.

Comments: It is crowded and there is limited maneuvering room. Summer is the time to visit, as winter is chilly. For things to do in the Rosarito area, please see page 80.

---

5. PLAYA ENCANTADA #2

Reference: **South of Rosarito; map A, grid b1.**

Campsites, facilities: There are pit toilets, but no other facilities. There is no water. Security is with a resident manager.

Tent camping is welcome. Obtain supplies in Rosarito.

Reservations, fees: All sites are first come, first served. The fee is moderate—$8 per night.

Who to contact: Drive in and talk to the owner.

Location: It is at Kilometer 30 on the free road, about one mile south of Rosarito.

Comments: Park on level land on a bluff above a very nice little beach between two points of land. You can lay back here and enjoy the ocean just below, but you had better come fully prepared for primitive camping as the facilities are limited. Summer is the time to visit, as winter is chilly. For things to do in the Rosarito area, please see page 80.

---

6.   COSTA DEL SOL

Reference: **South of Rosarito; map A, grid b1.**

Campsites, facilities: There are three campsites with full hook-ups and concrete pads. There are flush toilets, hot showers and a recreation hall. Don't drink the water. The park is secured with a fence. There is a night guard. Obtain supplies in Rosarito.

Reservations, fees: Reservations are accepted. Fees are moderate—$12 per night. Long-term rates are $85 per week and $202 per month.

Who to contact: Costa del Sol, P.O. Box 430852, San Ysidro, CA 92143; phone 011-52-661-2-0552.

Location: It is at Kilometer 30 on the free road, about one mile south of Rosarito.

Comments: Prepare to barbecue. This is mainly a trailer court for residents. Camping here is much like stumbling into suburbia. Summer is the time to visit, as winter is chilly. For things to do in the Rosarito area, please see page 80.

---

7.   POPOTLA TRAILER PARK

Reference: **South of Rosarito; map A, grid b1.**

Campsites, facilities: There are 33 campsites with full hookups and concrete pads. There are flush toilets and hot showers in clean, tiled restrooms, a pool and a restaurant. Don't drink the water. The park is secured with a guard gate. Obtain supplies in Rosarito.

Reservations, fees: Reservations are accepted. Fees are high—$14 per night. Long-term rates are $84 per week and $300 per month.

Who to contact: Popotla Trailer Park, Kilometro 33 Carretara Ensenada, Rosarito, Baja California, México; phone 011-52-661-2-1502; fax 011-52-661-2-1501.

Location: It is at Kilometer 33 on the free road, about three miles south of Rosarito.

Comments: This is primarily a residential park. The overnight spaces are in a separate area on the ocean with a little beach, which creates a pleasant setting. Summer is the time to visit, as winter is chilly. For things to do in the Rosarito area, please see page 80.

8.　　ALISITOS TRAILER PARK

Reference: **In La Misión; map A, grid c1.**

Campsites, facilities: There are pit toilets, but no other facilities. There is no water. The manager lives on the premises, so security is good. Tent camping is welcome. Obtain supplies in Rosarito.

Reservations, fees: All sites are first come, first served. The fee is low—$3.50 per night.

Who to contact: Drive in and talk to the owner.

Location: It is at Kilometer 59 on the free road, just north of the Hotel La Misión.

Comments: This is primitive camping on a flat area above a nice beach. The ocean is right below, creating a pleasant ambience. Summer is the time to visit, as winter is chilly. For things to do in the Rosarito area, please see page 80.

9.　　MAL PASO TRAILER PARK

Reference: **South of La Misión; map A, grid d1.**

Campsites, facilities: There are flush toilets in poor condition and cold showers. Don't drink the water. The owners live at the entrance of the compound, so security is good. It is made for tent camping. Obtain supplies in Rosarito.

Reservations, fees: All sites are first come, first served. The fee is low—$4 per night.

Who to contact: Drive in and talk to the owner.

Location: Drive 2.5 miles south of La Misión on the toll road. Cross the big creek bottom and the low ridge, then look for palms, trailers and cabins to the right of a pedestrian overpass. Slow down and turn off on a dirt road into the RV park at Kilometer 71, just before the overpass.

Comments: This is one of the few places where you can camp right on the beach—and a marvelous beach it is. They have hauled in soil on top of the sand to allow driving out to the high-tide line. The beach extends a short distance north and a long, long distance south. We spent a very enjoyable night here. Summer is the time to visit, as winter is chilly. For things to do in the La Misión area, please see page 80.

10.   OUTDOOR RESORTS OF BAJA

Reference: **South of La Misión; map A, grid d1.**

Campsites, facilities: There are 137 campsites with full hookups, including satellite TV and concrete pads. There are clean, tiled restrooms with flush toilets, hot showers, steam rooms and saunas, laundry, a pool and spa, a restaurant and bar, a store, a clubhouse, a recreation room, a game room, a reading room, two night-lighted tennis courts, a volleyball court, a horseshoe pit, horses and miniature golf. They can provide storage, safe-deposit boxes and transportation to Ensenada. The well water is brackish. Obtain purified water in the restaurant. There is a fence around the park, a guarded gate and 24-hour security inside. Obtain supplies at the park store.

Reservations, fees: Reservations are accepted. Fees are very high. Oceanfront sites are $30 per night and $150 per week in winter, $35 per night and $210 per week in summer.

Campsites inside the park are $24 per night and $120 per week in winter, $30 per night and $180 per week in summer. Long-term rates are available. There is an extra charge of $1 per night and $6 per week for pets.

Who to contact: Outdoor Resorts of Baja, 1177 Broadway, Suite #2, Chula Vista, CA 91911; phone (619) 422-2864; in California, phone (800) 982-BAJA; from elsewhere in the United States, phone (800) 356-BAJA.

Location: It is about three miles south of La Misión, at Kilometer 72 on the toll road. You can't miss it on the right on a long unobstructed stretch of highway. You will see the second pedestrian overpass 100 yards before the exit (the first one was back at Mal Paso Trailer Park). A big, high sign reads "Season's Restaurant & Cantina." A lower sign at ground level, partly hidden by plants, reads "Outdoor Resorts of America, Inc.—Baja Ensenada RV Resort & Beach Club."

Comments: This is a first-class resort on a long, long beautiful beach with all the amenities. We spent a night, just to experience the posh way of camping. Summer is the time to visit, as winter is chilly. For things to do in the La Misión area, please see page 80.

---

11. EJIDO RV PARK

Reference: **South of La Misión; map A, grid d1.**

Campsites, facilities: Once-functional restrooms are no longer useable. There is no water or security. Tent camping is welcome. Obtain supplies in El Sauzal.

Reservations, fees: All sites are first come, first served. The fee is low—$5 per night.

Who to contact: Drive in and talk to the manager at the little store alongside the highway.

Location: It is about five miles south of La Misión at Kilometer 75 on the toll road. Look for the sign and turn off. The "park" is downhill on the flat ground.

Comments: This is primitive camping in a field above the ocean, set among houses. There is nothing to attract anyone.

It is a desperation spot. Summer is the time to visit, as winter is chilly. For things to do in the La Misión area, please see page 80.

12. PLAYA SALDAMANDO

Reference: **North of Ensenada; map A, grid e1.**

Campsites, facilities: There are 100 campsites, none with hookups. The water is not potable—bring your own. There are toilets, cold showers and a dump station. Tent campers are welcome. There are two resident watchmen. Obtain supplies in El Sauzal.

Reservations, fees: All sites are first come, first served. The fee is low—$6 per night.

Location: It is reached by a one-half mile long, steep dirt road off the southbound side of the Tijuana-Ensenada toll road, about 10 miles north of Ensenada. The exit is marked by a sign. Heading south, start watching for the sign after passing the El Mirador viewpoint on the right side of the toll road.

Comments: Surfers, divers and fishermen come here. There is a rather sharp turn off the toll road onto the dirt road which must be taken slowly. The dirt road descends the precipitous slope of the mountainside. Small motor homes make it, but trailers and larger motor homes are not recommended. Summer is the time to visit, as winter is chilly. For things to do in the Ensenada area, please see page 84.

13. RANCHO SORDO MUDO

Reference: **North of El Sauzal on Tecate Highway 3; map A, grid d3.**

Campsites, facilities: There are 31 campsites, of which 20 are pull-throughs, 11 have full hookups and 20 have electricity and water. There are flush toilets, hot showers and laundry. The water is safe to drink. The isolated location affords security. Tent camping is welcome. Obtain supplies in Guadalupe.

Reservations, fees: Reservations are accepted. The fee is moderate—$12 per night.

Who to contact: Rancho Sordo Mudo, P.O. Box 1376, Chula Vista, CA 91912. There is no phone.

Location: It is about 19 miles north of El Sauzal at Kilometer 75 in the Guadalupe Valley, near the Domecq Winery.

Comments: This owners of this campground also run a school for deaf children to which all camping fees are donated. Staying here, you are within walking distance of the Domecq Winery. Tours of the winery are available only by prior arrangement through the operators of the campground. Summer is the preferred time to visit. For other things to do in the Ensenada area, please see page 84.

---

14. PANCHO'S RV PARK

Reference: **North of El Sauzal on Tecate Highway 3; map A, grid e2.**

Campsites, facilities: There are 20 pull-through campsites with full hookups. There are flush toilets, hot showers and a restaurant. Don't drink the water. There is no security. Obtain supplies in El Sauzal.

Reservations, fees: All sites are first come, first served. The fee is low—$5 per night.

Who to contact: Drive in and talk to the owner.

Location: From Ensenada, drive six miles north on Highway 1, then nine miles north on Tecate Highway 3. The camp is at Kilometer 93.

Comments: The park is shaded under large oak trees. It is a pleasant enough place to stay, but it is not a destination spot. Summer is the preferred time to visit. For things to do in the Ensenada area, please see page 84.

---

15. SAN MIGUEL VILLAGE

Reference: **In El Sauzal; map A, grid e1.**

Campsites, facilities: There are 100 campsites for tents and 30 sites for RVs with full hookups. There are flush toilets, hot showers, a dump station, a restaurant, a bar and a gift shop.

Don't drink the water. The manager lives on the premises, so it is secure. Obtain supplies in El Sauzal.

Reservations, fees: Reservations are accepted. Fees are moderate—$8 for tent camping, $10 for full hookup per night.

Who to contact: San Miguel Village, Apartado Postal 55, El Sauzal, Baja California, México; phone 011-52-617-4-6225.

Location: From the southern toll booth on the Tijuana-Ensenada toll road, it is one-half mile south on Highway 1D. From Ensenada, drive seven miles north on Highway 1.

Comments: The site is on a plateau above a rocky beach. The price is right and it is reasonably close to Ensenada. Summer is the best time to visit, as winter can get cold. For things to do in the Ensenada area, please see page 84.

---

16. CALIFORNIA TRAILER PARK AND MOTEL

Reference: **In El Sauzal; map A, grid f1.**

Campsites, facilities: There are 45 campsites with full hookups, some with concrete pads. There are flush toilets, hot showers and laundry. Don't drink the water. The park is secured with a gate. Obtain supplies in El Sauzal.

Reservations, fees: Reservations are accepted. Fees are moderate—$10 per night. Long-term rates are $150 per month.

Who to contact: California Trailer Park and Motel, Apartado Postal 262, Ensenada, Baja California, México; phone 011-52-617-4-6033.

Location: It is on the ocean side of Highway 1D just north of the Pemex plant. From Ensenada, drive six miles north on Highway 1.

Comments: There is an old, rundown RV place next door to the north under the same name and ownership. Don't confuse it with the nice new RV facilities within the motel compound. Summer is the preferred time to visit. For things to do in the Ensenada area, please see page 84.

17. RAMONA BEACH RV PARK & MOTEL

Reference: **In El Sauzal; map A, grid f1.**

Campsites, facilities: There are 50 pull-through campsites with full hookups and concrete pads. There are flush toilets, hot showers, a pool and a store. Don't drink the water. There is no security. Tent camping is welcome. Obtain supplies in El Sauzal.

Reservations, fees: Reservations are accepted. Fees are moderate—$8 per night. Long-term rates are $145 per month.

Who to contact: Ramona Beach RV Park and Motel, Apartado Postal 513, Ensenada, Baja California, México; phone 011-52-617-4-6045.

Location: It is on the ocean side of Highway 1D directly across from the Pemex plant. From Ensenada, drive six miles north on Highway 1.

Comments: Camping is on an unattractive site, a big, level area on the north side of the motel and store. The price is right, however, and it is fairly close to Ensenada. Summer is the preferred time to visit. For things to do in the Ensenada area, please see page 84.

18. KING'S CORONITA TRAILER PARK

Reference: **On the north side of Ensenada; map A, grid f1.**

Campsites, facilities: There are five pull-through campsites with full hookups and concrete pads. There are flush toilets and hot showers. Don't drink the water. The park is secured with a locked gate. You must ask the manager, who lives next to it, to unlock it for you. Obtain supplies in Ensenada.

Reservations, fees: Reservations are accepted. The fee is moderate—$10 per night.

Who to contact: King's Coronita Trailer Park, Apartado Postal 133, Ensenada, Baja California, México; phone 011-52-617-4-4540.

Location: It is on the ocean side of Highway 1D, just before the turn to the right into Ensenada around the waterfront. Watch for the sign south of the overpass to CICESE.

Comments: This park is occupied by permanents mainly and has a residential atmosphere. Summer is the preferred time to visit. For things to do in the Ensenada area, please see page 84.

---

19. CAMPO PLAYA RV PARK

Reference: **In Ensenada; map A, grid f1.**

Campsites, facilities: There are 90 pull-through campsites with full hookups and concrete pads. Note: The water is turned off from 2 p.m. to 11 p.m. There are clean, tiled restrooms with flush toilets and hot showers. Don't drink the water. It is fenced, but people can wander through. Tent camping is welcome. Any supplies you may need are nearby.

Reservations, fees: Reservations are accepted. The fee is high—$16 per night. Long-term rates are $98 per week and $200 per month.

Who to contact: Campo Playa RV Park, Apartado Postal 789, Ensenada, Baja California, México; phone 011-52-617-6-2918.

Location: It is on the corner of Las Dunas and Delante, which is across from the waterfront, a few blocks west of the Gigante Supermarket where Highway 1 takes a sharp right turn to the south. Street names in this area are hard to find and mapmakers disagree on what they are called. As you go through Ensenada, past the statue of the "three heads" in the Civic Plaza, keep looking to the left for Campo Playa. You can't miss it—really.

Comments: This is the best place to stay for fishing, dining and sightseeing in Ensenada. If you don't want to unhook and drive, you can call a cab. Restaurants are within walking distance, as is the Gigante Supermarket. The prominent, nearby 12-foot-high busts that people call "the three heads" are of the Mexican heroes Juárez, Carranza and Hidalgo. Summer is the preferred time to visit. For things to do in the Ensenada area, please see page 84.

20.   JOKER HOTEL, RV PARK & RESTAURANT

Reference: **In Ensenada; map A, grid g1.**

Campsites, facilities: There are 12 campsites with full hook-ups, including television. There are flush toilets, hot showers, a pool and a restaurant. The water is not drinkable. The park is secured with a guard. Obtain supplies in Ensenada.

Reservations, fee: Reservations are accepted. The fee is low—$5 per night.

Who to contact: Joker RV Park, Highway 1, Kilometer 12.5, Ensenada, Baja California, México. There is no phone.

Location: Take Highway 1 into the south side of Ensenada. It is south of the military base on the east side of Highway 1.

Comments: The campsites are narrow, short and difficult to get into. They are suitable only for vehicles under 23 feet without trailers. Summer is the best time to visit. For things to do in the Ensenada area, please see page 84.

21.   CORONA BEACH TRAILER PARK

Reference: **South of Ensenada; map A, grid f1.**

Campsites, facilities: There are 60 pull-through campsites with electricity and water. There are flush toilets, cold showers and a recreation hall. Don't drink the water. The park is secured with a fence. The owner lives on the premises. Tent camping is welcome. Obtain supplies at shops along Highway 1.

Reservations, fees: Reservations are accepted. The fees are moderate—$10 per night. Long-term rates are $260 per month.

Who to contact: Corona Beach Trailer Park, Apartado Postal 1149, Ensenada, Baja California, México. There is no phone.

Location: Take the Estero Beach Hotel turnoff from Highway 1 about 4.5 miles south of Ensenada. Go west on the paved street toward the beach, then turn right on the first paved road. When it turns to dirt, look north for a yellow water tower with "Corona Beach" painted on it.

Comments: This is a large, flat site on the beach of Bahía de Todos Santos, which normally has a very mild surf. It is a nice place to camp. Horses can be rented for rides on the beach; the going rate is $10 an hour. Try a gallop in the surf—it's fun! Summer is the preferred time to visit. For other things to do in the Ensenada area, please see page 84.

---

22. MONA LISA RV PARK

Reference: **South of Ensenada; map A, grid f1.**

Campsites, facilities: There are 17 campsites with full hookups and concrete pads. There are clean, tiled restrooms with flush toilets and hot showers, a restaurant, a curio store and horse rentals. Don't drink the water. The park is secured with a fence and the owner lives on the premises. Obtain supplies at shops along Highway 1.

Reservations, fees: Reservations are accepted. The fees are high—$17.50 per night. Long-term rates are $65 per week and $225 per month.

Who to contact: Mona Lisa RV Park, Apartado Postal 607, Ensenada, Baja California, México. There is no phone.

Location: Take the Estero Beach Hotel turnoff from Highway 1 about 4.5 miles south of Ensenada. Go west on the paved street toward the beach, then turn right on the first paved road. When that turns to dirt, you'll see the Mona Lisa sign to the left on the beach.

Comments: This is a very nice, neat, small compound with a homey atmosphere. It is required that you arrive with holding tanks empty, so as not to overload their septic system. The owner will turn you away if he suspects you are packing a full load. Visit in summer, since the winter can get cold. For things to do in the Ensenada area, please see page 84.

23. EL FARO BEACH MOTEL AND TRAILER PARK

Reference: **South of Ensenada; map A, grid f1.**

Campsites, facilities: There are 20 campsites with electricity and water on the beach, below the restaurant, and many more behind the sea wall to the right with no hookups. There are flush toilets, cold showers, a restaurant in the summer and a dump station. Don't drink the water—it is out of a cistern. The park is secured with a fence. Tent campers are welcome. Obtain supplies at shops along Highway 1.

Reservations, fees: Reservations are accepted. The fee is low— $8 per night.

Who to contact: El Faro Beach Motel and Trailer Park, Apartado Postal 1008, Ensenada, Baja California, México. There is no phone.

Location: Take the Estero Beach Hotel turnoff from Highway 1 about 4.5 miles south of Ensenada. Go west on the paved street toward the beach and continue west when it turns to dirt. You will see El Faro.

Comments: As this is a crowded place, it can get noisy. It is right on the beach, however, and we spent a very pleasant night there. Horses can be rented for rides on the beach; the going rate is $10 an hour. Try it. Summer is the preferred time to visit. For things to do in the Ensenada area, please see page 84.

24. ESTERO BEACH HOTEL AND RV PARK

Reference: **South of Ensenada; map A, grid f1.**

Campsites, facilities: There are 60 campsites with full hookups, plus an overflow area. The restrooms are clean, with flush toilets and hot showers. There is a restaurant, a launch ramp into the estero, a beach club with sailing, windsurfing, jetskiing, waterskiing and snorkeling, tennis courts, horses, bicycles, volleyball courts, a recreation center with billiards, ping-pong and games, a children's playground and shops.

Don't drink the water. The park is secured with a guard gate. Obtain supplies at shops along Highway 1.

Reservations, fees: Reservations are accepted. The fee is high—$18 per night.

Who to contact: Estero Beach Hotel and RV Park, Apartado Postal 86, Ensenada, Baja California, México; phone 011-52-617-6-6230, 6235 or 6225; fax 011-52-617-6-6925.

Location: Take the Estero Beach Hotel turnoff from Highway 1 about 4.5 miles south of Ensenada. Go west on the paved street and follow signs to the office to register. The RV park is on the bay a little farther on.

Comments: This is a full-fledged resort with all the amenities. The RV park has many shade trees and is on the edge of the estero with a wide variety of aquatic bird life, including loons, grebes, pelicans, cormorants, herons, egrets, hawks and coots. Estero Punta Banda is about 4.5 miles long and shaped somewhat like a dumbbell, with the north end about one mile wide and the south end about two miles wide. Punta Estero separates the estero from Bahía Todos Santos. There is a one-half mile gap between the north end of Punta Estero and the point of land housing the Estero Beach Hotel. This gap has a shallow bar beneath it which creates breakers at low tide and during storms. The resort rents equipment for all manner of water sports—you can get lessons if you want. Sailboarding is one of the more popular pursuits in the estero. In awe, we watched an elderly couple adroitly mount their individual boards at the ramp and sail off together with great aplomb. Fishermen launch their trailer boats here and brave the entrance sand bar for offshore fishing around Islas de Todos Santos—but they are careful to cross it at high tide each way. It can be dangerous, as friends of ours learned when bounced on the bottom between large swells. Summer is the best time to visit. For things to do in the Ensenada area, please see page 84.

25.   LA JOLLA BEACH CAMP

Reference: **In Punta Banda; map A, grid gØ.**

Campsites, facilities: There is plenty of room to camp on the beach without hookups in front of the permanent residences. There are flush toilets, hot showers, a restaurant, a dump station, a launch ramp and horse rentals. Don't drink the water. The park is secured with a guard gate. Tent camping is welcome. Obtain supplies in Punta Banda.

Reservations, fees: All sites are first come, first served. Fees are low—$6 per night for two people. Long-term rates are $140 per month.

Who to contact: Drive in and talk to the owner.

Location: Heading from Maneadero on the paved road to La Bufadora, drive eight miles. It is on the beach of Bahía Todos Santos at Kilometer 12.5.

Comments: On holidays, this park is jammed with tourists. It's a large place with lots of activity at any time of year. Small boats can be launched into the surf of Bahía de Todos Santos for fishing and diving around the Punta Banda peninsula. If you don't have your own boat, you can arrange to fish or scuba dive with Jessie and Sons for $20 per person. They're located one mile west of La Jolla Beach Camp on the paved road. La Bufadora Dive is located at La Bufadora. They charge $20 per person for a half-day, two-tank dive and $3 for an air fill. Contact Dale Erwin, Apartado Postal 102, Maneadero, Baja California, México. On the south side of the peninsula, you should visit La Bufadora or The Blowhole. Park in the cluster of curio shops at the end of the road and walk 100 yards to the viewing area. Every wave forces water into a narrow slot and upward onto the face of the cliff with a resounding boom. Summer is the best time to visit. For other things to do in the Ensenada area, please see page 84.

---

26.   VILLARINO RV PARK

Reference: **In Punta Banda; map A, grid gØ.**

Campsites, facilities: There are 35 campsites with full hookups. There are flush toilets, hot showers, a restaurant, a full-service store, boat rentals, tables, fire rings, grills, a playground, a volleyball court, a horseshoe pit, motorbike and hiking trails, horses and a launch ramp. Don't drink the water. The park is secured with a guard gate. Tent campers are welcome. Obtain supplies in Punta Banda.

Reservations, fees: Reservations are accepted. Fees are moderate—$5 per night per person. Discounts of 25- to 40-percent off per week are available, depending on the number of people camping. Long-term rates are $240 per month.

Who to contact: Villarino RV Park, Apartado Postal 842, Ensenada, Baja California, México; phone 011-52-617-6-4246; fax 011-52-617-6-1309.

Location: Heading from Maneadero on the paved road to La Bufadora, drive eight miles. It is on the beach of Bahía Todos Santos at Kilometer 12.5. It is next door to La Jolla Beach Camp.

Comments: There is a tree on each space. The place is well kept and is generally not as crowded as La Jolla Beach Camp. Summer is the best time to visit. For things to do in the Ensenada area, please see page 84 and for things to do on the Punta Banda peninsula, see Campground #25, La Jolla Beach Camp.

---

27.   EJIDO CAMPO #5

Reference: **West of Punta Banda; map A, grid gØ.**

Campsites, facilities: This is a primitive camping area with no facilities or security. There is no water available. Obtain supplies in Punta Banda.

Reservations, fees: All sites are first come, first served. Fees are very low.

Who to contact: Drive in to the entrance station.

Location: From Punta Banda, drive about 1.5 miles west on the paved road to La Bufadora.

Comments: The paved road to Punta Banda has climbed high on the intervening ridge and the dirt road down the mountainside to this primitive campground close to the ocean is very steep. Tent campers in small vehicles find the camping quite pleasant, but most drivers of larger rigs would not risk the hazard of getting here. Summer is the best time to visit. For things to do in the Ensenada area, please see page 84 and for things to do on the Punta Banda peninsula, see Campground #25, La Jolla Beach Camp.

---

28.   EJIDO CAMPO #7

Reference: **West of Punta Banda; map A, grid gØ.**

Campsites, facilities: This is a primitive camping area with no facilities or security. There is no water available. Obtain supplies in Punta Banda.

Reservations, fees: All sites are first come, first served. Fees are very low.

Who to contact: Drive in to the entrance station.

Location: From Punta Banda, drive about three miles west on the paved road to La Bufadora.

Comments: The paved road to Punta Banda has climbed high on the intervening ridge and the dirt road down the mountainside to this primitive campground close to the ocean is very steep. Tent campers in small vehicles find the camping quite pleasant, but most drivers of larger rigs would not risk the hazard of getting here. Summer is the best time to visit. For things to do in the Ensenada area, please see page 84 and for things to do on the Punta Banda peninsula, see Campground #25, La Jolla Beach Camp.

29. EJIDO CAMPO #8

Reference: **West of Punta Banda; map A, grid gØ.**

Campsites, facilities: This is a primitive camping area with no facilities or security. There is no water available. Obtain supplies in Punta Banda.

Reservations, fees: All sites are first come, first served. Fees are very low.

Who to contact: Drive in to the entrance station.

Location: From Punta Banda, drive about 4.5 miles west on the paved road to La Bufadora.

Comments: The paved road to Punta Banda has climbed high on the intervening ridge and the dirt road down the mountainside to this primitive campground close to the ocean is very steep. Tent campers in small vehicles find the camping quite pleasant, but most drivers of larger rigs would not risk the hazard of getting here. Summer is the best time to visit. For things to do in the Ensenada area, please see page 84 and for things to do on the Punta Banda peninsula, see Campground #25, La Jolla Beach Camp.

30. EL PALOMAR RV PARK

Reference: **In Santo Tomás; map A, grid i2.**

Campsites, facilities: There are 23 campsites, of which six are pull-throughs. Fifteen sites have full hookups and eight have electricity and water. There are rustic restrooms with flush toilets and hot showers, two pools, a restaurant, a curio store, barbecue pits, an area for off-road motorbikes, satellite TV, a gas station and hunting and fishing guides. Don't drink the water. The park is secured with a chain across the entrance road. Tent campers are welcome. Obtain supplies in Maneadero.

Reservations, fees: Reservations are accepted. Fees are moderate—$10 per night. Long-term rates are $150 per month.

Who to contact: El Palomar RV Park, Apartado Postal 595,

Ensenada, Baja California, México; phone 011-52-617-5-4011.

Location: From Maneadero, drive 18.5 miles south on Highway 1. The office is on the south side of the highway, while the actual campground is on the north side.

Comments: This park is set in a weekend recreation area for people from Ensenada who come for picnics, swimming and other activities. Quail hunters come to hunt on ranches up the valley of the Río Santo Tomás and fishermen come to angle in the ocean down the valley. At the north end of the olive grove below the highway, there is a small pile of melted adobe marking the last remains of the Misión de Santo Tomás de Aquino, which was built by the Dominicans in 1794. A note of warning: The entrance road down into the RV park is steep, which can be difficult coming up when you must look out for trucks and buses whizzing by on Highway 1. We had to go into four-wheel drive once to slowly crawl out into traffic with our 10,000-pound boat dragging behind us. Summer is the preferred time to visit. For things to do in the Ensenada area, please see page 84.

---

31. PUERTO SAN YSIDRO CAMPGROUND

Reference: **In Puerto San Ysidro; map A, grid jØ.**

Campsites, facilities: There are no developed facilities. Obtain supplies in Eréndira or San Vicente.

Reservations, fees: All sites are first come, first served. The fee is low—$3 per night.

Who to contact: Drive in and talk to the owner.

Location: Head seven miles north of San Vicente on Highway one, then 13 miles west. The campground is an unnamed spot on the bluff above the ocean, past Ejido Eréndira, then one-half mile beyond Castro's Camp where camping is allowed.

Comments: This is primitive camping on a bluff above the ocean. There is nothing you could call an amenity and very little space. It's a good place to use your camping equipment at very low cost. An alternative is to rent a cabin at Castro's

Camp. Kelp and bottom fishing is the big draw here. You can arrange for a panga for $25 per person at Castro's Camp. Summer is the preferred time to visit. For things to do in the Ensenada area, please see page 84.

32. MESÓN DON PEPE RV PARK AND RESTAURANT

Reference: **South of Colonia Vicente Guerrero; map B, grid e2.**

Campsites, facilities: There are 50 pull-through campsites with full hookups and concrete pads. There are simple, clean restrooms with flush toilets and hot showers and a restaurant. The water is safe to drink. There is no formal security, but there are no real problems. Tents are welcome. Supplies of all sorts can be found in San Quintín.

Reservations, fees: Reservations are accepted. Fees are low— tents are $3.50 per night, vans and campers are $6 and motor homes are $7.50. Long-term discounts of 10-percent off per week, 25-percent off per month and 40-percent off per year are available.

Who to contact: Mesón Don Pepe RV Park, Apartado Postal 7, Colonia Vicente Guerrero, Baja California, México; phone 011-52-616-6-2216.

Location: Head one mile south of Colonia Vicente Guerrero on Highway 1. Watch for the park's sign before the crest of the hill, north of the propane plant.

Comments: This is a regular stop for us when traveling to or from Guerrero Negro. The restaurant is dependably good. We are particularly fond of the fried rabbit. Anglers and surfers use nearby Playa San Ramon, which is 2.5 miles west of the campground on a sandy road. Fishing can be good for perch and corbina. In and around San Quintín there is a large agricultural community dedicated to growing tomatoes, most of which are shipped north to the United States. Summer is the best time to visit. For things to do in the San Quintín area, please see page 88.

33. POSADA DON DIEGO RV PARK, RESTAURANT AND BAR

Reference: **South of Colonia Vicente Guerrero; map B, grid e2.**

Campsites, facilities: There are 100 campsites, all with concrete pads, of which 40 have full hookups and 60 electricity and water. There are 15 pull-throughs. Restrooms suffer from a lack of maintenance, but they have flush toilets and hot showers. There are fire rings, tables, laundry, a restaurant, a bar, a dump station, a volleyball court and a horseshoe pit. The water is brackish from a well—don't drink it or cook with it. The owners live on the premises, so there are no problems with security. Tents are welcome. Obtain supplies in San Quintín.

Reservations, fees: Reservations are accepted. Fees are moderate—$9 per night. There is a 10-percent discount per week. Long-term rates are $160 per month.

Who to contact: Posada Don Diego RV Park, Apartado Postal 126, Colonia Vicente Guerrero, Baja California, México; phone 011-52-616-6-2181.

Location: Head one mile south of Colonia Vicente Guerrero on Highway 1. Watch for the sign on the crest of the hill, on the north side of the propane plant. It is one-half mile west, past Don Pepe's RV Park, on a dirt road.

Comments: The park covers a good deal of ground with big spaces and lots of room for large groups. We have stayed here many times when traveling south with groups of Vagabundos. Summer is the preferred time to visit. For information about nearby Playa San Ramon, see Campground #32, Mesón Don Pepe RV Park. For things to do in the San Quintín area, please see page 88.

34. THE OLD MILL MOTEL, RV PARK, RESTAURANT AND BAR

Reference: **South of San Quintín; map B, grid f1.**

Campsites, facilities: There are five pull-through spaces and 15 others, all with full hookups and concrete pads. There is also an overflow area with no hookups. The restrooms are clean and tiled, with flush toilets and hot showers. There are fire rings, grills, a restaurant, a bar, a small store, a launch ramp (no fee), a horseshoe pit and a volleyball court. They rent boats with guides. Don't drink the water in the RV park. The water served in the restaurant is pure, however. The manager lives on the premises, so there are no problems with security. Tents are welcome. San Quintín is the place for provisions.

Reservations, fees: Reservations are accepted. Fees are high— $10 per night for tents and $15 for RVs.

Who to contact: Phone (800) 479-7962 in California or (619) 428-2779; fax (619) 428-6269. There is no available mailing address.

Location: At the sign about 2.5 miles south of the military camp south of San Quintín, turn off Highway 1 and follow the signs 3.5 miles west on a graded dirt road to the shore of Bahía San Quintín.

Comments: This really is an old grist mill, left from a failed English farming attempt in the late 1800s. In front of the park, the embankment of an old railroad trestle narrows the tide through a raceway going into the upper bay. For decades, there were camping facilities known as Molino Viejo here, under different management. The park has been upgraded and expanded with first-class construction, making this a popular destination, particularly in summer. One major improvement: The owners have realigned and graded the access road. Hauling in big offshore boats like ours used to be a chore. Now it's a snap. The restaurant is excellent, but be forewarned: It serves big portions at big prices. The redone old mill that houses the restaurant and bar is very attractive.

Summer is the best time to visit. For things to do in the San Quintín area, please see page 88.

---

35.   CIELITO LINDO MOTEL AND RV PARK

Reference: **South of San Quintín; map B, grid g1.**

Campsites, facilities: Facilities are primitive and in disrepair. There is a main RV parking area, in addition to three or four RV spots at the motel which may not be available for overnight use. There is a restaurant at the motel. Don't drink the water. There is no security. This park is made for tent camping. Supplies can be obtained in San Quintín.

Reservations, fees: All sites are first come, first served. The fee is low—$5 per night.

Who to contact: Drive in, park and wait for someone to come to collect.

Location: Drive about eight miles south of San Quintín on Highway 1 to the La Pinta Hotel sign. Turn west on the paved road and continue about 3.5 miles past the hotel to Cielito Lindo. Watch for the signs. For the main RV parking area, continue past the motel toward the ocean and around a prominent concrete block.

Comments: This is a lovely location behind the dunes and close to the surf on one of the great beaches of Baja. Unfortunately, the campground is currently very uninviting. In its present state, it is primitive camping at its worst. There are toilets in the concrete brick building, but when we were there last, the drain water was bubbling up on the surface of the ground. The cold showers were unreliable, working only part of the day. All the facilities that were functioning many years ago have been allowed to disintegrate. The one small consolation is a good restaurant at the motel. Despite the disappointing campground, the spot itself is as lovely as ever. Playa Santa María extends for several miles to the south and offers good fishing for perch and corbina, as well as lots of Pismo clams. In years past, we were able to pick up big ones off the surface of the beach every morning after the waves of the night's high tide scooped them out of the sand for us. Fishing can be just as satisfying. While fishing one evening on the point between the beach and the inner bay, a dolphin came close, caught a large leopard shark and proceeded to toss it high in the air, catch it and toss it again. In one hour there that night, we caught a leopard shark, an angel shark, a bat ray, a sting ray and a guitarfish. All in all, it was a very memorable evening. Summer is the preferred time to visit. For more on the San Quintín area, please see page 88.

36. EL PABELLÓN RV PARK

Reference: **South of San Quintín; map B, grid g2.**

Campsites, facilities: There are many places to park at the edge of the dunes and farther back from them. There are six water faucets and sewer lines in a row on the south side of the restroom building, which is clean with flush toilets and hot showers. Don't drink the water. The park is guarded and secure. Tent campers revel in this place. San Quintín is the place to reprovision.

Reservations, fees: All sites are first come, first served. The fee is low—$5 per night.

Who to contact: Drive in and talk to the attendant.

Location: Proceed about nine miles south of San Quintín on Highway 1 from the La Pinta Hotel turnoff and look for the El Pabellón sign one mile south of the junction with the old highway—it comes in at a sharp angle on the right. Follow the dirt road one mile to the park on the beach.

Comments: This is a choice camping spot on magnificent Playa El Pabellón which runs for miles in both directions. When we asked the attendant where to park, he gave a wide sweep of his arm and with a huge smile bellowed, "Anywhere!" If you can, camp between widely-spaced rows of shrubs on the leveled-off area at the edge of the dunes. The shrubs break the wind and afford a little privacy. It is the best-run park operated by an ejido in Baja. Interestingly enough, it is not one of the old parks built for them by the government. Pangas can be chartered for fishing trips behind the breakers or out to Isla San Martín when they can get through the surf in front of the campground. Surf fishing can be good for perch and corbina. Summer is the preferred time to visit. For other things to do in the San Quintín area, please see page 88.

---

37. ENRIQUE'S RV PARK

Reference: **South of San Quintín; map B, grid g2.**

Campsites, facilities: There are 27 pull-through campsites with water and sewer hookups. There are clean restrooms with flush toilets and hot showers. Don't drink the water. A family lives on the premises for security. Tent campers are welcome. Obtain goods in San Quintín.

Reservations, fees: All sites are first come, first served. The fee is low—$5 per night.

Who to contact: Drive in and talk to the manager.

Location: Proceed about nine miles south of San Quintín on Highway 1 from the La Pinta Hotel turnoff and look for the El Pabellón sign one mile south of the junction with the old highway—it comes in at a sharp angle on the right. Turn off the highway there, but turn left at the rock portal over the road to El Pabellón. Follow Enrique's handmade signs for about two miles as the dirt road winds among fields to the park.

Comments: This used to be Honey's RV Park which had access to the beach one-quarter mile away. That access, as well as the original entrance road, has been cut off by El Pabellón. When you could drive down to the beach and park on high ground to see and hear the surf, it was a great spot. Now it is isolated and hard to find. Summer is the preferred time to visit. For things to do in the San Quintín area, please see page 88.

38. CONSTITUTION OF 1857 NATIONAL PARK

Reference: **East of Ensenada; map A, grid g6.**

Campsites, facilities: The camping is primitive. There are no developed facilities or services. There is no water. Obtain supplies in Ensenada.

Reservations, fees: All sites are first come, first served. There is no fee.

Who to contact: Drive in and camp.

Location: While you can access the park from either north or south, the most preferred access is from the south. Take Highway 3 southeast from Ensenada toward San Felipe about 25 miles to Ojos Negros. Turn left (north) on a short paved road into the village. At its end, turn right onto a graded dirt road. Continue eight miles then turn right at the junction. Go another 12 miles and turn left. The park is reached after about 27 miles, taking about two hours. Drive through the pines to Laguna Hanson, which may be dry, and pick a campsite. This road may be impassable after a rain. Pickup trucks are advised. Don't try this in a motor home or trailer without scouting it out. The northern route has some rough stretches of road and is used less. From Tecate, drive east on Highway 2 about 32 miles to El Condor where a graded dirt road heads south about 37 miles to the park. After about 16 miles, it joins another graded dirt road coming in from La Rumorosa on Highway 2, about 10 miles east of El Condor. The main road bears east passing El Topo Rancho, climbs a steep grade and enters the park. Use pickup trucks.

Comments: Camping in this park is uncrowded and can be a relaxing experience. It is a different way to enjoy Baja, which is usually identified by its coastal attractions. Those with a bent for exploring will enjoy visiting Constitution of 1857 National Park. Hiking is pleasant among the pines. Spring, summer and fall are the times to visit.

39. SIERRA SAN PEDRO MÁRTIR NATIONAL PARK

Reference: **Southeast of Ensenada; map B, grid d8.**

Campsites, facilities: The camping is primitive. There are no developed facilities or services. There is no water. Obtain supplies in Ensenada.

Reservations, fees: All sites are first come, first served. There is no fee.

Who to contact: Drive in and camp.

Location: The best access is from Highway 1 about eight miles south of Colonet in the village of San Telmo de Abajo, which is about 76 miles south of Ensenada. A sign to the village of San Telmo (about six miles) and the Meling Ranch (about 21 miles) marks the start of a graded dirt road going about 60 miles to the park, a drive of about three hours.

Comments: You can hike, fish, mountain climb and visit the National Observatory here. The road in from Highway 1 can be incredibly dusty—to a depth of several inches, enveloping the vehicle in clouds of the stuff, which penetrates every crack. There are some steep grades getting to the Meling Ranch and steeper ones beyond. Motor homes and trailers are not suited for this drive. The upper elevations of the mountains are covered by conifer trees interspersed with meadows (and aspen) generating year-round streams with a unique trout species—the Nelson rainbow trout. Camping is allowed wherever you wish. From the high points, sweeping views may be had of the desert plain around San Felipe, the Sea of Cortéz and the Sonoran coast on the Mexican mainland. It is pleasant to settle back against a towering Jeffrey pine and contemplate that arid region so far below baking in summer heat. Spring, summer and fall are the times to visit.

Northwest Baja Norte's
10 BEST BEACHES

❂ ❂ ❂ ❂

1. PLAYA ROSARITO

Reference: **In Rosarito; map A, grid b1.**
Location: It runs along the front of the city of Rosarito.
Comments: This long beach defining Rosarito has Campground #3, Coco Loco Trailer Park and Campground #4, Chuy's Trailer Park. This is a wide, clean beach with good surfing and fishing. While it is an urban beach which is heavily used, it is highly regarded by the people who flock to Rosarito because it is the first good beach below the border. Southern California beaches are so horribly crowded that Rosarito is greatly appreciated by those eager to spend weekends in a more attractive setting. Rosarito has everything you might need in the way of services or supplies. Summer is the preferred time to visit, as winter is chilly. For things to do in the Rosarito area, please see page 80.

2. CANTAMAR DUNES

Reference: **South of Rosarito; map A, grid c1.**
Location: The dunes are next to Highway 1 (free road) and extend for three miles between Kilometers 47 and 52, about 13 miles south of Rosarito. Exit the toll road at Cantamar.
Comments: There is a nice beach on the ocean below the dunes. The big activity here is driving all-terrain vehicles on the dunes. Obtain supplies in Rosarito. Summer is the preferred time to visit, as winter is chilly. For things to do in the Rosarito area, please see page 80.

3.   PLAYA LA FONDA

Reference: **South of Rosarito; map A, grid c1.**

Location: It is at Kilometer 59 on Highway 1, about 20 miles south of Rosarito. Take the Alisitos exit off the toll road.

Comments: The beach is first viewed from the bluffs above and is very enticing as it curves around the irregularities of the prominences. The sand is fine and clean. A night at Campground #8, Alisitos RV Park, which is on the bluff above it, takes full advantage of the moon's reflection on the sea and sand below—a romantic scene for any couple. This is a great place to stroll barefoot, letting the sand ooze between your toes, and to dash out in the receding wetness of the last wave. Get the things you need in Rosarito. Summer is the preferred time to visit, as winter is chilly. For things to do in the Rosarito area, please see page 80.

4.   PLAYA LA MISIÓN

Reference: **At La Misión; map A, grid c1.**

Location: The beach extends for about one mile north of the Río Guadalupe at Kilometer 69 on the toll road (the free road goes inland at La Misión just north). At La Misión, 24 miles south of Rosarito on Highway 1D, the free road (old Highway 1) crosses under the toll road (Highway 1D). Drive two miles south on the toll road to the parking area on the west side of the highway in the arroyo of Río Guadalupe.

Comments: We have enjoyed this wide, soft sand beach with friends who have a house in La Misión. The rocky prominence blocking the north end affords elevated spots for sitting and scanning the surf for the plumes of gray whales migrating south in the fall and north in the spring. During weekends, it can be very crowded near the south end. It is especially popular with locals. Surf fishing can produce perch and corbina. Obtain supplies in Rosarito. Summer is the preferred time to visit, as winter is chilly. For things to do in the La Misión area, please see page 80.

5.   PLAYA MAL PASO   ☀

Reference: **South of La Misión; map A, grid c1.**

Location: Access this lovely wide beach from Campground #9, Mal Paso RV Park at Kilometer 71, Campground #10, Outdoor Resorts of Baja at Kilometer 72, or La Salina, the salt pan, at Kilometer 73. It extends about 2.5 miles.

Comments: This beach is one of the most spectacular in all of Baja. It is wide with an unbroken sweep from one end to the other. Since there are only three access points, a little walking will bring as much solitude as a person may need. The sand is clean and soft and the beat of the surf soothing and relaxing. At Mal Paso RV Park, it is possible to drive out on imported clay soil and camp close to the surf line. Few beaches in Baja allow vehicular access so close to the surf. The soothing song of the sea lulls one into peaceful, restoring sleep. It is a beach where grunion might be seen during their frenzied nocturnal mating ritual—a startling sight for those who have never experienced it. These seven-inch smelt spawn through the spring and summer only on three or four nights following each full or new moon and then for a one- to three-hour period immediately after high tide. Females accompanied by several males swim onto the beach, dig themselves into the sand and lay their eggs. The males discharge their milt on the sand near the female and return to the water. The female frees herself and returns to the sea. The eggs remain buried in the sand for about 10 days, until the next series of high tides washes them out. As the baby grunion hatch and immediately swim off, fishermen dash about, scooping them up after each wave, filling their buckets. They are good broiled or battered and deep fried. A grunion run is an exciting and hilarious sight. The nearest supplies are in Rosarito. Summer is the preferred time to visit, as winter is chilly. For things to do in the La Misión area, see page 80.

6.   BAHÍA TODOS SANTOS BEACHES   ☀

Reference: **South of Ensenada; map A, grid f1.**

Location: Starting from Campground #21, Corona RV Park, on the north, the beaches extend about 1.5 miles past Campground #22, Mona Lisa RV Park, and Campground #23, El Faro RV Park, to Campground #24, Estero Beach Hotel and RV Park.

Comments: Even though we use the plural, this is really one long beach. Segments have various names, depending upon what is behind them. The bay is polluted near Ensenada but farther south, toward the estero, it is cleaner. This beach is very wide. We have had a great deal of enjoyment on these beaches riding horses, walking, wading in the surf or just sitting and watching the gulls and shorebirds as the waves roll in. Supplies can be picked up out on Highway 1 or on the side streets. Visit in summer, as winter gets chilly. For things to do in the Ensenada area, please see page 84.

7.   PLAYA PUNTA BANDA   ☀

Reference: **In Punta Banda; map A, grid g0.**

Location: It runs along the north side of the Punta Banda Peninsula. Take the Punta Banda road for about eight miles from Maneadero on Highway 1.

Comments: The beach in front of Campground #25, La Jolla Beach Resort, and Campground #26, Villarino RV Park, is very popular with campers. Small boats can be launched into the surf of the bay for fishing and diving along the point. Obtain supplies in Punta Banda or back at Maneadero. Visit in summer, as winter gets chilly. For things to do in the Ensenada area, please see page 84.

8.   PLAYA SAN ANTONIO DEL MAR   ☀

Reference: **West of Colonet; map B, grid b2.**

Location: Access is by a seven-mile dirt road leaving Highway 1 near the north end of the Colonet bridge. It is about 65 miles south of Maneadero.

Comments: There are dunes behind a large beach and room for camping. People like to cruise in their all-terrain vehicles in the dunes, surf and surf fish for perch and corbina. The road in is best handled by pickups or four-wheel-drive vehicles. Colonet has basic supplies. Summer is the time to visit, as winter is chilly.

9. PLAYA SAN RAMON

Reference: **Northwest and west of San Quintín; map B, grids e2 - f1.**

Location: Access is west of Campground #33, Posada Don Diego RV Park on a soft sand road to the dunes or by rough four-wheel-drive roads west of San Quintín.

Comments: A wide sand beach extends for about 12 miles south of the Río Santo Domingo, ending in cliffs. Surfers use the beach, there are lots of Pismo clams and there is good surf fishing for perch and corbina. Obtain supplies in San Quintín. San Quintín is the place to shop. Visit in summer. For things to do in the San Quintín area, please see page 88.

10. BAHÍA SANTA MARÍA BEACHES

Reference: **South of San Quintín; map B, grids g1 - h2.**

Location: The northern beach, Playa Santa María, is reached at Campground #35, Cielito Lindo RV Park. The southern beach, Playa Pabellón, is reached at Campground #36, Pabellón RV Park. Access is also by sandy roads off the road into Cielito Lindo and off Highway 1.

Comments: This magnificent stretch of continuous wide beach extends from the mouth of Bahía San Quintín for about 10 miles south to Arroyo Socorro. You'll find many Pismo clams. Surf fishing can be good for perch and corbina. Surfers enjoy the beach. San Quintín has a full array of supplies. Visit in summer. For things to do in the San Quintín area, please see page 88.

MAP C

BAJA MAP (general) .... see page 10
adjoining maps
NORTH .... California
3 CAMPGROUNDS   EAST .... Mexico mainland & Sea of Cortéz
Ø BEACHES   SOUTH (map D) .... see page 127
PAGES 126-159   WEST (maps A & B) .... see pages 76-77

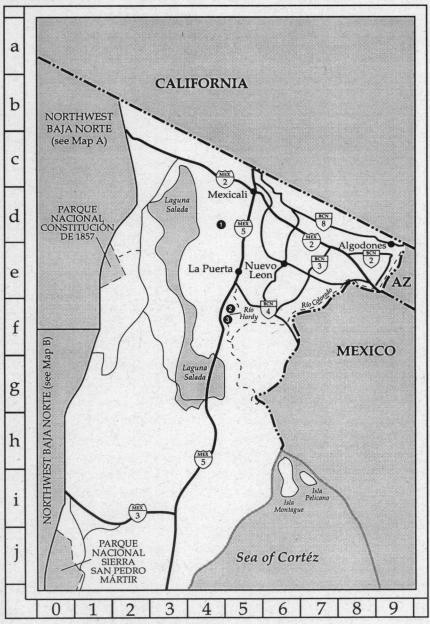

MAP D

30 CAMPGROUNDS
10 BEACHES
PAGES 126-159

BAJA MAP (general) .... see page 10
adjoining maps
NORTH (map C) .... see page 126
EAST ....: Sea of Cortéz
SOUTH (map E) .... see page 160
WEST (maps B & E) .... see pages 77 and 160

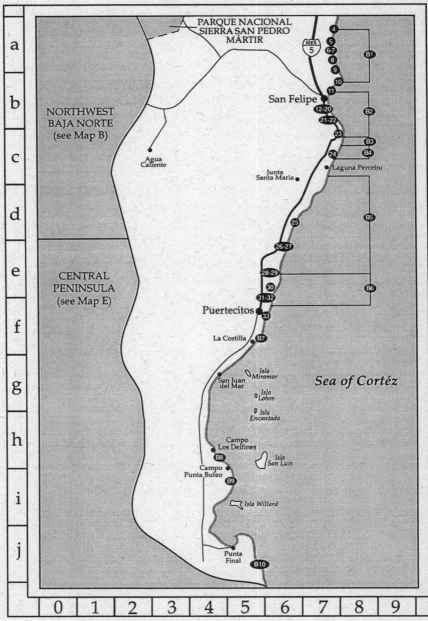

PARQUE NACIONAL
SIERRA SAN PEDRO
MÁRTIR

MEX 5

San Felipe

NORTHWEST
BAJA NORTE
(see Map B)

Agua
Caliente

Junta
Santa Maria

Laguna Percebu

CENTRAL
PENINSULA
(see Map E)

Puertecitos

La Costilla

Isla
Miramar

Sea of Cortéz

San Juan
del Mar

Isla
Lobos

Isla
Encantada

Campo
Los Delfines

Isla
San Luis

Campo
Punta Bufeo

Isla Willard

Punta
Final

NORTHEAST BAJA NORTE

❂ ❂ ❂ ❂

Readily accessible from Southern California through Mexicali, this section of the Baja California Peninsula is very popular. Winter is the prime season and summer the most uncomfortable with high desert temperatures. The area is easy to get to for long weekends, and even for short ones if you are willing to push it. San Felipe, the center of activity, is a mere 124 miles south of the border on Highway 5—the nearest Baja resort on the Sea of Cortéz.

The paved road on south to Puertecitos has its limitations. It is badly infected with potholes and has numerous small *vados* (dips into stream channels). Unlike elsewhere in Baja, these *vados* are not always announced to the driver by warning signs. The waterways they drop into are mostly narrow, creating a sudden drop and an equally sudden ascent on the other side. Popping into one at high speed could be disastrous. This road must be taken at moderate speed, preferably in daylight.

The large tourist population disperses itself into a huge collection of campos, playas and RV parks on the water between Río Hardy on the north and Puertecitos on the south. Pavement ends at Puertecitos and the rugged dirt road on south to Bahía Gonzaga and ultimately Highway 1 at Laguna Chapala is suitable only for high-clearance vehicles.

Sierra de Juárez area
(campground 1, page 133)

The Sierra de Juárez tilts gradually upward to the east, then drops precipitously down a 5,000-foot escarpment to the desert floor at sea level. The Rumorosa Grade on Highway 2 is steep, curvy and scenic, with startling vistas of the desert far below. The eastern slope has several palm-lined streams cut through solid rock, with water running from pool to pool. Exploring is best done in winter, as the rock-lined canyons become oven-like in the summer heat.

Río Hardy area
(campgrounds 2-3, pages 134-135)

The Río Hardy is about 40 miles south of the border and 80 miles north of San Felipe. It is not on the Sea of Cortéz and, accordingly, people go there for different activities—freshwater fishing, game-bird hunting and waterskiing. The river is fed mainly by agricultural drain water.

San Felipe and Puertecitos areas
(campgrounds 4-33, pages 135-153)

Originally a fishing village, San Felipe has had nearly 45 years of paved roads to stimulate development of a strong tourist clientele. With the *totuava* fish population depleted and protected, the shrimp fishery all but moribund and commercial fishing closed by presidential decree in the northernmost reaches of the Sea of Cortéz, tourism, including sportfishing, supports the local economy. The growth of hotels, campgrounds and resort developments is continuous. The great beaches are the main attraction.

Starting about 10 miles north of San Felipe and continuing another 54 miles south to Puertecitos, there is a series of campos and playas on the Sea of Cortéz, each with its own sign and access road off Highway 5. Even when they adjoin each other, there are separate access roads. Along some stretches of highway such roads occur every quarter of a mile.

While most of these campos lease sites by the year and do not serve overnight travelers, some indicate on their signs that they have camping facilities. These vary from nothing except a place to pitch a tent or park a rig to full-service establishments.

Frequent campers check them out, then settle into a favorite and return year after year. Newcomers with nothing to guide them are completely befuddled and can exhaust all their available time driving down one access road after another.

The camping experience in Puertecitos is out of the ordinary and requires an attitude. The large number of visitors who seek out this area are imbued with the ambience of simple desert living on a Baja beach away from the trappings of urbanized society. Sunrises and sunsets take on special significance; the comings and goings of the extreme daily tides become endlessly fascinating. The satisfying pleasures of life are oriented to natural phenomena rather than contrived amusements. There is much opportunity for intriguing activities, but there is no need to do anything. Camping here can touch the essence of mañana land and create a great refreshing of the spirit, or it can be the epitome of privation in a primitive existence. Those who are oriented to it would be nowhere else, while those who are not find it appallingly stark and unsettling.

Things to Do

Fishing

In Puertecitos, you'll find corvina, bay bass, triggerfish, barracuda, sierra, pargo and grouper in the vicinity. In San Felipe, you can expect corvina, croaker and different types of bass. If you don't have your own boat, you can rent a *panga* wherever there are local commercial fishermen. Ask other campers who have been there awhile how the fishing is, as it comes and goes.

Alex's (Alejandro's) Sportfishing in San Felipe has a good reputation with foreign residents. His office is on the Malecón (the city waterfront) and he is usually nearby. He speaks good English and has fair prices for half-day trips—$55 for two people, $65 for three people and $85 for four people. Half-day rental runs from 6:30 a.m. to noon. A full-day trip to Roca Consag costs $125 for three people. Use these prices for comparison when dealing with *panga* operators elsewhere.

Boating

Many visitors bring car-top or small trailer boats to San Felipe and Puertecitos for fishing. Others bring large trailer boats to begin an extended cruise of the Sea of Cortéz—at times with their destination Cabo San Lucas or mainland México ports such as Bahía Kino, San Carlos, Guaymas or points even farther south. Starting from San Felipe or Puertecitos can save many miles of highway trailering farther into Baja or onto the mainland.

Boaters must learn to deal with the special conditions created by the area's extreme tidal ranges. They must coordinate launching and retrieving with high tide and avoid anchoring in shallow water at high tide. Boats can be launched by a special vehicle at Campground #14, Ruben's RV Park. Four launch ramps can be used at high tide—Ruben's, El Cortéz Motel and Club de Pesca RV Park (Campground #20) in San Felipe and the launch ramp in Puertecitos—for about $5 each. There are no longer any free launch ramps.

Off-roading

Running around the desert and on the beaches in various types of off-road vehicles (ORVs) is a major outdoor activity in these areas. People use all types of vehicles, many of them homemade. A common denominator is they are lightweight and use soft, fat tires. There are motor scooters, trail bikes, dune buggies, sand rails, all-terrain vehicles (ATVs), two-wheelers, three-wheelers, four-wheelers and so on.

Tidepooling

The high tidal range of 20 feet or more exposes hundreds of yards of sea floor at low tide, inviting exploration. The incoming tide moves swiftly enough to warrant attentiveness and brisk walking to avoid being dunked, however.

Mountaineering

West of San Felipe and Puertecitos are the two northernmost

ranges of the many mountains that form the high spine of the peninsula—the northern Sierra de Juárez and the southern Sierra San Pedro Mártir. The great eastern escarpment of Baja's highest peak, the 10,154-foot El Picacho del Diablo, looms up behind San Felipe, offering a mountain climbing adventure, but one which is for experts only. It is an extremely grueling and dangerous climb.

The eastern canyons of both ranges are steep with hidden pools and palm groves. Huge boulders and smooth water-worn rock faces are difficult and risky to surmount. Summer heat can turn these canyons into ovens. Exploring them for their hidden nooks is best done in the cool of winter. You might observe some other mountaineers, desert bighorn sheep, in these canyons.

Excursions

If you don't have the equipment to get off the pavement and on the water, you can have someone take you for a fee. Enchanted Island Excursions in San Felipe offers cruises of up to three days to the Enchanted Islands and remote beaches. Contact them at 233 Paulin #8512, Calexico, CA 92123; phone 011-52-657-7-1431 in Baja or (619) 342-4193 in the United States.

1. GUADALUPE CANYON HOT SPRINGS AND CAMPGROUND

Reference: **West of Mexicali; map C, grid d4.**

Campsites, facilities: There are 10 large campsites for two to five vehicles each which have private cement and rock hot tubs with valves to control the temperature of natural geothermal mineral water, picnic tables, barbecue pits and palapas. There are also two small campsites for single vehicles. Tent camping is very popular. There are hot showers, toilets, a pool with natural 80°F water, a restaurant open on weekends, a small store, gas and oil and cellular phone service. There are no electric, water or sewer hookups. All water is mineral. Potable water, ice and firewood must be brought in by campers.

Reservations, fees: Reservations are recommended on weekends. Fees are $15 a night for the small campsites and $30 for the large ones. There are discounts by week, month or year.

Who to contact: Guadalupe Canyon Hot Springs and Campground, P.O. Box 4003, Balboa, CA 92661; (714) 673-2670.

Location: It is about 66 miles east of Tecate on Highway 2 and about 28 miles west of Mexicali on Highway 2, then south on a graded dirt road at a "Cañon de Guadalupe" sign near Kilometer 28. After about 27 miles, turn right (west) at a large sign, then about six miles on a winding dirt road and a final two miles over a bad road not recommended for motor homes or trailers.

Comments: The camp is open all year and is busiest on weekends. There is guide service to Indian caves and rock art for $20, waterfalls to visit, hiking, rock climbing and, of course, the hot springs. Motor homes under 28 feet and tent trailers have been accommodated, but very careful and slow driving is required. Heavy rains can wash the road out, another reason to call before going.

2. CAMPO SONORA

Reference: **South of Mexicali; map C, grid f4.**

Campsites, facilities: There are seven campsites with palapas, very dirty toilets and a small restaurant that is open in summer for drinks and snacks. Tent camping is welcome. Don't drink the water. The park is secured with a chain at the entrance to the parking lot.

Reservations, fees: All sites are first come, first served. The fee is low—$7 per night.

Who to contact: Drive in and talk to the owner.

Location: Head about 40 miles south of the border on Highway 5. The park is at Kilometer 58.

Comments: The good news? This camp is set on the river, where you can fish for carp and perch. There are also nearby hunting opportunities for waterfowl and white-winged dove. The bad news? This is a very minimal facility and it is poorly maintained at that. Noise from the adjacent highway can be disturbing. A note of warning: It is difficult to find a place to purchase things you might need without going back to Mexicali, so it's best to enter México fully supplied for your entire trip if you are staying here. Visit in winter, as summer can be hot.

3. CAMPO MOSQUEDA

Reference: **South of Mexicali; map C, grid f4.**

Campsites, facilities: There are 50 campsites, of which 20 have electricity. There are clean restrooms with flush toilets and cold showers, a restaurant and a lake. Tent camping is welcome. Don't drink the water. The owner lives on the premises, so security is good.

Reservations, fees: All sites are first come, first served. The fee is low—$7 per night.

Who to contact: Drive in and talk to the owner.

Location: It is about 40 miles south of the border. Turn off Highway 5 at Kilometer 60, which is well marked with a large sign, and drive one mile.

Comments: Being so close to the border makes this a very convenient destination. It is a large, attractive campground with lots of trees and palms. Some of the campsites are on a small, pretty, man-made lake. If you like freshwater fishing, it is also stocked with catfish and both largemouth and smallmouth bass. Fees are $1 per rod and $3 per kilogram of fish caught. Waterskiing and bird hunting for waterfowl and white-winged dove are also excellent. A note of warning: It is difficult to find a place to purchase goods without going back to Mexicali, so it's best to enter México fully supplied for your entire trip if you are staying here. Visit in winter, as summer can be hot.

---

4.   CAMPO LOS AMIGOS

Reference: **North of San Felipe; map D, grid a7.**

Campsites, facilities: Hot showers are available for $1 and there are toilets and a few palapas and tables. Tent camping is welcome. Don't drink the water. The manager lives on the premises, so security is good. Obtain supplies in San Felipe.

Reservations, fees: All sites are first come, first served. Fees are low—$2 for day use and $5 for overnight camping.

Who to contact: Drive in and talk to the manager.

Location: Drive about 10 miles north of San Felipe, then one mile east of Highway 5 at Kilometer 172 on a wide, hard-packed dirt road.

Comments: This campground is at the northern end of the string of campos and playas along the Sea of Cortéz north of San Felipe. The shoreline to the north turns into extensive mud flats extending south from the mouth of the Colorado River. To the south there is a fine beach. Winter is the time to come, as summer is hot. For things to do in the San Felipe area, please see page 129.

5. PLAYA GRANDE

Reference: **North of San Felipe; map D, grid a7.**

Campsites, facilities: There are showers for $1, pit toilets and 14 palapas. Tent camping is welcome. Don't drink the water. The manager lives on the premises, so security is good. Obtain supplies in San Felipe.

Reservations, fees: All sites are first come, first served. The fee is low.

Who to contact: Drive in and talk to the manager.

Location: Drive about 10 miles north of San Felipe, then one mile east of Highway 5 at Kilometer 173 on a good dirt road.

Comments: The beach is very nice and warrants the name, extending north and south in front of the camp. Camping here is enjoyable. Winter is the time to come, as summer is hot. For things to do in the San Felipe area, please see page 129.

6. PETE'S EL PARAISO CAMP

Reference: **North of San Felipe; map D, grid a7.**

Campsites, facilities: There is a lot of space for RV and tent camping on the beach. There are hot showers for $1, flush toilets, laundry, a restaurant, a bar, a gym and an RV dump station. Ask for drinking water. The manager lives on the premises and it is well populated with permanent residents, so security is good. Obtain supplies in San Felipe.

Reservations, fees: All sites are first come, first served. The fee is moderate—$8 per night.

Who to contact: Drive in and talk to the manager.

Location: Drive about eight miles north of San Felipe on Highway 5. Head east for one mile on the good dirt road at Kilometer 178.

Comments: This is an old campground with a substantial following. It was crammed full on the weekend we were there, while the other campgrounds north of San Felipe were empty. It can be boisterous, as the clientele is heavily oriented to beach vehicles and partying. Winter is the time to come, as summer is hot. For things to do in the San Felipe area, please see page 129.

---

7. LA PLAYA ENCANTADA

Reference: **North of San Felipe; map D, grid a7.**

Campsites, facilities: There are 30 palapas, showers and flush toilets. Tent camping is welcome. Don't drink the water. At the time we were there, it was new and there was no apparent security, but we expect there will be a resident manager once it is fully operational. Obtain supplies in San Felipe.

Reservations, fees: All sites are first come, first served. When we visited, there was no one to ask about the fee, nor was it posted. We expect it will be moderate once the park is up and running.

Who to contact: Drive in and talk to the manager.

Location: Drive about eight miles north of San Felipe on Highway 5. Head east for one mile on the good dirt road at Kilometer 178.

Comments: This beach camp adjoins Pete's El Paraiso Camp across a fence. The restrooms are well constructed and new. The road down to the beach is a bit narrow and steep. Be forewarned: The camping area is so narrow it would be difficult for a truck and trailer to turn around. Winter is the season to visit, as summer is hot. For things to do in the San Felipe area, please see page 129.

---

8. CAMPO LOS COMPADRES

Reference: **North of San Felipe; map D, grid a7.**

Campsites, facilities: There are pit toilets and several palapas. Don't drink the water. The manager lives on the premises, so security is good. Obtain supplies in San Felipe.

Reservations, fees: All sites are first come, first served. The fee is moderate—$10 per night.

Who to contact: Drive in and talk to the manager.

Location: Drive about seven miles north of San Felipe on Highway 5. Head east for one mile on the good dirt road at Kilometer 180.

Comments: Camping is on a gentle slope leading to a nice beach with plenty of room for rigs or tents. The beach is wide and goes far in both directions. We spent a pleasant night watching the tide come in and go out and enjoyed poking around in little tidepools among the boulders. We also admired the profuse fireworks launched skyward from Pete's El Paraiso Camp to the north and marveled at the variety and number of beach vehicles coming and going. A little boy was sent down to collect the fee, which he stoutly insisted was $2 more than we had been told upon arrival. We didn't have the heart to complicate his life by arguing. Winter is the best season to come, as summer is hot. For things to do in the San Felipe area, please see page 129.

9. SAN DIEGO BEACH

Reference: **North of San Felipe; map D, grid a7.**

Campsites, facilities: There are hot showers and palapas. Tent camping is welcome. Don't drink the water. The manager lives on the premises, so security is good. Obtain supplies in San Felipe.

Reservations, fees: All sites are first come, first served. The fee is low—$7 per night.

Who to contact: Drive in and talk to the manager.

Location: Drive about six miles north of San Felipe on Highway 5. Head east for one mile on the fair dirt road at Kilometer 182.

Comments: This is a small, tight, nice beach with little maneuvering room. It is only for small rigs and tents—don't try it with a trailer. Winter is the time to come, as summer is hot. For things to do in the San Felipe area, please see page 129.

10. PLAYA BLANCA

Reference: **North of San Felipe; map D, grid b7.**

Campsites, facilities: There are rundown toilets and some

palapas. Don't drink the water. There is no security. Obtain supplies in San Felipe.

Reservations, fees: All sites are first come, first served. The fee is moderate—$10 per night.

Who to contact: Drive in and talk to the manager.

Location: Drive about five miles north of San Felipe on Highway 5. Take the turnoff at Kilometer 183 and drive 1.5 miles to the Sea of Cortéz.

Comments: This is a wide beach going far in both directions. It offers some trees and plenty of room for RV and tent camping. An abandoned one-story hotel sits in the dunes above a nice beach, attracting the occasional sightseer. The open camping area is astride a beach-vehicle route, so it can get loud. Winter is the time to come, as summer is hot. For things to do in the San Felipe area, please see page 129.

---

11.   CAMPO NUMERO UNO

Reference: **In San Felipe; map D, grid b7.**

Campsites, facilities: There are eight palapas and nothing else. Don't drink the water. The camp is secured by a guard. Obtain supplies in San Felipe.

Reservations, fees: All sites are first come, first served. When we visited, there was no one to ask about the fee, nor was it posted. We expect it is moderate.

Who to contact: Drive in and talk to the manager.

Location: Take Highway 5 into San Felipe; it is 124 miles south of Mexicali. In San Felipe, the park is up against the hill on Avenida Mar de Cortéz. All the other northside beach parks are on the waterfront street east of Avenida Mar de Cortéz. Follow the signs.

Comments: This is the northernmost campground on the beach in San Felipe. It is a pleasant location for roughing it in tents or RVs. Being off the beaten track, it is not well known. Winter is the time to come, as summer is hot. For things to do in the San Felipe area, please see page 129.

12. MARCO'S RV PARK

Reference: **In San Felipe; map D, grid b7.**

Campsites, facilities: There are 15 campsites with full hookups, concrete pads, palapas and tables. There are flush toilets and hot showers. Don't drink the water. The park is secured with a gate. Obtain supplies in San Felipe.

Reservations, fees: All sites are first come, first served. Fees are moderate—$8 per night. Long-term rates are $50 per week and $200 per month.

Who to contact: Drive in and talk to the manager.

Location: Take Highway 5 into San Felipe; it is 124 miles south of Mexicali. In San Felipe, the park is on the land side of the waterfront street, just north of Ruben's RV Park (a landmark by virtue of being the largest RV park in that neighborhood).

Comments: The Sea of Cortéz is in front of the properties on the other side of the street, so Marco's lacks the main attraction in this area—the beach. It has a loyal clientele, however, who like the privacy. Winter is the time to come, as summer is hot. For things to do in the San Felipe area, please see page 129.

13. PLAYA BONITA RV PARK

Reference: **In San Felipe; map D, grid b7.**

Campsites, facilities: There are 32 spaces with full hookups, concrete pads, palapas and tables. There are flush toilets and cold showers. Don't drink the water. The park is secured with a gate. Obtain supplies in San Felipe.

Reservations, fees: Reservations are accepted. Fees are moderate—$12 per night. Long-term rates are $70 per week.

Who to contact: Playa Bonita RV Park, 529 South Alvarado Street, Los Angeles, CA 90057; phone 011-52-657-7-1215 in San Felipe or (909) 595-4250 in the United States for reservations.

Location: Take Highway 5 into San Felipe; it is 124 miles

south of Mexicali. In San Felipe, the park is on the north side of Ruben's.

Comments: This is a very nice little park on the wide, extensive beach. Since it fills up in winter, the early birds settle into the few choice campsites overlooking the water. Visit in winter, as summer is hot. For things to do in the San Felipe area, please see page 129.

14. RUBEN'S RV PARK

Reference: **In San Felipe; map D, grid b7.**

Campsites, facilities: There are 50 pull-through campsites with full hookups, tables and shade structures with balconies on top giving ocean views. There are flush toilets, hot showers, a restaurant and boat launching by an ancient four-wheel-drive Army truck. Don't drink the water. The park is well populated and is secured with a gate. Obtain supplies in San Felipe.

Reservations, fees: Reservations are accepted. Fees are moderate—$12 per night. Long-term rates are $70 per week, $225 per month and $1,400 per year.

Who to contact: Campo Ruben, Apartado Postal 196, San Felipe, Baja California, México. There is no phone.

Location: Take Highway 5 into San Felipe; it is 124 miles south of Mexicali. In San Felipe, the park is on the beach, on the waterfront street on the north side of town.

Comments: There is a great beach in front, making this a very popular spot. Tents are often pitched on top of the balconies. It is a large campground and can be a beehive of activity. Boats can be launched by special vehicle at just about any tide for $20 to $40, depending on the size of the boat, and there is a launch ramp. Winter is the time to come, as summer is hot. For things to do in the San Felipe area, please see page 129.

15.　　　NO NAME RV PARK

Reference: **In San Felipe; map D, grid b7.**

Campsites, facilities: There are 21 campsites with full hookups, concrete pads, balconies and tables. There are flush toilets and hot showers. Don't drink the water. A manager lives on the premises and the park is secured with a gate. Obtain supplies in San Felipe.

Reservations, fees: All sites are first come, first served. Fees are moderate—$12 per night on the beach and $10 back from it.

Who to contact: Drive in and talk to the manager.

Location: Take Highway 5 into San Felipe; it is 124 miles south of Mexicali. In San Felipe, the park is on the beach on the north waterfront street, adjoining Ruben's on the south.

Comments: This is a very nice little RV park on the same big beach as Ruben's. The people staying there urged us not to tell anyone about it and no one knew of a name. There is no sign and it appears to be part of Ruben's, but it is not. Mysterious, no? Winter is the time to come, as summer can sizzle. For things to do in the San Felipe area, please see page 129.

16.　　　VISTA DEL MAR RV PARK

Reference: **In San Felipe; map D, grid b7.**

Campsites, facilities: There are 20 campsites with full hookups, concrete pads, tables, barbecues and palm trees. There are flush toilets and hot showers. Don't drink the water. A manager lives on the premises and the park is secured with a gate. Obtain supplies in San Felipe.

Reservations, fees: Reservations are accepted. Fees are moderate—$12 per night or $10 without electricity.

Who to contact: Phone 011-52-657-7-1252. There is no available mailing address.

Location: Take Highway 5 into San Felipe; it is 124 miles south of Mexicali. In San Felipe, the park is at the corner of Avenidas Mar de Cortéz and Puerto Vallarta.

Comments: This is a very clean park on a slope with a brick driveway and a well-manicured appearance. Though it has an ocean view, it is not on the beach—which is the main attraction in San Felipe. Winter is the time to come, as summer is hot. For things to do in the San Felipe area, please see page 129.

17.   LA JOLLA RV PARK

Reference: **In San Felipe; map D, grid b7.**

Campsites, facilities: There are 55 pull-through campsites with full hookups and palapas. Tents are welcome. There are flush toilets, hot showers, laundry, a pool and a jacuzzi. Don't drink the water. A manager lives on the premises. Obtain supplies in San Felipe.

Reservations, fees: Reservations are accepted. The fee is high—$15 per night.

Who to contact: La Jolla RV Park, Post Office Box 978, El Centro, CA 92244; phone 011-52-657-7-1222.

Location: It is in the middle of San Felipe at Avenidas Manzanillo and Mar Bermejo.

Comments: The park is situated in a quiet residential neighborhood. However, it is not on the beach which is the main attraction in San Felipe. Visit in winter, as summer can be hot. For things to do in the area, please see page 129.

18.   PLAYA DE LAURA RV PARK

Reference: **In San Felipe; map D, grid b7.**

Campsites, facilities: There are 45 pull-through campsites with electricity, water, concrete pads and palapas, 20 of which also have sewer hookups. There are flush toilets and hot showers. Don't drink the water. The park is well populated and secure. Obtain supplies in San Felipe.

Reservations, fees: Reservations are accepted. The fees are high—$13 to $15 per night.

Who to contact: Playa de Laura RV Park, P.O. Box 130,

Calexico, CA 92231. There is no phone.

Location: Take Highway 5 into San Felipe; it is 124 miles south of Mexicali. In San Felipe, the park is on the beach in the southern part of town on Avenida Mar de Cortéz.

Comments: This is a popular and crowded park. We have stayed in it and appreciated the large beach and its proximity to restaurants. It was a bit too congested for us, however, and can be raucous. Winter is the time to come, as summer is hot. For things to do in the San Felipe area, please see page 129.

---

19.   VICTOR'S RV PARK

Reference: **In San Felipe; map D, grid b7.**

Campsites, facilities: There are 50 pull-through campsites with full hookups and concrete pads. There are flush toilets and hot showers. Don't drink the water. The park is secure. Obtain supplies in San Felipe.

Reservations, fees: Reservations are accepted. The fees are high—$15 per night. Long-term rates are $75 per week, $200 per month and $2,000 per year.

Who to contact: Victor's RV Park, P.O. Box 1227, Calexico, CA 92232; phone 011-52-656-1-8324.

Location: Take Highway 5 into San Felipe; it is 124 miles south of Mexicali. In San Felipe, the park is on the beach in the southern part of town on Avenida Mar de Cortéz.

Comments: This is a very popular park with a number of permanents, which gives it a residential atmosphere. It fills up quickly. It is a little tight for maneuvering, however. Visit in winter, as summer is hot. For things to do in the San Felipe area, please see page 129.

---

20.   CLUB DE PESCA RV PARK

Reference: **In San Felipe; map D, grid b7.**

Campsites, facilities: There are 40 campsites with electricity, water, palapas and concrete pads. The campsites away from the beach have sewer hookups. There are flush toilets, hot showers, a dump station, a recreation room, a launch ramp and a store. Don't drink the water. There is 24-hour security. Obtain supplies in San Felipe.

Reservations, fees: Reservations are accepted. The fees are high—$17 per night on the beach and $12 in back. If you stay a week, you get one day free and 30 percent off if you stay a month. Long-term rates are $1,560 per year.

Who to contact: Club de Pesca RV Park, P.O. Box 9001, Suite 217, Calexico, CA 92231; phone 011-52-657-7-1180.

Location: Take Highway 5 into San Felipe; it is 124 miles south of Mexicali. In San Felipe, the park is on the beach in the southern part of town at the south end of Avenida Mar de Cortéz.

Comments: The beach is wide and enjoyable. It is primarily a residential park with private and mobile homes. Though campers do fit in, the residential atmosphere seems a bit incompatible with the tourist experience. Boat launches cost about $5. Winter is the time to come, as summer is hot. For things to do in the San Felipe area, please see page 129.

---

21.   MAR DEL SOL RV PARK

Reference: **In San Felipe; map D, grid b7.**

Campsites, facilities: There are 106 campsites with concrete pads, of which 85 have full hookups and 21 have no hookups. There are flush toilets and hot showers in clean restrooms, laundry, a pool, a restaurant and brick walkways. Don't drink the water. Tent campers are welcome. The park is secured with a gate. Obtain supplies in San Felipe.

Reservations, fees: Reservations are accepted. Fees are very high—$23 per night on the beach with full hookup, $20 back from the ocean with full hookup and $13 for no hookup.

Who to contact: Mexico Resorts International, P.O. Box 120637, Chula Vista, CA 91912; phone (800) 336-5454.

Location: Take Highway 5 into San Felipe; it is 124 miles south of Mexicali. In San Felipe, the park is on the beach in the southern part of town off the paved road to the airport, just north of the harbor and south of Las Misiones Hotel. Watch for the sign.

Comments: Overnighters can camp in the front row in full view of the water and beach, which is very enjoyable. This is a well-maintained, first-class operation. The beach in front is wide, with lots of room for running dune buggies and other off-road vehicles—a plus if you like cruising along the waterfront, a minus if you're trying to take a siesta. Eventually, the small trees and palms on the grounds will grow to shade-giving proportions. We have found this to be a very clean and comfortable place to stay, though short on tranquility, given all the vehicular activity. Winter is the time to come, as summer is hot. For things to do in the San Felipe area, please see page 129.

22. SAN FELIPE MARINA RESORT AND RV PARK

Reference: **South of San Felipe; map D, grid b7.**

Campsites, facilities: There are 143 campsites with full hook-ups (30- and 50-amp electrical outlets), cable TV, concrete pads and palapas. There are flush toilets and hot showers in clean restrooms, laundry, a pool and a restaurant. Don't drink the water unless they have begun treating it (they plan to do so). There is 24-hour security. Obtain supplies in San Felipe.

Reservations, fees: Reservations are accepted. The fees are very high—$25 per night from June through October and $35 from November through May. Long-term rates are $140 per week in summer and $195 in winter, $490 per month in summer and $695 in winter, all subject to availability and change.

Who to contact: San Felipe Marina Resort and RV Park, Kilometer 4.5 Carretera Aeropuerto, San Felipe, Baja California, México; phone 011-52-657-7-1435 in San Felipe or (619) 558-0295 in the United States.

Location: From San Felipe, take Highway 5 south 2.5 miles. It is adjacent to the paved airport road well above the beach.

Comments: The wide beach below the elevated camping area is Playa San Felipe, which extends another 7.5 miles south. Beach vehicles can run the entire 10-mile stretch between San Felipe and Punta Estrella. The owners of San Felipe Marina Resort and RV Park want to make this an exclusive private membership resort and they will undoubtedly attain their goal. When they do, the park will no longer have spaces available for non-members. Winter is the time to come, as summer is hot. For things to do in the San Felipe area, please see page 129.

---

23. EL FARO RV PARK

Reference: **South of San Felipe; map D, grid c7.**

Campsites, facilities: There are 135 pull-through campsites with full hookups and concrete pads. There are flush toilets, hot showers and a pool. Don't drink the water. The park is secured with a gate. Obtain supplies in San Felipe.

Reservations, fees: Reservations are accepted. The fee is high—$23 per night.

Who to contact: El Faro RV Park, Apartado Postal 107, San Felipe, Baja California, México. There is no phone.

Location: Drive about nine miles south of San Felipe on the paved road to Puertecitos. Take the turnoff at Kilometer 15 and continue a few hundred yards to the park. Watch for the sign.

Comments: This is one of the more upscale campgrounds in the San Felipe area. It is a bit remote from restaurants, fishing charters and so forth, however. Below it is the northern part of beautiful, wide Playa Punta Estrella. Visit in winter, as summer is hot. For things to do in the San Felipe area, please see page 129.

24.   RANCHO VISTA HERMOSA

Reference: **South of San Felipe; map D, grid c7.**

Campsites, facilities: Tent camping is welcome. There are toilets. Don't drink the water. There is no security. Obtain supplies in San Felipe.

Reservations, fees: All sites are first come, first served. The fee is low—$5 per night.

Who to contact: Drive in and talk to the manager.

Location: Drive about 12 miles south of San Felipe on the paved road to Puertecitos. The park is on the beach a few hundred yards off the road. Watch for the sign.

Comments: This is the northernmost of the string of beach campos and playas on the Sea of Cortéz between San Felipe and Puertecitos. Campers who come here regularly find the campground that suits their tastes, then stick with it. Many eventually bring in a trailer and leave it parked in a campsite leased on an annual basis to return to, trip after trip, year after year, gradually adding improvements so that it becomes a permanent fixture on the landscape. Winter is the time to come, as summer is hot. For things to do in the San Felipe area, please see page 129.

25.   CAMPO GARCÍA

Reference: **North of Puertecitos; map D, grid d6.**

Campsites, facilities: Tent camping is welcome. There are toilets. Don't drink the water. The manager lives on the premises. Obtain main supplies in San Felipe. Limited groceries and fuel can be obtained in Puertecitos, which has a Pemex station and a small store.

Reservations, fees: All sites are first come, first served. The fee is moderate—$10 per night.

Who to contact: Drive in and talk to the manager.

Location: It is about 31 miles south of San Felipe on the beach one-half mile off the paved road to Puertecitos. Watch for the sign.

Comments: The entrance road is in good shape. Family camping is stressed. Winter is the best time to come, as summer is hot. For things to do in the Puertecitos area, please see page 129.

---

26.   PUNTA BAJA

Reference: **North of Puertecitos; map D, grid e6.**

Campsites, facilities: Tent camping is welcome. There is no security. Obtain main supplies in San Felipe. Limited groceries and fuel can be obtained in Puertecitos, which has a Pemex station and a small store.

Reservations, fees: All sites are first come, first served. The fee is low.

Who to contact: Drive in and talk to the manager.

Location: It is about 38 miles south of San Felipe on the beach one mile off the paved road to Puertecitos. Watch for the sign.

Comments: Expect primitive camping here. The beach goes far in both directions. Puertecitos is closer than San Felipe. Winter is the time to come, as summer is hot. For things to do in the Puertecitos area, please see page 129.

---

27.   CAMPO TURISTICO VALLARTA

Reference: **North of Puertecitos; map D, grid e6.**

Campsites, facilities: There are five palapas with concrete pads. Tent camping is welcome. There are pit toilets. Obtain main supplies in San Felipe. Limited groceries and fuel can be obtained in Puertecitos, which has a Pemex station and a small store.

Reservations, fees: All sites are first come, first served. The fee is moderate—$8 per night.

Who to contact: Drive in and talk to the manager.

Location: It is about 38 miles south of San Felipe on the beach 1.5 miles off the paved road to Puertecitos. Watch for the sign.

Comments: This camp fronts on sand dunes behind a rock beach. The entrance road is a little longer than to the campgrounds to the north, as the highway swings inland. Winter is the time to come, as summer is hot. For things to do in the Puertecitos area, please see page 129.

---

28.   RANCHO EL ZIMARRÓN

Reference: **North of Puertecitos; map D, grid e6.**

Campsites, facilities: Tent camping is welcome. Don't drink the water. There is no security. Obtain main supplies in San Felipe. Limited groceries and fuel can be obtained in Puertecitos which has a Pemex station and a small store.

Reservations, fees: All sites are first come, first served. While there was no one to collect the fee when we visited, we expect it is low.

Who to contact: Drive in and talk to the manager.

Location: It is about 45 miles south of San Felipe on the beach one mile off the paved road to Puertecitos. Watch for the sign.

Comments: Expect primitive camping. The highway has come closer to the shore, so that means there is a shorter drive in and also fewer camps. Puertecitos is only nine miles farther south. Winter is the time to come, as summer is hot. For things to do in the Puertecitos area, please see page 129.

---

29.   CAMPO LA VIOLETA

Reference: **North of Puertecitos; map D, grid e6.**

Campsites, facilities: Tent camping is welcome. There are toilets, boat rental and trailer storage. Don't drink the water. The manager lives on the premises. Limited groceries and fuel can be obtained in Puertecitos, which has a Pemex station and a small store.

Reservations, fees: All sites are first come, first served. The fee is low.

Who to contact: Drive in and talk to the manager.

Location: It is about 49 miles south of San Felipe on the beach one mile off the paved road to Puertecitos. Watch for the sign.

Comments: This is in a cluster of campos and playas near Puertecitos. Winter is the time to come, as summer is hot. For things to do in the Puertecitos area, please see page 129.

---

30. JACARANDA

Reference: **North of Puertecitos; map D, grid e6.**

Campsites, facilities: Tent camping is welcome. Don't drink the water. There is no security. Limited groceries and fuel can be obtained in Puertecitos, which has a Pemex station and a small store.

Reservations, fees: All sites are first come, first served. There is no fee.

Who to contact: Drive in and talk to the manager.

Location: It is about 51 miles south of San Felipe on the beach off the paved road to Puertecitos. Watch for the sign.

Comments: This is primitive camping. Talk to the locals about fishing techniques. Winter is the time to come, as summer is hot. For things to do in the Puertecitos area, please see page 129.

---

31. SPEEDY'S CAMPO

Reference: **North of Puertecitos; map D, grid e6.**

Campsites, facilities: Tent camping is welcome. There are pit toilets and a little store. Don't drink the water. There is no security. Limited groceries and fuel can be obtained in Puertecitos, which has a Pemex station and a small store.

Reservations, fees: All sites are first come, first served. There is no fee.

Who to contact: Drive in and talk to the manager.

Location: It is about 52 miles south of San Felipe on the beach off the paved road to Puertecitos. Watch for the sign.

Comments: This campground is set in a little cove, but it's just off the highway. There's not much in the way of privacy as people seem to be constantly pulling in off the road. Speedy runs the little store by the campground; we're not sure why there is no fee to camp here, unless it's because he's more interested in selling goods to campers than in charging them to camp. Winter is the time to come, as summer is hot. For things to do in the Puertecitos area, please see page 129.

---

32.   OCTAVIO'S CAMPO PLAYA ESCONDIDA

Reference: **North of Puertecitos; map D, grid e6.**

Campsites, facilities: Tent camping is welcome. There are pit toilets and cold showers. Don't drink the water. There is no security. Limited groceries and fuel can be obtained in Puertecitos, which has a Pemex station and a small store.

Reservations, fees: All sites are first come, first served. The fee is low—$5 per night.

Who to contact: Drive in and talk to the manager.

Location: It is about 53 miles south of San Felipe on the beach one-half mile off the paved road to Puertecitos. Watch for the sign. Puertecitos is a mere mile away.

Comments: This campground is in a small cove with a nice beach. You can rent pangas for fishing here; the standard price is whatever you can negotiate. The commercial fishermen are often happier to take a tourist out for a fee than struggle with their nets for less. If a *pangero* is not catching much, he'll take you out for a reasonable fee. If he is catching a lot, he won't take you at all. Fishing charter businesses are different—they set prices, though they are always negotiable. Winter is the time to come, as summer is hot. For things to do in the Puertecitos area, please see page 129.

---

33.   PUERTECITOS CAMPGROUND

Reference: **In Puertecitos; map D, grid f6.**

Campsites, facilities: There are 14 campsites with electricity (three to four hours a day), concrete pads and beach palapas.

Tent camping is welcome. There are toilets, a restaurant, a store and a launch ramp. Don't drink the water. The camp is secured with a fence and a 24-hour guard. Limited groceries and fuel can be obtained in Puertecitos, which has a Pemex station and a small store.

Reservations, fees: All sites are first come, first served. The fee is low—$5 per night.

Who to contact: La Familia Orozco, P.O. Box 2268, Heber, CA 92249. There is no phone.

Location: It is in Puertecitos, next to the only restaurant in town.

Comments: The local commercial fishermen will charter pangas for reasonable rates and guide you to fishing grounds around Islas de Las Encantadas. The Islas are five islands and exposed rocks about 15 miles south offshore of Puertecitos. You'll find great fishing for white sea bass, bay bass, triggerfish, sierra, yellowtail, dorado, skipjack and grouper. If you're hauling your own boat, the steep, rough, concrete and rock launch ramp at the point is suitable for large craft—it's also free. There is a hot sulfur spring near the ramp on the north side of the point, about one-quarter mile from the RV park. At low tide, it creates several hot pools in natural depressions in the rocky beach in which you can dunk yourself. They can best be enjoyed during maximum tidal action at full and new moons. Tides can have a range of 20 feet or more. Visit in winter, as summer is hot. For more information on things to do in the Puertecitos area, please see page 129.

Northeast Baja Norte's
10 BEST BEACHES

✸ ✸ ✸ ✸

1.　　　　PLAYA LAS ALMEJAS　　　✸

Reference: **North of San Felipe; map D, grid a7 - b7.**

Location: Heading 10 miles north of San Felipe on Highway 5, you can access the beach in many places via dirt roads.

Comments: This is the extremely popular eight-mile beach north of San Felipe, roughly between Campground #4, Campo Los Amigos, on the north and Campground #10, Playa Blanca, on the south. Fishing is fair for corvina, croaker and bass. You may find it difficult to secure privacy, due to all the off-road-vehicle traffic, however. The beach can be driven from one end to the other by beach vehicles. Pick up supplies in San Felipe. Winter is the time to come, as summer is hot.

2.　　　　PLAYA SAN FELIPE　　　✸

Reference: **In San Felipe; map D, grid b7 - c7.**

Location: Take Highway 5 into the town of San Felipe. You can access the beach by highway vehicle at several RV parks and numerous other places.

Comments: This is the mainstay of San Felipe's attraction for tourists. It runs through town and beyond for about 10 miles to Punta Estrella. Beach vehicles can drive along most of the beach. Fishing is fair for corvina, croaker and bass. Pick up supplies in San Felipe. Winter is the best season to visit, as summer is hot.

3.　　　　PLAYA PUNTA ESTRELLA　　✸

Reference: **South of San Felipe; map D, grid c7.**

Location: Highway vehicles can access it at Campground #23,

El Faro RV Park, and Campground #24, Rancho Vista Hermosa. Sand tracks allow access by four-wheel-drive vehicles and beach vehicles can run the beach.

Comments: Extending about five miles south from Punta Estrella to Punta Diggs, this is a wide sand beach about 11 miles south of San Felipe that is popular for camping and fishing. The Huatamote Wash enters the Sea of Cortéz about one-half mile north of Punta Diggs creating a lagoon that can interrupt the beach. The slope of land is very shallow along this stretch of coast. At low tide, the water can recede more than one-quarter mile, creating a vast expanse of exposed flats to explore. Fishing is fair for corvina, croaker and bass. Pick up supplies in San Felipe. Winter is the time to come, as summer is hot.

4. PLAYA EL PROVENIR ☀

Reference: **South of San Felipe; map D, grid c7.**

Location: It is accessible by four-wheel-drive vehicles over sand tracks from Campground #24, Rancho Vista Hermosa.

Comments: Extending south of Punta Diggs for about four miles, this is a wide sand beach about 15 miles south of San Felipe with extensive low tidal flats. The Parra Wash may create a lagoon about two miles south of Punta Diggs which can interrupt vehicle traffic along the beach. Punta Diggs and other points in this area are low and not very prominent. Fishing is fair for corvina, croaker and bass. Pick up supplies in San Felipe. Winter is the time to come, as summer is hot.

5. BEACHES BETWEEN BAHÍA SANTA ☀ MARIA & PUNTA SAN FERMIN

Reference: **North of Puertecitos; map D, grid c7 - e6.**

Location: Highway vehicles can reach them via campgrounds between Campground #25, Campo García and Campground #28, Rancho El Zimarrón. Four-wheel-drive vehicles can use numerous sand tracks and beach vehicles can navigate the beaches.

Comments: An almost continuous wide sand beach with hundreds of yards of tidal flats extends from Bahía Santa María (about 25 miles south of San Felipe) for about 24 miles to Punta San Fermín. The land here is level, with few distinguishing features. The north half has numerous camps along the beach which are easily accessible from the paved road one-half mile or less away, leading to congestion on popular weekends. The south half is more remote and less populated as the highway is farther inland and there are only a couple of camps. Fishing is fair for corvina, croaker and bass. Pick up supplies in San Felipe. Winter is the time to come, as summer is hot.

6. BEACHES BETWEEN PUNTA SAN ☀ FERMIN & OCTAVIO'S CAMP

Reference: **North of Puertecitos; map D, grid e6 - f6.**
Location: Highway vehicles can use access roads between Campground #28, Rancho El Zimarrón, and Campground #32, Octavio's Camp, which is one mile north of Puertecitos. There are many sand tracks for four-wheel-drive vehicles.
Comments: Beaches are nearly continuous for about four miles between these two points. These wide, sand beaches are backed by low-lying land and fronted by extensive tidal flats, as is common north to Punta Estrella. You can fish for corvina, bay bass, triggerfish, barracuda, sierra, pargo and grouper in the vicinity. Limited groceries and fuel can be obtained in Puertecitos, which has a Pemex station and a small store. Winter is the time to come, as summer is hot.

7. PLAYA LA COSTILLA ☀

Reference: **South of Puertecitos; map D, grid f5.**
Location: This beach is six miles south of Puertecitos, on the graded road heading south to Bahía San Luis Gonzaga.
Comments: The beach is protected by an offshore reef which makes it nice for swimming. Shore fishing is good for bass,

corvina, barracuda and triggerfish. Security is provided for by a resident manager. The only facilities are pit toilets. Pick up major supplies in San Felipe. Limited groceries and fuel can be obtained in Puertecitos. A word of warning: The road south of Puertecitos becomes very rough and requires high-clearance vehicles going dead slow. It can damage motor homes and trailers. Winter is the time to come, as summer is hot.

---

8. PLAYA BUFEO ☀

Reference: **South of Puertecitos; map D, grid h4.**

Location: Head 38 miles south of Puertecitos on a very rough road or 43 miles north of Highway 1 at Laguna Chapala on a somewhat better road. Turn east on a dirt road and continue to the beach for three-quarters of a mile.

Comments: This is a very nice white sand beach. Fishing is good for bass, corvina, grouper, pargo, yellowtail, sierra and triggerfish. The Punta Bufeo Resort, a restaurant and an air-strip are near the beach. The wide beach is in a gently curving cove that extends about two miles north of the rocky outcrop of Punta Bufeo. The point provides protection from southerly and easterly winds. Come in fully supplied. Emergency necessities can be scrounged at Bahía Gonzaga about eight miles south. Winter is the time to come, as summer is hot.

---

9. PLAYA EL FARO ☀

Reference: **South of Puertecitos; map D, grid i5.**

Location: Drive 42 miles south of Puertecitos or 39 miles north of Highway 1 at Laguna Chapala. The beach is three miles north of Punta Willard (Bahía Gonzaga area) on the Puertecitos-to-Bahía San Luis Gonzaga road.

Comments: This beautiful beach is very good for swimming. Fishing is good for bass, yellowtail, pompano, grouper, barracuda and triggerfish. Emergency supplies can be scraped up around Bahía Gonzaga. Come fully stocked. Winter is the time to come, as summer is hot.

10.   BAHÍA CALAMAJUE ☼

Reference: **South of Puertecitos; map D, grid j5.**

Location: Leave Highway 1 at Laguna Chapala and drive 12 miles north to the Calamajue road, then 27 miles northeast to Calamajue.

Comments: The nice sand beach is at the south end and require four-wheel drive. Fishing is good for bass, yellowtail, grouper and triggerfish. Come fully stocked. It is a long way from anywhere. Winter is the time to come, as summer is hot.

Campo Los Compadres on the Sea of Cortéz north of San Felipe is on magnificent Playa Las Almejas (see pages 137 and 154).

MAP E

BAJA MAP (general) .... see page 10
adjoining maps
NORTH (maps B & D) .... see pages 77 and 127
EAST (map D) .... see page 127
SOUTH (map F) .... see page 161
WEST .... Pacific Ocean

3 CAMPGROUNDS
Ø BEACHES
PAGES 160-185

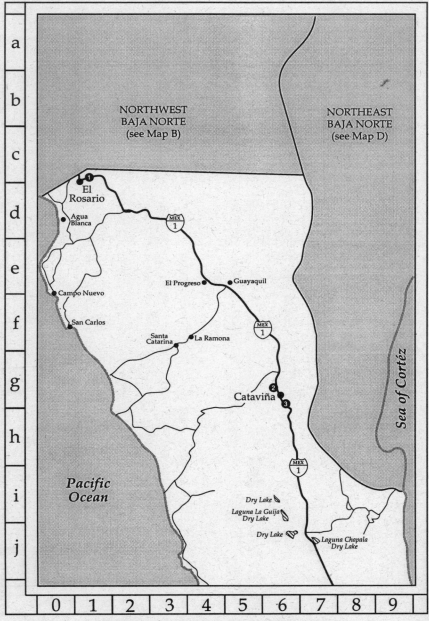

MAP F

BAJA MAP (general) .... see page 10
adjoining maps
NORTH (map E) .... see page 160
EAST .... Sea of Cortéz
SOUTH (map G) .... see page 162
WEST .... Pacific Ocean

9 CAMPGROUNDS
8 BEACHES
PAGES 160-185

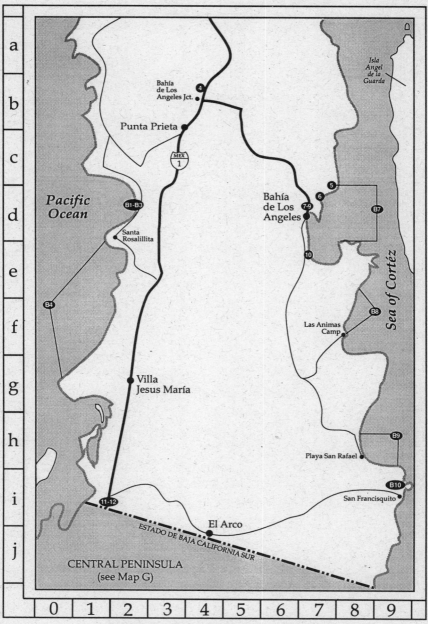

a

b

Bahía
de Los
Angeles Jct. ●④

Punta Prieta ●

MEX 1

c

Pacific
Ocean

B1-B3

⑤
⑥
Bahía
de Los
Angeles
7-9

d

Santa
Rosalillita ●

B7

⑩

e

Sea of Cortéz

B4 ●

f

Las Animas
Camp

B8

g

Villa
Jesus María ●

h

B9

Playa San Rafael ●

i

11-12

B10

San Francisquito ●

El Arco ●

j

ESTADO DE BAJA CALIFORNIA SUR

CENTRAL PENINSULA
(see Map G)

Isla
Angel
de la
Guarda

| 0 | 1 | 2 | 3 | 4 | 5 | 6 | 7 | 8 | 9 |

MAP G

BAJA MAP (general) .... see page 10
adjoining maps
NORTH (map F) .... see page 161
EAST .... Sea of Cortéz
SOUTH (map H) .... see page 186
WEST .... Pacific Ocean

5 CAMPGROUNDS
2 BEACHES
PAGES 160-185

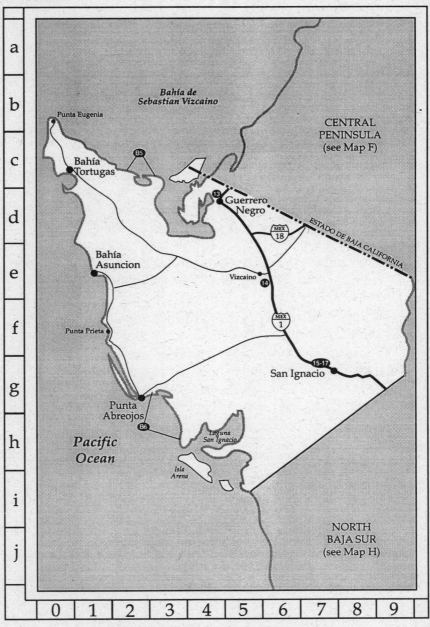

Bahía de Sebastian Vizcaino

CENTRAL PENINSULA (see Map F)

Punta Eugenia

B5

Bahía Tortugas

13

Guerrero Negro

MEX 18

ESTADO DE BAJA CALIFORNIA

Bahía Asuncion

Vizcaino

14

MEX 1

Punta Prieta

15-17

San Ignacio

Punta Abreojos

B6

Pacific Ocean

Laguna San Ignacio

Isla Arena

NORTH BAJA SUR (see Map H)

a b c d e f g h i j

0 1 2 3 4 5 6 7 8 9

CENTRAL PENINSULA

❄ ❄ ❄ ❄

The middle portion of the Baja Peninsula has the least amount of tourist developments. It is essentially wild, remote country with Highway 1 traversing its length. Bahía de Los Angeles is the one concentration of campgrounds and activities.

Some of the most unusual plants to be found anywhere can be seen while driving Highway 1 through this part of Baja. A few miles east of El Rosario, the first *cirios* come into view. These plants are at the extreme edge of their range and seem stunted, though it is difficult to know just what constitutes normality with these odd-balls. Tapering from a plump base to wispy, whip-like branches, their tan bark studded with tiny stubs of branchlets, they resemble nothing familiar. Following rains, small green leaves and delicate white flowers pop out, the plant sucks up all the water it can, then drops leaves and flowers and harbors its internal water supply until the next irrigation. The only other place in the world that *cirios* are found is in a small patch in Sonora—another proof that the Baja Peninsula was once firmly attached to mainland México.

The first giant *cardón* cacti appear at about the same place. These in the "fringe" habitat are hardly giants, but farther inland they become so. Their appearance is much like that of the more familiar saguaro of Arizona, though they have multiple trunks. *Cardón* have strong internal hardwood rods supporting their mass, which serve as stout building material. In dry times, their flesh shrinks inward with pronounced ribbing. Following rain they swell up with water and appear almost round.

Farther south on Highway 1 the third member of Central Baja's most prominent plants appears—the elephant tree. It actually looks like branched, spreading trees the world over, except its trunk and limbs are grossly round and fat. It may seem a bit shriveled in dry times. There are two large versions of these in Baja—one gray, the other pinkish.

Around Cataviña, midway between the Pacific Ocean and the Sea of Cortéz, is the Desert Natural Park. For miles, Highway 1 threads its way between massive piles of enormous rounded boulders, among which are scattered magnificent specimens of *cirio, cardón* and elephant trees, along with a full array of other Baja desert vegetation.

The scenery is on a grand scale, bluish distant mountains across vast desert plains and Highway 1 stretched far out in front of you. Many dirt side roads beckon off-road explorers, but crews of large RVs must continue on their pilgrimage to distant coastlines offering other things to do. The delights of Bahía de Los Angeles are in mind for many.

Fuel can be a problem between El Rosario and Guerrero Negro, so top off all tanks at El Rosario, Cataviña and Bahía de Los Angeles junction. The latter two Pemex stations may be temporarily out of fuel or out of service.

Highway 1 area (campgrounds 1-4, 11-17, pages 167-169, 173-178)

For most people, the stretch of Highway 1 extending from El Rosario past San Ignacio is little more than a corridor of travel to the enticing camping areas south on the Sea of Cortéz. There are a few scattered campgrounds along the 300-plus miles of essentially inland travel to accommodate weary travelers for a night. Those with eyes that see more than the black ribbon rolling beneath their vehicle will be entranced by the area's odd plants and rock formations and will find the long drive fascinating.

Bahía de Los Angeles area (campgrounds 5-10, pages 169-173)

This area can be reached in one long day's drive from San Diego. At times, the 42-mile paved road in from Highway 1 deteriorates and can be slow going until you reach a repaired stretch again. One of the most stunning views in Baja is the first sight of Bahía de Los Angeles from high in the hills. The reds and browns of the many islands in the bay contrast vividly with the bright blues of sky and water.

The small town has the basic necessities, including both Nova and Magna Sin gasoline. However, there are perennial problems with electricity and water. Camping here is somewhat more rustic than in other Baja locales, but for those of us who are captivated by the place, it is worth the extra effort. The most magnificent stand of *cirios, cardóns* and elephant trees we have seen is along the road in from Highway 1. Spring flowers are exquisite.

Things to Do

Fishing

This narrowed midriff area of the Sea of Cortéz with its numerous islands creates upwellings of nutrient-rich water that supports a resident fin whale population, sportfish and migratory game fish plus myriad sea birds. Fishing is the main activity for tourists. Most people bring their own boats and launch them at one of the three ramps, which is an unusually high concentration in launch-ramp-poor Baja.

Bahía de Los Angeles is famous for its feeding frenzies, with sharp-toothed game fish driving huge balls of bait to the surface, attracting hundreds of birds that dive madly into the maelstrom. Fishing is good for grouper, yellowtail, bass, barracuda, sierra and triggerfish. At times, huge schools of yellowfin tuna enter the midriff area and provide great fishing.

Guillermo's rents boats and guides for $75 to $100 for four

fishermen, cost depending on how far they want to go. Boats leave at 7 a.m. and return at 3 p.m. (See page 172 for more information on Guillermo's.)

Diaz rents *pangas* for $80, four people, from 6 a.m. to 1 p.m. (See page 172 for Diaz RV Park.)

Off-roading

There are some interesting side roads to take into the mountains behind the village and south toward San Francisquito if you are prepared to take on rugged and hazardous desert conditions.

Sightseeing

English-speaking naturalist Raul Espinosa guides tours for $85 a day with six to eight people in a 26-foot panga to explore islands and view whales, dolphins and sea birds. He also guides land tours to Indian pictographs, desert flora and fauna and to Misión de San Francisco de Borja. In the United States, phone him at (818) 899-7876. In Baja, he can be located in Bahía de Los Angeles at Campo Turístico La Ventana on the road to La Gringa. There is a sign.

Guillermo's takes groups of up to six people out by boat.

In the village, there is a very interesting archaeological museum that is a must-see.

1. SINAI RV PARK

Reference: **In El Rosario; map E, grid c1.**

Campsites, facilities: There are 30 campsites with no hookups at present. They may have electricity and water in the future. There are flush toilets, hot showers, laundry and a restaurant. Don't drink the water. The owner lives on the premises. Tents are welcome. Obtain supplies in El Rosario.

Reservations, fees: All sites are first come, first served. Fees are moderate—$10 per night and $50 per week.

Who to contact: Drive in and talk to the owner.

Location: As you head south on Highway 1, follow the sharp left turn the highway makes in El Rosario. Look for the park in about one mile on the left.

Comments: El Rosario is not a prime tourist destination. In fact, until this RV park was developed recently, there was no campground in the vicinity. Still, you should take a look at the ruins of one of two separate missions bearing the name Misión Nuestra Señora del Santísimo Rosario Viñadaco. The location where the mission was founded in 1774 flooded out and, in 1802, the mission was relocated, then abandoned in 1832. The relocated mission has only a few remnants of adobe walls left, but is easily seen about a mile west of town on the south side of the stream. It is alongside the dirt road going west. A sign tells about its history. (The first mission's ruins have melted down and can't be seen at all.) In the fall, look for masses of red chiles drying on the south-facing hillsides south of town on the highway. It is a very colorful display. Top off fuel tanks here—the next gas stations down the line may be out. Winter is the time to visit, as summers are hot.

2. CATAVIÑA TRAILER PARK (ejido)

Reference: **In Cataviña; map E, grid g6.**

Campsites, facilities: There are 67 pull-through campsites, a few of which may have electricity. There are flush toilets and hot showers. Don't drink the water. The park is secured, with a gate and a surrounding fence. A resident family also provides security. Tents are welcome. Obtain supplies in El Rosario.

Reservations, fee: All sites are first come, first served. The fee is low—$7 per night.

Who to contact: Drive in and talk to the manager.

Location: Drive about 76 miles south of El Rosario on Highway 1. The park is in Cataviña, just north of the La Pinta Hotel.

Comments: This trailer park is within the Desert Natural Park (Parque Natural del Desierto Central), which is a jumbled mass of enormous old, old granite boulders as big as houses. *Cirio* trees, giant *cardón* cacti and elephant trees grow throughout the area. There are some Indian rock art sites and running streams with tall palms. It is a fascinating place in which to poke around and explore, with exciting photographic opportunities at every turn. Top off fuel tanks here, as it is about 65 miles to the next gas station at the Bahía de Los Angeles junction, which is often not operating. From there, it is about another 59 miles to the next gas station at Villa Jesús María.

---

3. RANCHO SANTA YNEZ

Reference: **South of Cataviña; map E, grid g6.**

Campsites, facilities: There is a large, level parking area next to a restaurant. The water is not drinkable. Being at the ranch headquarters affords security. Tent campers are welcome. Obtain supplies in El Rosario.

Reservations, fee: Camping is first come, first served. The fee is very low—$2 per night.

Who to contact: Drive in and park. There is no phone number.

Location: It is one-half mile south of Cataviña on Highway 1, then three-quarters of a mile east.

Comments: This was one of the original stopping places for travelers long before the highway was paved. Old-timers enjoy the nostalgia of stopping for the excellent tacos. Winter is the time to visit, as summers are very hot. For things to do in the Cataviña area, please see Campground #2, Cataviña Trailer Park.

---

4. BAHÍA DE LOS ANGELES JUNCTION RV PARK (ejido)

Reference: **At the junction of Highway 1 and the road to Bahía de Los Angeles; map F, grid b4.**

Campsites, facilities: There are 40 pull-through campsites with concrete pads and no hookups. The park is secured with a gate and a surrounding fence. A resident family also provides security. Tents are welcome. Obtain supplies in El Rosario or Guerrero Negro.

Reservations, fee: All sites are first come, first served. The fee is low—$5 per night.

Who to contact: Drive in and talk to the manager.

Location: From El Rosario, follow Highway 1 about 141 miles south. The park is at the junction of Highway 1 and the road to Bahía de Los Angeles, one-quarter mile north of the Pemex station.

Comments: This park provides a place to pull into, if night sneaks up on you. Other than that, few tourists have reason to stop here. There is an interesting cactus garden to examine among the RV spaces. Top off fuel tanks if the Pemex is operating. Winter is the popular time to visit, as summers are hot.

---

5. PLAYA LA GRINGA

Reference: **North of Bahía de Los Angeles; map F, grid c7.**

Campsites, facilities: There are no facilities. Obtain supplies in Bahía de Los Angeles.

Reservations, fees: All sites are first come, first served. There is no fee.

Who to contact: Drive in and camp.

Location: The beach is at the end of the dirt road north of Bahía de Los Angeles village, which is about 183 miles south of El Rosario. Coming into town, make a sharp left turn at the Conasupa sign onto the dirt road to the airport. At eight-tenths of a mile, turn right at the Brisa Marina RV Park sign. After a half mile, turn left at the Reuben's sign. You are now on a wide, washboard dirt road that will take you past numerous turnoffs to private beach camps in sight on the beach. Some of the signs announce camping for a small fee—$2 or so. La Gringa is six miles north at the end of the road.

Comments: There are camping spots all along the beach and a fish camp just short of a narrow spit of land going out to Punta La Gringa. (The beach was named for an American woman who tried to establish a camping operation here years ago. You can still see the ruins of a concrete restroom she built.) A narrow road goes on through a low saddle between hills and ends on a rocky beach facing Isla Smith. This is such a scenic location that it is pleasant just to be here. While kicking back here, one of our friends saw a whale shark cruise by. Fishermen with small boats that can be launched across the beach do well, since they are close to prime fishing grounds around Isla Smith. Winter is the best time to visit, as it is very hot in summer. For things to do in the Bahía de Los Angeles area, please see page 164.

---

6.   BRISA MARINA RV PARK (ejido)

Reference: **North of Bahía de Los Angeles; map F, grid d7.**

Campsites, facilities: There are 50 pull-through campsites with no hookups. Pitch tents wherever you want. Purchase supplies in Bahía de Los Angeles.

Reservations, fees: All sites are first come, first served. There is no fee.

Who to contact: Drive in and camp.

Location: Follow directions to Campground #5, Playa La Gringa, but don't turn left at the Ruben's sign—instead continue straight for another two-tenths of a mile to the beach.

Comments: You can park here, but you'll be closer to the water if you go in front of the park, to the side of the turtle ponds. They're maintained by Tony Resendez, who lives 100 yards north. You can camp in his compound for a small fee if you ask. Winter is the best time to visit, as it is very hot in summer. For things to do in the Bahía de Los Angeles area, please see page 164.

7. VILLA VITTA RV PARK

Reference: **In Bahía de Los Angeles; map F, grid d7.**
Campsites, facilities: There are 100 pull-through campsites with electricity and sewage disposal. There are flush toilets and hot showers at the hotel, also a pool, a restaurant, a bar, a store and a launch ramp. Don't drink the water. The park is secured with a gate. Tents are welcome. Obtain supplies in Bahía de Los Angeles.
Reservations, fee: The fee is moderate—$10 per night.
Who to contact: Villa Vitta RV Park, 509 Ross Drive, Escondido, CA 92029; (619) 741-9583.
Location: It is across the road from the Villa Vitta Hotel and Restaurant on the beach. Register in the hotel office.
Comments: The camping area is shadeless and unattractive. The restroom building located there was non-functional the last time we saw it, necessitating a hike across the road to use the facilities in the hotel—which was considerably inconvenient. Still, Villa Vitta has the best launch ramp in Bahía de Los Angeles. They charge $10 for launching, which includes both putting in and taking out. The owner has plans for improvements, including a gas pump on the pier. Hopefully these will materialize. Winter is the best time to visit, as it is very hot in summer. For things to do in the Bahía de Los Angeles area, please see page 164.

8. GUILLERMO'S HOTEL, RV PARK, RESTAURANT, BAR & STORE

Reference: **In Bahía de Los Angeles; map F, grid d7.**

Campsites, facilities: There are 40 pull-through campsites with full hookups. There are flush toilets, hot showers, a restaurant, a bar, a store and a launch ramp. The water is on only part of the day. Don't drink it. There is no security. Tents are welcome. Obtain supplies in Bahía de Los Angeles.

Reservations, fee: Reservations are accepted. The fee is low—$4 per person per night.

Who to contact: Phone 011-52-617-6-4946. There is no available mailing address.

Location: It is south of Villa Vitta on the beach.

Comments: We have stayed at Guillermo's several times over the years and find it suits our needs. The owners are gracious and helpful and the restaurant is very good. One nice bonus: The launch ramp is free for guests of the hotel and RV park. Visit in winter, summer is very hot. For things to do in the Bahía de Los Angeles area, please see page 164.

9. DIAZ RV PARK

Reference: **In Bahía de Los Angeles; map F, grid d7.**

Campsites, facilities: There are five campsites with full hookups. There are poorly-maintained flush toilets and cold showers, a restaurant, a store and a launch ramp for $5, free for guests. Don't drink the water. The spigot near the gas station is supposed to have drinking water from the spring. Other water is piped in from elsewhere. There is no security. Obtain supplies in Bahía de Los Angeles.

Reservations, fee: All sites are first come, first served. The fee is low—$5 per night.

Who to contact: Drive in and register at the restaurant.

Location: It is in Bahía de Los Angeles, on the south side of the gas station.

Comments: This park is not being maintained well and is in disrepair at this time. For things to do in the Bahía de Los Angeles area, please see page 164.

10. GECKO CAMP

Reference: **South of Bahía de Los Angeles; map F, grid e7.**

Campsites, facilities: There are 10 campsites with palapas but no hookups. There are toilets, hot showers and a little ramp for small boats. Don't drink the water. There is no security. Obtain supplies in Bahía de Los Angeles.

Reservations, fee: All sites are first come, first served. The fee is low—$3 to $5 per night.

Who to contact: Drive in and talk to the attendant.

Location: Coming into the village, turn right when the rock wall is dead ahead, then take the first left turn to go about 3.5 miles south on a rough dirt road to the camp on the beach.

Comments: This secluded camp offers more privacy than in town. Some people prefer it for that reason. It is a good place for tent camping. Visit in winter, summer is very hot. For things to do in the Bahía de Los Angeles area, please see page 164.

11. LA ESPINITA RESTAURANT & RV PARK

Reference: **North of Guerrero Negro; map F, grid i2.**

Campsites, facilities: There is a restaurant with restrooms and a parking lot. (The owner may even let you use the shower, if you ask.) Obtain supplies in Guerrero Negro.

Reservations, fee: Parking is first come, first served. There is no fee.

Who to contact: Drive in and park.

Location: It is on Highway 1, about one-half mile north of the big steel eagle marking the Baja Norte-Baja Sur State line. Guerrero Negro is about 222 miles south of El Rosario on Highway 1.

Comments: Several people have told us about spending the night in the parking lot here. Beyond that, we have yet to see the "RV Park" part of the name. The latest word is that improvements are slowly being made. It may actually come into being before too long—at least the intention is there. The owner has been very helpful to tourists with mechanical breakdowns and we hope his blossoming business will be successful. For things to do in Guerrero Negro, please see Campground #13, Malarrimo RV Park.

12. GUERRERO NEGRO RV PARK (ejido)

Reference: **North of Guerrero Negro; map F, grid i2.**

Campsites, facilities: There are 40 pull-through campsites with concrete pads. Some in the west and south portions of the park have full hookups. There are modest restrooms with flush toilets and cold showers. Don't drink the water. The park is secured, with a gate and a surrounding fence. A resident family also provides security. Tents are welcome. Obtain supplies in Guerrero Negro.

Reservations, fee: All sites are first come, first served. The fee is low—$5 per night.

Who to contact: Drive in and talk to the manager.

Location: It is on Highway 1 at the Baja Norte-Baja Sur state line, next to the La Pinta Hotel. Guerrero Negro is about 222 miles south of El Rosario on Highway 1.

Comments: The local ejido makes an effort to keep facilities working, but the cost of electricity can exceed income. Over the years, it has been hit or miss. Sometimes there are hookups and the restrooms work, but other times nothing works—or the park is closed altogether. Guerrero Negro is a convenient place to stop on pilgrimages south and this park does the job when it is open. For things to do in Guerrero Negro, please see Campground #13, Malarrimo RV Park.

13. MALARRIMO MOTEL, RV PARK, RESTAURANT AND BAR

Reference: **In Guerrero Negro; map G, grid d4.**

Campsites, facilities: There are 20 campsites with full hookups and concrete pads. There are clean, modest restrooms with flush toilets and hot showers, a pool table and a restaurant. Don't drink the water. The park is behind the restaurant and motel. A guard provides security. Tents are welcome. Reprovision in Guerrero Negro, which has a wide selection of stores and supplies.

Reservations, fee: Reservations are accepted. The fee is low— $8 per night.

Who to contact: Malarrimo Motel and RV Park, Guerrero Negro, Baja California Sur, México; 011-52-115-7-0250.

Location: It is on the right as you enter Guerrero Negro. The town is about 222 miles south of El Rosario on Highway 1.

Comments: We have gravitated to staying here, as it's the most dependable campground in the area. The restaurant is widely renowned for its good food. Catch the Friday night fiesta. An additional plus is that owner Enrique Achoy is very helpful with whatever you need in Guerrero Negro. Though this is a company town devoted to producing salt—and said to be the largest such operation in the world—tourism is becoming more of a business here. Winter whale watching in nearby Scammon's Lagoon is attracting more and more tourists. Whale-watching trips in pangas can be booked by phone through the restaurant. Ask for Enrique. (You can reach the lagoon by driving about eight miles south of Guerrero Negro on Highway 1 to a sign, then about 17 miles south on a graded dirt road, which has too much soft sand for motor homes and trailers.) Many people also come for the winter birdwatching in the extensive marshes west of town, where you might see gulls, shorebirds, ducks and ospreys. A word about the weather: The climate is better in summer, but getting to Guerrero Negro involves driving through hot desert.

Winter can be chilly. Many times we have come north from the southern peninsula in shorts and T-shirts and have had to bundle up in long pants and jackets once in Guerrero Negro. It can be a shock.

---

14.   KADAKAAMÁN RV PARK

Reference: **In Vizcaíno; map G, grid e6.**

Campsites, facilities: There are five campsites with electricity and water. There are flush toilets and hot showers. Meals can be taken in the owner's home, which adjoins the park. Don't drink the water. The park is secure, as it is next door to the owner's home. Tents are welcome. Obtain supplies in Guerrero Negro.

Reservations, fee: All sites are first come, first served. The fee is low—$5 per night.

Who to contact: Drive in and talk to the manager.

Location: It is on Highway 1, on the east side of Vizcaíno, about 45 miles south of Guerrero Negro.

Comments: This would be a convenient place to pull off if you're caught on the road at nightfall. Other than that, there is nothing much to do unless you are leaving Highway 1 here for Malarrimo Beach to the west—not a trip for motor homes or trailers.

---

15.   SAN IGNACIO RV PARK (ejido)

Reference: **In San Ignacio; map G, grid g7.**

Campsites, facilities: There are 20 pull-through campsites with full hookups that sometimes work. There are modest restrooms with flush toilets and cold showers. Don't drink the water. The park is secure, with a gate and a surrounding fence. A resident family also provides security. Tents are welcome. Obtain supplies in San Ignacio.

Reservations, fee: All sites are first come, first served. The fee is low—$6 per night.

Who to contact: Drive in and talk to the manager.

Location: From Guerrero Negro, head south on Highway 1 about 89 miles to San Ignacio. The park is in town, behind the Pemex station.

Comments: This is a noisy spot, being right behind and above the gas station. There is no reason to stay here save desparation. For things to do in San Ignacio, see Campground #17, El Padrino RV Park.

16. MANUEL QUEZADA RV PARK

Reference: **In San Ignacio; map G, grid g7.**

Campsites, facilities: There is one water spigot and a pit toilet. Don't drink the water. The park is secure, with a gate and a surrounding fence. Tents are welcome. Obtain supplies in San Ignacio.

Reservations, fee: All sites are first come, first served. The fee is very low—$2 per night.

Who to contact: Drive in and park. Manuel will come around to collect.

Location: From Guerrero Negro, head south on Highway 1 about 89 miles to San Ignacio. Heading into town, watch for the handmade sign on the left. Turn and go about three-quarters of a mile from the highway. Open the gate and drive in.

Comments: Some would call this primitive camping. Others would call it sleeping in a parking lot. Either way, it's a pleasant spot, set in a date palm grove. We have used it with enjoyment. Tent campers like it, for they are likely to have it all to themselves. For things to do in San Ignacio, see Campground #17, El Padrino RV Park.

17. EL PADRINO RV PARK, RESTAURANT AND BAR

Reference: **In San Ignacio; map G, grid g7.**

Campsites, facilities: There are 22 campsites, of which seven have full hookups and the rest have no hookups. There are flush toilets, hot showers, a restaurant and a bar. Don't drink the water. The park is secure, with a gate and a surrounding fence. Tents are welcome. Obtain supplies in San Ignacio.

Reservations, fees: All sites are first come, first served. Fees are low—$5 per night with no hookups and $6 with hookups.

Who to contact: El Padrino RV Park, Carretera Peninsular 1/2 Kilometro, San Ignacio, Baja California Sur, México; phone 011-52-115-4-0089.

Location: From Guerrero Negro, head south on Highway 1 about 89 miles to San Ignacio. The park is about 1.25 miles from town. Watch for the prominent sign.

Comments: The dammed lake on the way into San Ignacio is fed by a powerful spring, a natural wonder. It gives life to an enormous expanse of date palms. The many blessings visited on San Ignacio seem to have influenced its citizens, who are exceptionally gracious and hospitable. Stay a few days and absorb as much of it as you can. You will be better for the experience. San Ignacio is a lovely town for strolling. The town square is unique, dominated by huge, ancient Indian laurel trees. The shade they cast is dense. Be sure to visit the magnificent Misión de San Ignacio Kadakaamán across the street from the square. If you are taking the rough road south past Laguna San Ignacio to Ciudad Insurgentes and Highway 1, San Ignacio is the take-off point. If you're inclined, make arrangements for whale watching in Laguna San Ignacio and for seeing the famous giant cave paintings in the Sierra de San Francisco to the north on day trips. Contact Oscar Fischer at Motel La Posada, Avenida Carranza 22, Pueblo Nuevo, San Ignacio, Baja California Sur, México; phone 011-52-115-4-0313. Ask directions if you are in town.

Central Peninsula's
10 BEST BEACHES

☼ ☼ ☼ ☼

---

1.   BAHÍA FALSA BEACH   ☼

Reference: **On the Pacific Ocean, north of Guerrero Negro; map F, grid d2.**

Location: It is about four miles long between Punta Cono on the north and Punta María on the south. Access is about 35 miles up the coast from the Santa Rosalillita road. Leave Highway 1 near Kilometer 38 about 16 miles south of Punta Prieta at the Santa Rosalillita sign. It is about 10 miles on a good dirt road to Santa Rosalillita. About 1.5 miles short of the village, turn north on a good dirt road, which turns into typical rough country roads with many branches.

Comments: This is a nice, big beach—worth the trip in. Fishing for halibut, corvina, perch and bass can be good. Surfers and boardsailors like this beach. Take only pickups, vans or four-wheel-drive vehicles. The latter will give greater peace of mind, for there can be bad stretches and it is remote. Obtain supplies in El Rosario or Guerrero Negro. Summer is the best time to visit, as winter can be cool.

---

2.   PLAYA MARIA   ☼

Reference: **On the Pacific Ocean, north of Guerrero Negro; map F, grid d2.**

Location: It is about seven miles long between Punta María on the north and Punta Lobos on the south. Access is about 30 miles up the coast from the Santa Rosalillita road. See route description for Bahía Falsa Beach.

Comments: This is a big, pretty beach. Fishing for halibut, corvina, perch and bass can be good, as is clamming. It is very

---

popular with surfers and boardsailors. Take only pickups, vans or four-wheel-drive vehicles as the road in can get rough. Obtain supplies in El Rosario or Guerrero Negro. Summer is the best season to visit, as winter can be cool.

---

3. PLAYA EL MARRON

Reference: **On the Pacific Ocean, north of Guerrero Negro; map F, grid d2.**

Location: It is on the south side of Punta Negra (Prieta). Access is about 17 miles up the coast from the Santa Rosalillita road. See route description for Bahía Falsa Beach.

Comments: It is a beautiful crescent beach about two miles long. Fishing for halibut, corvina, perch and bass can be good. Surfers and boardsailors like it. Take only pickups, vans or four-wheel-drive vehicles as the road in can get rough. Obtain supplies in El Rosario or Guerrero Negro. Visit in summer, as winter can be cool.

---

4. ROSALILLITA BEACHES

Reference: **On the Pacific Ocean, north of Guerrero Negro; map F, grid e1 - g∅.**

Location: Access these beaches by the good side road at the Santa Rosalillita sign near Kilometer 38 on Highway 1, about 16 miles south of Punta Prieta. It is about 10 miles in. Four-wheel-drive roads go south to Highway 1 between kilometers 62 and 63, about seven miles south of Rosarito. Coming in that way, the dirt road (pickups, vans and four-wheel-drives only) goes three miles to a shingle beach, then north to the sand beaches around Punta Rosarito and farther north to Santa Rosalillita. You'll find a third access by dirt road from Highway 1 at Kilometer 73, about 10 miles south of Rosarito. It goes three miles to El Tomatal (Miller's Landing), where there is a shingle beach. A fourth access is by paved road from the sign to Morro Santo Domingo at Kilometer 96, Jesus María, on Highway 1. After one mile, turn left on a gravel road and drive another 6.5 miles to Laguna Manuela. To reach the extensive beaches, drive north around Morro Santo Domingo over four-wheel-drive roads in soft sand to harder sand on the beaches.

Comments: These beaches extend for about 30 miles south of Punta Santa Rosalillita (Santa Rosalía) to Morro Santo Domingo. They are all especially popular with surfers and boardsailors and offer good fishing for halibut, croaker, corbina, bass and corvina. If you're a digger, you'll find plenty of clams to keep you busy. Large motor homes and trailers are not recommended. Obtain supplies in El Rosario or Guerrero Negro. Visit in summer, as winter can be cool.

---

5.   MALARRIMO BEACH ☀

Reference: Northwest of Guerrero Negro, on the south shore of Bahía de Sebastian Vizcaíno; map G, grid c2.

Location: Turn west at Vizcaíno on Highway 1, about 43 miles south of Guerrero Negro. The first 22 miles of the some 70 miles to the turnoff to Malarrimo is paved and the next 48 miles is well graded and ready for paving. If you have arrived at San José del Castro, you have gone a half mile too far. Turn north at the turnoff and continue for another 27 miles on a road best navigated by four-wheel-drive vehicles due to soft sand. Another access suitable for pickups is north and east by dirt road out of Bahía Tortugas, which reaches the north-facing coast about 10 miles west of Malarrimo proper.

Comments: If you're a scavenger at heart, you'll love this beach. The peninsula on the south shore of Bahía de Sebastian Vizcaíno sticks out into the ocean like a hook, catching flotsam and jetsam from the North Pacific, burying it in sand and adding more beach in front of it. Junk of the ages can be picked up on the beach and mined from the dunes well back from the present shore. You'll find anything that ever floated—Japanese blown-glass net floats, ship wreckage, flotsam and jetsam from ships (plastic bottles by the thousands), logs from Canada, you name it. Obtain supplies in Guerrero Negro. Visit in summer, as winter gets chilly.

---

6. ABREOJOS BEACHES ☼

Reference: **On the Pacific Ocean, south of Guerrero Negro and east of Punta Abreojos; map G, grid g3.**

Location: Access is from Kilometer 98 on Highway 1, 71 miles south of Guerrero Negro. There is a sign and a restaurant at the turnoff. Continue on a dirt road for about 50 miles.

Comments: These beaches extend for about 10 miles from Punta Abreojos south to Estero de Coyote, accessible by road, and for another 14 miles across the entrance to the estero on south to Laguna San Ignacio, accessible by boat. Large motor homes and trailers are not recommended. There is good fishing in the ocean for barracuda, mackerel, bass, bonito, yellowtail, dorado, corvina and grouper and in the esteros for halibut, grouper, bass, corvina, triggerfish and sierra. Pismo clams abound. A friend in the Baja Sur state government told us of sending two assistants to Abreojos, a small fishing village not geared to tourists, on business. Finding no restaurant, they began knocking on doors to arrange for dinner. After several unsuccessful attempts, one lady tentatively offered but explained that she had only the simple fare they ate every day, which may not be appealing. When asked what that simple fare was, she replied, "Just lobster and abalone." Obtain supplies in Guerrero Negro. Summer is the time to visit, as winter can be cool.

---

7. BAHÍA DE LOS ANGELES BEACHES ☼

Reference: **On the Sea of Cortéz, around Bahía de Los Angeles; map F, grid d8.**

Location: From Cataviña, drive 65 miles south on Highway 1 to Bahía de Los Angeles junction. Turn east and head 40 miles to Bahía de Los Angeles.

Comments: These beaches extend from Punta La Gringa on the north all the way around the bay more than 10 miles to the south end. Fishing is good for grouper, bass, triggerfish, yellowtail, barracuda and sierra. Obtain supplies in Bahía de Los Angeles. Winter is when to come, as summer can be very hot.

---

8.   PLAYA DE LAS ANIMAS

Reference: **On the Sea of Cortéz, south of Bahía de Los Angeles; map F, grid e8 - f8.**

Location: Drive about 28 miles south of Bahía de Los Angeles on a rough dirt road to the marked turnoff, then about seven miles to a fork. Take the north branch, go about another four miles to an old ranch on the shore, which is rocky and not good for camping. Drive one-half mile north to a wide sand beach. You can hike about one mile farther north to another wide sand beach.

Comments: Your vehicle must have four-wheel-drive, due to soft sand en route. There is about two miles of beach north of the old rancho. Obtain supplies in Bahía de Los Angeles.

---

9.   PLAYA SAN RAFAEL

Reference: **On the Sea of Cortéz, south of Bahía de Los Angeles; map F, grid h8 - h9.**

Location: Drive about 45 miles south of Bahía de Los Angeles on a rough dirt road to the marked turnoff, then about one-quarter mile to the beach.

Comments: There is three miles of white sand beach accessible by road north toward Punta San Rafael and another 15 miles of beach south of that toward Punta San Francisco, which is accessible by foot. Fishing is good for bass, grouper, halibut and yellowtail. Four-wheel-drive is best from Bahía de Los Angeles, due to soft sand en route. Obtain supplies in Bahía de Los Angeles. Winter is the season to come, as summer can be very hot.

10.   PLAYA SAN FRANCISQUITO ☀

Reference: **On the Sea of Cortéz, south of Bahía de Los Angeles; map F, grid i9.**

Location: Drive about 85 miles south of Bahía de Los Angeles on a rough dirt road, keeping to the left near Rancho El Progreso about 12 miles from the beach in Cala San Francisquito. A more difficult route, with a very steep and rocky hill to overcome, is about 80 miles from Highway 1 via El Arco, south of Guerrero Negro.

Comments: The cove *(cala)* is small and well protected. Fishing is good for bass, barracuda and grouper. This is very remote country and it is best to travel in a group for safety. You are completely on your own. Obtain supplies in Bahía de Los Angeles or Guerrero Negro.

The strange cirios and cardón cacti can be seen along the Transpeninsular Highway.

MAP H

BAJA MAP (general) .... see page 10
adjoining maps
NORTH (map G) .... see page 162
EAST .... Sea of Cortéz
SOUTH (map I) .... see page 187
WEST .... Pacific Ocean

15 CAMPGROUNDS
4 BEACHES
PAGES 186-219

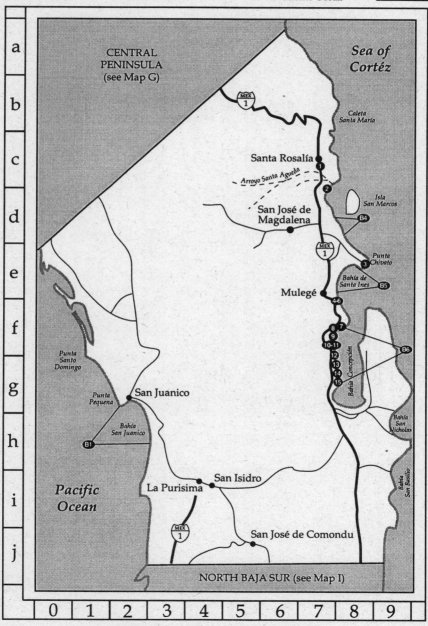

a

b

c

d

e

f

g

h

i

j

CENTRAL
PENINSULA
(see Map G)

Sea of Cortéz

MEX 1

Caleta Santa María

Santa Rosalía ①

② *Arroyo Santa Agueda*

Isla San Marcos

San José de Magdalena ●

B4

MEX 1

Punta Chivato

③

Bahía de Santa Ines

B5

Mulegé ● 4-6

8 ⑦
9
10-11
12
13
14
15

Bahía Concepción

B6

Punta Santo Domingo

Bahía San Nicholas

Punta Pequena

San Juanico ●

Bahía San Juanico

B1

San Isidro ●

La Purisima ●

Bahía San Basilio

Pacific Ocean

MEX 1

San José de Comondu ●

NORTH BAJA SUR (see Map I)

0 1 2 3 4 5 6 7 8 9

MAP I

BAJA MAP (general) .... see page 10
adjoining maps
NORTH (map H) .... see page 186
EAST .... Sea of Cortéz
SOUTH (map J) .... see page 220
WEST .... Pacific Ocean

9 CAMPGROUNDS
6 BEACHES
PAGES 186-219

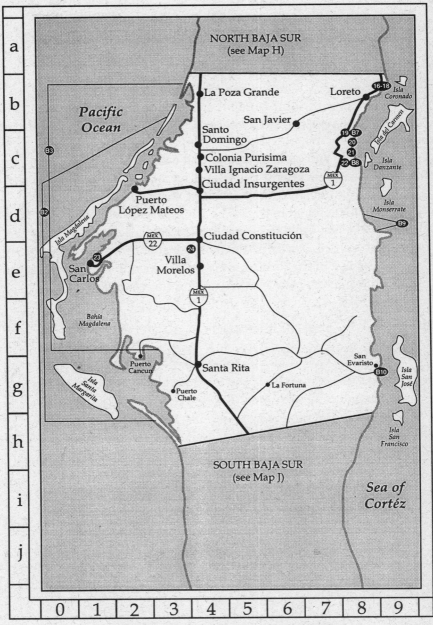

NORTH BAJA SUR
(see Map H)

Pacific
Ocean

La Poza Grande

Loreto

16-18   Isla
        Coronad

San Javier

Santo
Domingo

19 B7

Isla del Carmen

Colonia Purisima

20

Villa Ignacio Zaragoza

21

Ciudad Insurgentes

22 B8

Isla
Danzante

MEX
1

B3

Puerto
López Mateos

Isla
Monserrate

B2

B9

Isla Magdalena

MEX
22

Ciudad Constitución

24

23

Villa
Morelos

San
Carlos

MEX
1

Bahía
Magdalena

San
Evaristo

Puerto
Cancun

Santa Rita

B10

Isla San
José

Isla
Santa
Margarita

Puerto
Chale

La Fortuna

Isla
San
Francisco

SOUTH BAJA SUR
(see Map J)

Sea of
Cortéz

| 0 | 1 | 2 | 3 | 4 | 5 | 6 | 7 | 8 | 9 |

a b c d e f g h i j

NORTH BAJA SUR

✹ ✹ ✹ ✹

This section of the Baja California Peninsula is very enticing for campers. Excitement builds while descending the Santa Rosalía Grade and reaches a crescendo as the Sea of Cortéz comes into view with Isla San Marcos prominent in the scene. There is an irresistible certainty that the best part of the trip is about to begin—balmy air, warm water, white sand beaches, great fishing and relaxation.

There are numerous RV parks and campsites for both tents and RVs on beaches off Highway 1 on the Sea of Cortéz. Punta Chivato and Bahía Concepción offer some of the most stunning scenery to be found in Baja. The Pacific Ocean side of this portion of the peninsula has some outstanding beaches, but access to most of them is a bit difficult. There are persistent rumors of developing a better road from La Purisima north to San Ignacio, which would improve access to a long stretch of coastline.

Santa Rosalía-Mulegé area (campgrounds 1-6, pages 196-200)

Santa Rosalía is a company town without a company. It is reorienting itself toward tourism by preserving its small-town atmosphere and protecting its marina. While it is not a prime travel destination, its narrow, shaded streets are pleasant for strolling.

Fishing

There are no boat launching facilities in Santa Rosalía, nor has a sport fishery developed. However, there are commercial panga fishermen and it is always possible to engage one for a day's fishing if he is not otherwise occupied. Fishing north or south of town and off Isla San Marcos can be quite good. Las

Palmas RV Park is the place to stay for fishing north and south of Santa Rosalía. You can catch grouper, bass, triggerfish, yellowtail, dorado, barracuda, sierra and skipjack and the panga fishermen know better than anyone else what is biting where at any given time.

Waters north to Islas Santa Inéz, south of Mulegé along the shore and off Punta Concepción can be good for grouper, yellowtail, sierra and bass. Commercial panga fishermen are always willing to be engaged for a day's fishing, if they are not otherwise occupied.

Sightseeing

Santa Rosalía was founded in 1885 by Compañia del Boleo to allow the exploitation of rich copper deposits. Remains of the smelter, an old steam engine and other mining equipment which was used for 100 years are still present. The unique preconstructed metal Church of Santa Bárbara, designed by Gustave Eiffel, was installed in 1897 on the main street, several blocks west of the waterfront. A few blocks east of it is a renowned bakery, El Boleo, which produces marvelous bread. The French Hotel on the northern mesa above the main street is worth a visit. It is in restored French colonial style and reflects French tastes introduced to Santa Rosalía when the mining company started in the last century.

Mulegé has a lot to offer, which is why so many foreigners have selected it for their winter quarters. Among its many charms are its vast number of date palms and its spring-fed river, Rio Mulegé, which give the town an exotic tropical appearance.

Mulegé is a charming village tightly crammed between the river and steep hills to the north. Don't drive in with a trailer or large motor home. You can't believe how narrow the streets are. They are pleasant to explore on foot, however.

The restored Misión Santa Rosalía de Mulegé on a hill west of town and the old territorial prison on the north side are well worth visiting.

You can arrange excursions out of Mulegé to see Indian rock art through the Serenidad Hotel.

Boating

Small boats can be launched into the river, which is quite shallow, but it does give access to the Sea of Cortéz for those who know the channel. Large boats can be launched at high tide on the ramp, just east of the airstrip in Mulegé. You must thread your way around the Serenidad Hotel to get there, however, taking special care at the sharp right turn on the northwest corner of the hotel to avoid a power pole and cable.

Diving and snorkeling

Mulegé Divers on General Martínez, the main street through town, charges $30 for a boat and an underwater guide if you bring your own equipment, $40 for a two-tank dive with tanks and weight belt provided, and $50 with regulator, depth gauge and buoyancy compensator provided. They also rent wet suits. A Certification Card is required. Snorkeling is $20 per person if you bring your own equipment and $25 with mask, fins and snorkle provided. They lead snorkeling excursions outside Punta Concepción or to Islas Santa Inéz. Contact Miguel and Claudia Quintana at General Martínez s/n, Mulegé, Baja California Sur, México; phone their store at 011-52-115-3-0059 or their home at 011-52-115-3-0134.

Kayaking

You can spend an interesting day on Bahía Concepción with Bahía Tropicales Island Kayak Adventures from Playa Santispac. For fee and reservation information, see page 191 in "Bahía Concepción area."

Dining

There are some very fine restaurants in Mulegé, Serenidad, Las Casitas and El Nido among them.

Bahía Concepción area
(campgrounds 7-15, pages 200-206)

This bay is one of the great beauty spots of Baja California. The first view of it coming from the north is absolutely stunning. Many people decide this is just what they have been looking for and park on the first beach spot they can find, then luxuriate in the delights of tranquil water and opulent colors—tans and reds of the rocky shores and islands set against bright blues of sea and sky with fringes of glistening white sand beaches.

Fishing

At times, you can find sierra, barracuda, bass and triggerfish, but the netters have pretty well cleaned out the bait fish that the bigger ones need for food. If you want to hire a panga fisherman, ask the management of one of the RV parks for assistance.

Boating

Small boats can be launched over the firm sand and anchored close inshore.

Diving and snorkeling

The water can be quite clear and there are colorful fish to watch. If you have tanks, Mulegé Divers can refill them. Try the eastern shore of the bay. You should have no trouble finding butter and chocolate clams, pen shells (the adductor muscle makes great scallops) and big rock scallops.

Kayaking

Spend an interesting day on Bahía Concepción with Bahía Tropicales Island Kayak Adventures from Playa Santispac. The fee is $35 per person, which includes clam digging, refreshments and a specially prepared clam feast. For reservations, contact Baja Tropicales, Apartado Postal 60, Mulegé, Baja California Sur, México; phone 011-52-115-3-0019; fax 011-52-115-3-0340. If you're in town and want to just drop in, see Roy and Becky at Palapa #17, Playa Santispac on Bahía Concepción.

Other Activities

Sailboarding and waterskiing are popular in these protected waters.

Loreto area
(campgrounds 16-22, pages 206-211)

This part of Baja is nearly as attractive as Bahía Concepción. Isla Carmen lies off Loreto and heads a whole string of islands that continue all the way south to La Paz and beyond. The vista from the highway overlook north of Puerto Escondido is every bit as good as that of Bahía Concepción from the high point on the highway north of Santispac.

Fishing can be exceptional around the islands, cruising is great and the beaches attract many campers. Puerto Escondido, with its exceptional harbor, first-class launch ramp and Tripui RV Park, #20 (see page 209), is a focal point of activity.

Fishing

With your own boat, opportunities are unlimited. Anglers will find good fishing offshore for dorado, yellowtail, grouper, bass, barracuda, sierra, jack crevalle and bonito. Get to know some of the resident experts at Tripui. If you don't have your own boat, you can charter one in Loreto.

Andres Cota Arce is one of the many *pangeros* who work for hotels, the two big fleets or on their own. We happened to meet this fellow at the harbor in Loreto, where he hangs out with others. His operation is typical. He owns a 22-foot panga with a 65-horsepower outboard. He has life jackets, but no sun shades. He charges $90 for three people to fish for three hours, plus $5 for a rod and $2 for each live bait. He also has lures.

Alfredo's Sportfishing Boats has an office on the Malecón south of the harbor. Alfredo also runs the restaurant next door,

Pacific Coast area
(campgrounds 23-24, pages 211-212)

The Pacific Coast area of North Baja Sur is dominated by Bahía Magdalena, a huge mangrove-lined bay that few people know much about. One of those few experts, Dwight (Chino) Suitter, a fellow Vagabundo who spends winters on the bay, helped us with his hard-won information. The two towns— Puerto San Carlos and Puerto López Mateos—are commercial ports and not particularly oriented to tourism. There are few places for people in highway vehicles to camp. Off-roaders have a wide choice of sandy roads to run out and remote beaches on which to camp, both north and south of Bahía Magdalena, however.

Fishing

This is the main attraction in Bahía Magdalena. There is an unusual fishing opportunity for people with small boats that can be maneuvered up the small channels, though it takes local knowledge. Expect to catch grouper, halibut, bass, snapper, corvina, mackerel, snook and pompano. Puerto San Carlos is the launching point for adventurous fishing trips 50 miles off-shore to Thetis Banks, a target for the long-range boats out of San Diego for striped marlin and wahoo. You can find butter and chocolate clams easily at low tide.

Other activities

Puerto López Mateos is developing a tourist business for whale watching. The grays are in from January through April. This may develop into as popular an area as Scammon's La-goon and Laguna San Ignacio once people learn that whales can be approached as closely here as anywhere and that a good paved road leads to Puerto López Mateos.

1.   LAS PALMAS RV PARK

Reference: **South of Santa Rosalía; map H, grid c7.**

Campsites, facilities: There are 30 campsites with grass, palms and other trees, all with full hookups. There are well-maintained flush toilets, hot showers and laundry. Don't drink the water. The park is secured with a gate. The manager lives on the premises. Tent campers are welcome. Obtain supplies in Santa Rosalía.

Reservations, fees: Reservations are accepted. Fees are moderate—$10 per night with full hookups and $6 without, with discounts by the week or month. The annual fee is $1,000.

Who to contact: Las Palmas RV Park, Apartado Postal 123, Santa Rosalía, Baja California Sur, México; phone 011-52-115-2-2070; fax 011-52-115-2-2270.

Location: Go 2.4 miles south of Santa Rosalía on Highway 1 to the park.

Comments: This is a good place to spend the night, or to stay longer if you are drawn to Santa Rosalía or are waiting for the ferry to Guaymas. Keep in mind that you cannot depend upon obtaining the Temporary Vehicle Import Permit required to enter the mainland of México in Santa Rosalía. Plan ahead and obtain it in Tijuana at Customs just inside the border. Otherwise, you may have to go on to La Paz for it (see Travel Tips—Licenses and Permits on page 56, also Ferries on page 73, for further details). Winter is the time to visit here, as summer is hot. For things to do in the Santa Rosalía area, please see page 188.

2.   SAN LUCAS COVE RV PARK

Reference: **South of Santa Rosalía; map H, grid c7.**

Campsites, facilities: There are 20 campsites on the water and room for about 40 more behind, in a large lot. There are a few palapas on the water and barely minimal restrooms with a single old flush toilet and a single, cold headless shower in each. A restaurant and bar may or may not be open; the management is unreliable. Don't drink the water. There is no security. Tent campers are welcome. Obtain supplies in Santa Rosalía.

Reservations, fees: All sites are first come, first served. The fee is low—$6 per night.

Who to contact: San Lucas Cove RV Park, Apartado Postal 50, Santa Rosalía, Baja California Sur, México. There is no phone.

Location: Head nine miles south of Santa Rosalía on Highway 1. The access road is at Kilometer 182. Watch for the sign on the left. The exit off Highway 1 is steep and sharp at the sign, but there is a gentler exit on a short frontage road just to the north. Go slow as you approach Kilometer 182 so you can get off gently. The park is one-half mile east.

Comments: In spite of the primitive facilities, this is a popular location. Set on the water in a protected cove with a few palms and mesquite trees, the waterfront ambience is very pleasant. Swimming is comfortable in the protected cove. Small boats can be launched over the firm beach and safely anchored just offshore. If you want to fish, Isla San Marcos, five miles away, can be very good for grouper, bass, triggerfish, yellowtail, dorado, barracuda, sierra and skipjack. You'll find plenty of other fishing opportunities along the coast, both north and south. Arrange to hire a guide and panga through the park or by asking around. Mostly, this is a good spot for kicking back. On a hot, muggy July night, we were entertained by a marvelous sound and light show over the Sea of Cortéz. Sunrise colors seem to be exceptionally intense and varied here. Winter is the time to visit—avoid the summer heat. For other things to do in and around Santa Rosalía, please see page 188.

---

3.   PUNTA CHIVATO BEACH

Reference: South of Santa Rosalía; map H, grid e8.

Campsites, facilities: There are pit toilets, cold showers and some palapas. Buy drinking water in one-liter plastic jugs at the little store near Punta Chivato Hotel. There is no security. It is a great spot for tent camping. Obtain major supplies in Santa Rosalía.

Reservations, fees: All sites are first come, first served. The fee is low—$5 per night on the beach east of the hotel. Pay at the hotel.

Who to contact: Punta Chivato Hotel, Apartado Postal 18, Mulegé, Baja California Sur, México; phone 011-52-115-3-0188.

Location: From Santa Rosalía, head 25 miles south on Highway 1 to Kilometer 156. Turn east onto the washboard road and continue about 12 miles to the beach.

Comments: The view toward the peninsula is delightful. This is considered by many tourists to be one of the prettiest locations in Baja. A launch ramp west of the hotel is suitable at high tide for large boats. Small boats can be launched across the beach. Fishing can be quite good nearby around Islas Santa Inéz for yellowfin tuna, yellowtail, dorado, skipjack, grouper, sierra, pargo and barracuda, though a trip north to Isla San Marcos often produces better results. Winter is the time to visit here, as summer is hot. For more on things to do in the Mulegé area, please see page 188.

4.   ORCHARD (HUERTA SAUCEDO) RV PARK

Reference: In Mulegé; map H, grid f7.

Campsites, facilities: There are 43 campsites, of which 25 are pull-throughs, a few with concrete pads, all with full hookups. There are palapas and clean restrooms with flush toilets and hot showers. The water is safe to drink. A resident guard provides security. Tent camping is welcome. Obtain supplies in Mulegé.

Reservations, fees: Reservations are accepted. Fees are moderate—$14 per night with full hookups, $6 for tents with two people. Long-term rates are $84 per week and $244 per month.

Who to contact: Orchard RV Park, Apartado Postal 24,
Mulegé, Baja California Sur, México; 011-52-115-3-0300.

Location: The park is on the south side of the river off Highway 1, about one mile south of the turnoff into Mulegé.
Watch for the sign.

Comments: This is a very pleasant and well-kept park with lots
of space, though the riverfront is completely taken up with
permanent residences. Many trees provide lots of shade.
Winter is the time to visit here, as summer is hot. For things
to do in the Mulegé area, please see page 188.

---

5.   VILLA MARÍA RV PARK

Reference: **In Mulegé; map H, grid f7.**

Campsites, facilities: There are 24 pull-through campsites on
grass, all with full hookups. There are clean restrooms with
flush toilets and hot showers, laundry, a dump station and a
pool. The water is safe to drink. The owner lives on the premises. Tent camping is welcome. Obtain supplies in Mulegé.

Reservations, fees: Reservations are accepted. Fees are moderate—$10 per night with full hookups. Lower fees for tent
camping can be arranged. Long-term rates are $60 per week
and $275 per month.

Who to contact: Villa María RV Park, Apartado Postal XX,
Mulegé, Baja California Sur, México; phone or fax 011-52-
115-3-0246.

Location: The park is on the south side of the river off Highway 1 about 1.5 miles south of the turnoff into Mulegé.
Watch for the sign.

Comments: A bakery in the park has been closed, but it's expected to reopen. The pool here is great. The park is primarily residential, but a designated area is reserved for travelers.
Winter is the time to visit here, as summer is hot. For things
to do in the Mulegé area, please see page 188.

6.   SERENIDAD HOTEL AND RV PARK

Reference: **In Mulegé; map H, grid f7.**

Campsites, facilities: There are nine campsites in a concrete-walled compound, all with full hookups. (Check to be sure electricity and water work and that the sewer line doesn't empty into the parking area.) There are restrooms with flush toilets and cold showers. In the hotel, there is a pool, a restaurant and a bar. The water is safe to drink. The compound is well secured. Obtain supplies in Mulegé.

Reservations, fees: Reservations are accepted. Fees are moderate—$10 per night with full hookups. Long-term rates are $50 per week and $200 per month. Pay at the hotel.

Who to contact: Serenidad Hotel, Apartado Postal 9, Mulegé, Baja California Sur, México; phone 011-52-115-3-0111.

Location: The turnoff is on the south side of the river off Highway 1 about 2.5 miles south of the turnoff into Mulegé. Watch for the sign. It is about one-half mile on the dirt road adjoining the western edge of the airstrip.

Comments: This camp has its ups and downs. The downs are lack of shade, poor restrooms and undependable electrical outlets. Before settling in, check to be sure you have one that works. On the up side, the adjoining hotel's restaurant hosts a Wednesday night Mexican buffet and a Saturday night pig roast with dancing, which are renowned. When you arrive, turn into the walled compound on the southern side of the hotel and back your vehicle against the south wall. Winter is the time to visit here, as summer is hot. For things to do in the Mulegé area, please see page 188.

7.   CAMPO PLAYA PUNTA ARENA

Reference: **On Bahía Concepción; map H, grid f8.**

Campsites, facilities: The toilets are marginal. Don't drink the water. There is no security. Tent camping is welcome. Obtain supplies in Mulegé.

Reservations, fees: All sites are first come, first served. Fees are low—$3 to park for the night and $5 per night for a palapa on the water.

Who to contact: Drive in and talk to the manager.

Location: Drive about 10 miles south of Mulegé on Highway 1. At Kilometer 119, near the north end of the bay, look for the sign and turn left onto a fairly rough dirt road. Continue for about two miles, taking right turns where there are signs. Don't be concerned if you don't see the beach on your approach—it is out of sight to the south.

Comments: This is a very pretty beach facing south with a beautiful view. Several permanents are lined up along the water's edge, but there is plenty of room for transients in RVs or tents. Winter is the favored season to visit here, as summer is hot. For things to do in the Bahía Concepción area, please see page 191.

---

8.   PLAYA SANTISPAC

Reference: **On Bahía Concepción; map H, grid f8.**

Campsites, facilities: There are two restaurants, pit toilets for $1, cold showers for $1 and a dump station. Don't drink the water. There is no security. Tent camping is welcome. Obtain supplies in Mulegé.

Reservations, fees: All sites are first come, first served. Fees are low—$4 per night for a small palapa on the water and $5 for a large one.

Who to contact: Drive in and talk to the manager.

Location: It is on Highway 1 at Kilometer 114, about 13 miles south of Mulegé.

Comments: This is such a well-protected spot and the view is so pleasant that a great number of people spend the entire winter here. The early birds get their choice of spots. RVers must have a great tolerance for elbow-to-elbow living, but tent campers can find plenty of room. There are two restaurants—Anna's Restaurant, Bar and Bakery and Maru Restaurant. Winter is the best time to visit here, as summer is hot. For things to do in the Bahía Concepción area, please see page 191.

9. POSADA CONCEPCIÓN RV PARK

Reference: **On Bahía Concepción; map H, grid f8.**

Campsites, facilities: There are eight spaces near the highway
for overnighters, all of which have full hookups. There are
palapas, flush toilets, hot showers and sulfur hot springs.
Don't drink the water, which is hauled in and not treated.
The owner lives on the premises. Obtain supplies in Mulegé.

Reservations, fees: All sites are first come, first served. The fee
is moderate—$10 per night. There is a 10 percent discount if
you stay a month.

Who to contact: Drive in and talk to the owner.

Location: Drive about 14 miles south of Mulegé on Highway 1.
The park is at Kilometer 112.

Comments: Occupied mostly by permanents, this park is a
place to get off the highway when overtaken by dark and
there is nowhere else to go. It's all right, as long as you don't
mind camping in the middle of a residential community well
back from the one attraction—the beach. For things to do in
the Bahía Concepción area, please see page 191.

10. PLAYA LOS COCOS

Reference: **On Bahía Concepción; map H, grid f8.**

Campsites, facilities: There are pit toilets and a dump station.
There is no water and no security. Obtain supplies in Mulegé.

Reservations, fees: All sites are first come, first served. Fees
are low—$4 per night. Long-term rates are $105 per month.

Who to contact: Drive in and park. Someone will be around to
collect the fee.

Location: Drive about 15 miles south of Mulegé on Highway 1.
The beach access is at Kilometer 111. Go slow and watch for
the dirt road to the left, then proceed a few hundred yards.

Comments: This is a glistening white, soft-sand beach lapped
by crystal-clear water that rarely has a ripple in it and has a
gorgeous light green color from the white sand a few inches
beneath the surface. Tent camping is delightful here, with

camps pitched inches from the water's edge, enabling one to take a few steps from the shade of a palm tree, cool off with a quick dip and return to deep contemplation. Small boats can be launched over the sand and anchored just offshore. Photos of this place would make a great promo for a South Sea island vacation. Many people come early and spend the winter. Makes perfect sense—summer is just too hot. For things to do in the Bahía Concepción area, please see page 191.

---

11.   PLAYA EL BURRO

Reference: **On Bahía Concepción; map H, grid f8.**

Campsites, facilities: There are palapas, toilets and a dump site. There is no water and no security. Obtain supplies in Mulegé.

Reservations, fees: All sites are first come, first served. Fees are low—$3 per night. The long-term rate is $60 per month. The south end is under different management and there is usually no charge.

Who to contact: Drive in and park. Someone will come around to collect the fee.

Location: Drive about 16 miles south of Mulegé on Highway 1. The beach is at Kilometer 109.

Comments: As you round the hill to the north on the highway, check out the beach down below. It is a popular spot in a protected cove. You can launch small boats over the sand and anchor them in front of your rig. A group of regulars spend their winters here. We have heard that years ago there was a lame burro colt that lived near the beach, which is perhaps the source of its name. Caravaners led by the Vagabundos del Mar uniformly like to stay at El Burro and tent camping here is delightful. Winter is the favored season to visit, as summer is hot. For things to do in the Bahía Concepción area, please see page 191.

12.   PLAYA EL COYOTE

Reference: **On Bahía Concepción; map H, grid f8.**

Campsites, facilities: There are a few palapas right off the high-way. There is no water and no security. Obtain supplies in Mulegé.

Reservations, fees: All sites are first come, first served. The fee is low—$5 per night.

Who to contact: Drive in and park. Someone will come around to collect the fee.

Location: Drive about 17 miles south of Mulegé on Highway 1. The beach is at Kilometer 108, at the south end of Bahía Coyote. A rough road takes off to the south along the water's edge against a rocky slope and leads to a larger, more open area with some nice trees.

Comments: This protected cove is a good spot for tent camping, especially if you're looking for a little solitude—it's not as popular as the other beaches on Bahía Concepción. Winter is the favored season to visit here, as summer is hot. For things to do in the Bahía Concepción area, please see page 191.

13.   PLAYA BUENAVENTURA

Reference: **On Bahía Concepción; map H, grid g8.**

Campsites, facilities: There are pit toilets, palapas, hot showers at $3 for eight minutes, a restaurant, a bar, a mini-market and a concrete launch ramp into the surf. Don't drink the water. There is no security. Tent camping is welcome. Obtain major supplies in Mulegé.

Reservations, fees: All sites are first come, first served. The fee is low—$6 per night.

Who to contact: Drive in and talk to the manager.

Location: Drive about 25 miles south of Mulegé on Highway 1. The beach is at Kilometer 94.

Comments: This is an exposed location that is not popular. Expect high prices at George's Olé Restaurant and Bar on the beach. Winter is the best season to visit here. For things to do in the Bahía Concepción area, please see page 191.

14. PLAYA EL REQUESON

Reference: **On Bahía Concepción; map H, grid g8.**

Campsites, facilities: There are pit toilets. There is no water and no security. Obtain supplies in Mulegé.

Reservations, fees: All sites are first come, first served. The fee is low—$2 per night.

Who to contact: Drive in and park. Someone will come around to collect the fee.

Location: Drive about 26 miles south of Mulegé on Highway 1. The beach access is at Kilometer 92. Go slow and watch for the dirt road going off to the left. It is a little rough, but only a few hundred yards and everyone makes it easily.

Comments: The site is a beautiful sand spit with a beach and water on each side. Don't drive out on the really narrow part—at high tide it goes under. This is one of the old-time campsites that is popular with locals as well as tourists. If you love beaches, what could be better than two beaches all at once? The cove on the north side is great for playing around and clamming. Winter is the favored season to visit here, as summer is hot. For things to do in the Bahía Concepción area, please see page 191.

15. PLAYA ARMENTA

Reference: **On Bahía Concepción; map H, grid g8.**

Campsites, facilities: There are some small palapas and a pit toilet. There is no water and no security. Obtain supplies in Mulegé.

Reservations, fees: All sites are first come, first served. There is no fee.

Who to contact: Drive in and camp.

Location: Drive about 27 miles south of Mulegé on Highway 1. The beach access is at Kilometer 91. Turn off the highway at the sign and follow the dirt road around a bluff to a small beach.

Comments: This is not one of the better beaches. It will do, however, in a pinch. It's best for tent camping. Winter is the favored season to visit here, as summer is hot. For things to do in the Bahía Concepción area, please see page 191.

16.   EL MORO RV PARK

Reference: **In Loreto; map I, grid b9.**

Campsites, facilities: There are 14 campsites with full hookups. There are flush toilets and hot showers. The water is safe to drink. The park is secured with a gate and a night watchman. Tent campers are welcome. Obtain supplies in Loreto.

Reservations, fees: Reservations are accepted. Fees are moderate—$10 per night. Long-term rates are $60 per week and $180 per month.

Who to contact: El Moro RV Park, Rosendo Robles #8, Loreto, Baja California Sur, México; phone 011-52-113-5-0542.

Location: From Mulegé, drive about 84 miles south to Loreto on Highway 1. The park is in town one block from the Malecón. Go through town to the waterfront on Calle Salvatierra, which becomes Calle Miguel Hidalgo. Turn left on Rosendo Robles at the sign just before the La Misión Hotel.

Comments: There is a launch ramp four blocks away in the boat harbor. The park is convenient to everything in town. Dogs and chickens next door can disturb at night, however. Winter is the favored season to visit here, as summer is hot. For things to do in the Loreto area, please see page 192.

17.   VILLAS DE LORETO RV PARK

Reference: **In Loreto; map I, grid b9.**

Campsites, facilities: There are 13 campsites with full hookups, three of which are pull-throughs. There are flush toilets, hot showers, laundry, a pool, a small store, a dump station and a launch ramp. The water is safe to drink. The park is in a walled compound with a large wrought-iron gate, a resident caretaker and a guard dog. Tent campers are welcome. Obtain supplies in Loreto.

Reservations, fees: Reservations are accepted. Fees are high— $13 per night for full hookups and $11 for tents.

Who to contact: Villas de Loreto, Antonio Mijares y Playa, Colonia Zaragosa, Loreto, Baja California Sur, México; phone or fax 011-52-113-5-0586.

Location: From Mulegé, drive about 84 miles south to Loreto on Highway 1. The park is on the south side of town on the beach. Go through town on Salvatierra and turn right on Francisco Madero, continuing across the big arroyo until you see the sign.

Comments: This newly opened RV park is situated in what was once, years ago, the Flying Sportsmen's Lodge. The campsites are against the wall on the street, away from the water. The compound has many large palms and other trees and a large lawn. There are also motel rooms in front of the campground area which face the Sea of Cortéz. Winter is the favored season to visit here, as summer is hot. For things to do in the Loreto area, please see page 192.

---

18. LOREMAR RV PARK

Reference: **In Loreto; map I, grid b9.**

Campsites, facilities: There are 36 pull-through campsites with full hookups. There are clean restrooms with flush toilets and hot showers, laundry and a restaurant. The water is safe to drink. There is no security. Tent campers are welcome. Obtain supplies in Loreto.

Reservations, fees: Reservations are accepted. Fees are moderate—$11 per night for two people and $3 for each additional person.

Who to contact: Loremar RV Park, Apartado Postal 56, Colonia Zaragoza, Loreto, Baja California Sur, México; phone 011-52-113-5-0711.

Location: From Mulegé, drive about 84 miles south to Loreto on Highway 1. The park is on the south side of town on the beach. Go through town on Salvatierra and turn right on Francisco Madero, continuing across the big arroyo until you see the sign.

Comments: RV spaces are behind a large multiple-dwelling building which blocks the view of the Sea of Cortéz. In years past, camping was on the beach, but economics have pushed it back to the current undesirable location. Winter is the favored season to visit here, as summer is hot. For things to do in the Loreto area, please see page 192.

---

19. JUNCALITO BEACH

Reference: **South of Loreto; map I, grid c8.**

Campsites, facilities: There are only trash barrels. There is no water and no security. Obtain supplies in the store in Tripui RV Park.

Reservations, fees: All sites are first come, first served. There is no fee.

Who to contact: Drive in and park.

Location: It is about 14 miles south of Loreto on Highway 1 (about one mile north of the turnoff to Tripui RV Park and Puerto Escondido), then one-half mile down a rough dirt road to the beach on the southern end of Bahía Juncalito. The village of Juncalito occupies the northern waterfront. Look for the sign on the highway shortly after descending the grade to north.

Comments: This is a popular beach with primitive camping. Why is it so popular? Because it is free in a very attractive area. Tripui RV Park is only about 2.5 miles south where there is a restaurant, a store, laundry, toilets, showers and a pool that can be made use of. The scenery is great, the beach is in a somewhat protected cove, fishing is fantastic around several islands offshore and boats can be anchored close to the beach. While tent campers will be very pleased, RVers most likely won't. Before going in with a large motor home or trailer, walk it out. It probably isn't for you. Winter is the favored season to visit here, as summer is hot. For things to do in the Loreto area, please see page 192.

---

20.   TRIPUI RV PARK

Reference: **South of Loreto at Puerto Escondido; map I, grid c8.**

Campsites, facilities: There are 30 campsites with full hookups along the paved road in an area with its own entrance, just before the main entrance to Tripui. Go in the main entrance and register at the office, then return. Ask about campsites inside the main park. All are leased, but some are rented out when the owners are not there. They have more shade. There are good restrooms with flush toilets and hot showers, laundry, a pool, a restaurant, a store and a launch ramp down at the harbor. The water is safe to drink. The park is secured by a gate and a guard who lives on the premises. Tents are welcome. Obtain supplies in the park store.

Reservations, fees: Reservations are accepted. Fees are high— $14 per night, $16.50 inside the main park. Long-term rates are $83 per week, $336 per month and $2,615 per year.

Who to contact: Tripui RV Park, Apartado Postal 100, Loreto, Baja California Sur, México; phone 011-52-113-3-0818; fax 011-52-113-3-0828.

Location: Head 15 miles south of Loreto on Highway 1. Watch for the signed turnoff. Turn east and continue 1.5 miles east on pavement to the park.

Comments: This is one of the better parks in Baja California Sur. We have spent many happy weeks playing here. The islands offshore are great for cruising, dinghying to nice sand beaches and fishing for dorado and yellowtail. Skipjack are abundant and great sport to catch, but not good to eat. Live mackerel can be caught early in the morning off the entrance to Puerto Escondido. The excellent launch ramp at Puerto Escondido about one mile down the road is one of the best in Baja. Any size boat can be launched on this fine concrete ramp into the protected water of the harbor. Winter is the favored season to visit here, as summer is hot. For more information on things to do in the Loreto area, please see page 192.

---

21. TRIPUI BEACH

Reference: **South of Loreto; map I, grid c8.**

Campsites, facilities: There is no water and no security. Obtain supplies in Loreto.

Reservations, fees: All sites are first come, first served. There is no fee.

Who to contact: Drive in and park.

Location: The turnoff is about 15 miles south of Loreto on Highway 1 at a sign, then 1.25 miles east on pavement to the westernmost fence of Tripui RV Park camping area. Turn right (south) on a good gravel road and drive about 1.5 miles past the airport and dump on the right, around the hill southeast of Tripui RV Park to the beach.

Comments: You can camp on some sandy portions of the rocky beach. The allure of this spot is privacy on the water. There is ample room for a number of rigs on firm ground within 150 feet of the water. Boats can be launched at the excellent ramp in Puerto Escondido and moored off your camp on a buoy of your own making. Winter is the favored season to visit here, as summer is hot. For things to do in the Loreto area, please see page 192.

---

22. PLAYA LIGUI

Reference: **South of Loreto; map I, grid c8.**

Campsites, facilities: There is a pit toilet and trash barrels. There is no water and no security. Obtain supplies in the Tripui RV Park store.

Reservations, fees: All sites are first come, first served. There is no fee.

Who to contact: Drive in and park.

Location: Drive about 22 miles south of Loreto on Highway 1 (about six miles south of Tripui RV Park and Puerto Escondido). At the fence, ignore the *Propriedad Privada* sign (Private Property), but look closely at the small "Trailer Park E. Blanca" sign. It has a rough map showing the turn to take to the low ridge at the south end of the beach and the most accessible camping area. Drive down the dirt road straight east of Highway 1 about three-quarters of a mile to the beach, then take the last right turn and follow the signs marked "Playa" for another three-quarters of a mile. The rest of the beach immediately to the north is used by the local fishermen for their pangas.

Comments: This is not for trailers or larger rigs. There is thorny brush to scratch against, soft sand and a small beach—but it is pretty. Additional beaches about two miles north and two miles south to Ensenada Blanca can be reached by sand roads suitable only for pickups, vans or four-wheel-drive vehicles. Inflatable or car-top boats can be carried or dragged across the beach for a lot of fun fishing and snorkeling around the many little islands. The small ones that stick straight up are called Los Candeleros (The Candles). There are some very nice coves down the coast to explore, well within the range of such small boats. Diving and snorkeling around the islands is delightful, with lots of colorful reef fish. We spent a week doing that out of a tent and loved it. Winter is the favored season to visit here, as summer is hot. For things to do in the Loreto area, please see page 192.

---

23.   LA CURVA BEACH

Reference: **North of San Carlos; map I, grid e1.**

Campsites, facilities: There is no water and no security. Obtain supplies in Ciudad Constitución or San Carlos.

Reservations, fees: All sites are first come, first served. There is no fee.

Who to contact: Drive in and park.

Location: About 2.5 miles north of San Carlos on Highway 22, there is an abandoned disco and restaurant on the right. Turn and drive to a long beach which turns to mud at low tide.

Comments: This is primitive camping which tent campers will enjoy especially. It is heavily used by people from Ciudad Constitución on weekends. You'll find fishing and whale watching opportunities here. Winter is the season to visit, as summer tends to scorch. For more information on activities in the area, please see page 195.

24. CAMPESTRE LA PILA

Reference: **South of Ciudad Constitución; map I, grid e4.**

Campsites, facilities: There are 32 pull-through campsites with electricity and water. There are flush toilets, hot showers, a pool and a dump station. Don't drink the water. The park is secured with a chain. The manager lives on the premises. Tent campers are welcome. Obtain supplies in Ciudad Constitución.

Reservations, fees: All sites are first come, first served. The fee is low—$8 per night.

Who to contact: Drive in and go to the office.

Location: From the northern outskirts of Ciudad Constitución at Highway 22 going west to San Carlos, drive south through the city on Highway 1 for about 1.5 miles to the big Campestre La Pila sign on the southern outskirts of Ciudad Constitución, then turn west for about one-half mile to the campground.

Comments: The ground is bare and dusty. There are a few small trees. In other words, there is not a lot to recommend this spot, except as a port of refuge if you're on the road and it's getting dark. It is a recreation area for the local people, but it is not geared to tourism. If you do find yourself here, however, Ciudad Constitución is a good place to shop for those hard-to-find items. It is a farming community and many items can be purchased there that are difficult to find south of Ensenada. If you need any major vehicle repairs, this is the place. Winter is the time to go, as summer is hot. For more on the Pacific Coast area, please see page 195.

North Baja Sur's
10 BEST BEACHES

❀ ❀ ❀

---

1. SAN JUANICO BEACH ❀

Reference: **On the Pacific Coast, north of Puerto López Mateos; map H, grid g2 - h2.**

Location: Drive about 60 miles north of Ciudad Insurgentes on the paved road ending near La Purisima, then on the washboard dirt road to San Juanico. People with large motor homes and trailers will have to decide how much shake, rattle and roll they are comfortable with. You can also come south from San Ignacio on a worse road which is suitable only for pickups, vans and four-wheel drives.

Comments: Well-known to surfers for years, San Juanico has one of the most beautiful beaches in Baja Sur, running about eight miles south. Most of it is along high sand bluffs and is driveable only at low tide. Fishing is good for halibut, grouper, pargo, snook, sierra, corbina and corvina. All-terrain vehicles and four-wheel drives can do a loop south and back to San Juanico. There may be camping at Scorpion Ranch Preserve at San Juanico, though we have not been able to confirm that it is currently in operation.

---

2. BAHÍA MAGDALENA
BARRIER ISLAND BEACHES ❀

Reference: **On the Pacific Coast, in the Bahía Magdalena complex; map I, grid b3 - h3.**

Location: The beach on Isla Las Animas can be reached by a small boat from a graded sand road west of La Poza Grande, which is 36 miles north of Ciudad Insurgentes on the paved highway. Small boats can go from both La Banqueta (17 miles north of Ciudad Insurgentes, then 1.5 miles west of the highway through Santo Domingo on good hard sand) and Puerto López Mateos to Isla Santo Domingo. Both Puerto López Mateos and Puerto San Carlos offer small-boat access to Isla Magdalena. Small boats can also go from Puerto Chale (about 15 miles from Highway 1 at Santa Rita, which is about 32 miles south of Ciudad Constitucíon) to Isla Creciente.

Comments: Most of the barrier islands of the Bahía Magdalena complex have exciting, pristine beaches, particularly on the ocean side. They are Islas Las Animas, Santo Domingo, Magdalena and Creciente. In total, the islands extend about 100 miles from north to south. They don't just offer tiny sand coves—Isla Magdalena has two long Pacific beaches, 45 miles from the northern tip of the island at Boca Soledad south to Cabo San Lázaro and 22 miles south of Cabo San Lázaro to Cabo Corso. Isla Santo Domingo has 11 miles of beach. Once reached by small boat, you can explore these marvelous ocean beaches by foot, an all-terrain vehicle or a motorcycle. Adventurous explorers have a rare opportunity here to go where few men have trod.

3. BAHÍA MAGDALENA BAY BEACHES ☀

Reference: **On the Pacific Coast, in the Bahía Magdalena complex; map I, grid b4 - f3.**

Location: These beaches are accessible on sand roads with pickups, vans or four-wheel drives. Some north of Puerto López Mateos are Playa Santa Elenita, which is about four miles north of the Mateos-Insurgentes paved road, and Playas Las Vacas and Los Prados, which are about eight miles north. Others north to La Poza Grande can be reached off the paved road north to La Purisima and the main dirt road north to La Poza Grande. You'll also find beaches south of Puerto López Mateos, such as the one at Curva del Diablo, about 10 miles south of the Mateos-Insurgentes paved road, then about 15 miles west. This is where the tides from north and south meet. Campground #23, La Curva Beach, is another. The beach at Puerto Cancun on Bahía Almeja can be reached from Kilometer 173 on Highway 1 about 25 miles south of Ciudad Constitución, then about 16 miles west on a dirt road. Again, don't try these roads with big rigs.

Comments: Shellfish are abundant everywhere along these beaches and fishing is good for grouper, corvina, bass, snapper, halibut, mackerel and pompano. It is an all-terrain vehicler's paradise with tidal flats and sand roads. One note of caution: The hard sand turns to mud at low tide. Visit in winter, as summer is hot. For more on the Bahía Magdalena area, please see the previous beach listing.

4.　　　　SAN BRUNO BEACHES

Reference: **On the Sea of Cortéz, south of Santa Rosalía; map H, grid d7 - d8.**

Location: The beaches extend for five miles south of San Bruno, which is one mile east of Highway 1 at Kilometer 173, about 14 miles south of Santa Rosalía.

Comments: These beaches are white sand and reachable by off-road vehicles. Winter is the time to go, as summer is hot. For more on the Santa Rosalía area, please see page 188.

5.　　　　PUNTA CHIVATO BEACHES

Reference: **On the Sea of Cortéz, south of Santa Rosalía; map H, grid e8.**

Location: They are most easily reached about 12 miles east of Highway 1 at Kilometer 156, about 25 miles south of Santa Rosalía, off the washboard road to the Punta Chivato Hotel. Starting with the northernmost beach, Playa La Palmita west of the airstrip, Playas Mapachito and El Chivato extend about 10 miles south along the western shore of Bahía Santa Inéz.

Comments: Playa La Palmita is readily accessible by pickups and vans on several dirt roads down small gullies. It takes four-wheel-drive vehicles to work farther south from La Palmita or to access the southern beaches off of Highway 1 north of Mulegé. Fishing off the beach you might find roosterfish. It is a great place for seeking out sea shells. We spent a delightful four days on Playa La Palmita following the shade around the camper, reading books, enjoying the sweeping view and dipping into the placid bay a hop away to keep cool. Winter is the time to go, as summer is hot. For more on the Santa Rosalía-Mulegé area, please see page 188.

6. BAHÍA CONCEPCIÓN BEACHES

Reference: **On the Sea of Cortéz, south of Mulegé; map H, grid f8 - g8.**

Location: The northernmost beach, Campground #7, Campo Playa Punta Arena, is about 10 miles south of Mulegé. It is about 20 miles from there to the southernmost, Campground #15, Playa Armenta, with seven other campgrounds in between.

Comments: This is the greatest aggregation of uniformly lovely beaches, all with stunning views and fronting on placid waters, to be found in Baja, the rest of México or anywhere else in the world we have been, heard of or read about. In other words, go. If fishing's your thing, you may be disappointed, but clamming is great. Winter is the best time to visit, as summer gets scorching. For more on things to do in the Bahía Concepción area, please see page 191.

7. JUNCALITO BEACH

Reference: **On the Sea of Cortéz, south of Loreto; map I, grid c8.** Please see the listing for Campground #19 in this chapter, page 208.

8. LIGUI BEACHES

Reference: **On the Sea of Cortéz, south of Loreto; map I, grid c8.** Please see the listing for Campground #22 in this chapter, page 210.

9.   AGUA VERDE BEACHES

Reference: **On the Sea of Cortéz, south of Loreto; map I, grid d8.**

Location: From Kilometer 63 on Highway 1, about 35 miles south of Loreto, it is about 25 miles on a dirt road. The final pitch is steep with sharp switchbacks and is for pickups, vans or four-wheel drives only—no motor homes or trailers.

Comments: Remember that you have to come back up. Playa San Cosme is at the bottom of the grade. There are low sandy beaches between rock outcrops for about 1.5 miles on the north side of Punta San Cosme. Campsites can also be found elsewhere along the eight miles of road to Agua Verde village. Fishing is fair for grouper and barracuda near the shore. The view of Agua Verde Cove is worth the trip. It has long been a favored anchorage for cruising boats. Now you can enjoy it, too. We anchored there overnight with a group of Vagabundo boats and were delighted. Winter is when you should visit.

10.   SAN EVARISTO BEACHES

Reference: **On the Sea of Cortéz, north of La Paz; map I, grid g8.**

Location: The village of San Evaristo is about 45 miles north of San Juan de La Costa on a rough dirt road (about 80 miles north of La Paz). A paved road leads 24 miles into San Juan de La Costa from Kilometer 17 on Highway 1, about 10 miles north of La Paz. Another, but worse, route is about 50 miles in from Highway 1 at Las Pocitas, which is about 27 miles south of Santa Rita and about 62 miles south of Ciudad Constitución.

Comments: You need a four-wheel-drive vehicle to get to San Evaristo by either route. Pickups and vans can get to El Mechudo, about 10 miles south of San Evaristo, on the San Juan de La Costa route, but four-wheel drive is necessary from El Mechudo on. We went in some years ago, shortly after this road was completed, with a friend who owns the salt works at San Evaristo and Isla San José. It was a fascinating trip, but up and back from La Paz in one day was too much. The cove at San Evaristo is a favored anchorage for cruisers and has a very nice little beach. Other beaches are between San Evaristo and El Mechudo. Fishing can be good for bass, grouper, snapper, pargo, roosterfish, dorado and sierra, improving the farther north you go.

This small cove is one of many idyllic settings in Coyote Bay on Bahía Concepción (see page 216).

MAP J

11 CAMPGROUNDS
3 BEACHES
PAGES 220-263

BAJA MAP (general) .... see page 10
adjoining maps
NORTH (map I) .... see pages 187
EAST .... Sea of Cortéz
SOUTH (map K) .... see page 221
WEST .... Pacific Ocean

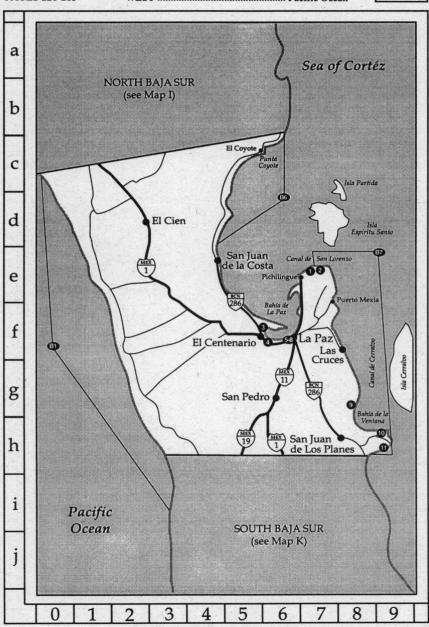

MAP K

19 CAMPGROUNDS
7 BEACHES
PAGES 220-263

BAJA MAP (general) .... see page 10
adjoining maps
NORTH (map J) .... see page 220
EAST .... Sea of Cortéz
SOUTH .... Pacific Ocean
WEST .... Pacific Ocean

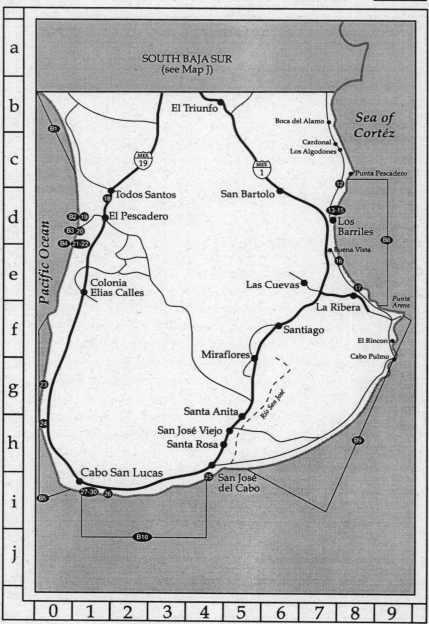

SOUTH BAJA SUR
(see Map J)

El Triunfo

Sea of Cortéz

Boca del Alamo

Cardonal
Los Algodones

MEX 19

MEX 1

Punta Pescadero

12

Todos Santos

San Bartolo

18

B2 19

El Pescadero

13-15

Los Barriles

B3 20

B8

B4 21-22

Buena Vista

16

Pacific Ocean

Colonia
Elias Calles

Las Cuevas

17

Punta Arena

La Ribera

Santiago

El Rincon

Miraflores

Cabo Pulmo

Río San José

23

Santa Anita

San José Viejo

24

Santa Rosa

B9

Cabo San Lucas

25

San José del Cabo

B5 27-30 26

B10

SOUTH BAJA SUR

❈ ❈ ❈ ❈

The southern part of the Baja Peninsula has a special allure. For one thing, the tip of the peninsula is officially in the tropics—south of the Tropic of Cancer. It is a long enough drive, 1,000 miles from the border to Land's End, to constitute a major trip with a substantial commitment of time—five days the way we do it. Anything less than a month leaves precious little time for savoring all the delightful experiences that await. We find something of interest wherever we are and the time just melts away.

La Paz area
(campgrounds 1-11, pages 236-244)

La Paz enjoys a unique standing in Baja's history—it is where Cortéz first landed 460 years ago. The romance of divers endangering their lives seeking riches among beds of pearl oysters, spurred on by legends of black pearls, permeates its image. It is a cosmopolitan city, the seat of the state government and the commercial center for the young 20-year-old state of Baja California Sur. It is a mix of antiquity and modernity with a laid-back lifestyle that natives cherish. It will never succumb to the breakneck frenzy of México City or its U.S. counterpart, New York City. Though tourist dollars are important, there is a conscious effort to avoid turning La Paz into another Cabo San Lucas. As our friend, a young businessman, once observed, "La Paz is a sedate matron, but we would like her to lift her skirts a little." We enjoy being there.

Fishing
While fishing can be good out of La Paz, it is not as consistent as in the Cape or East Cape areas. North toward Isla Espiritu Santo, you'll find pargo, dorado, sierra, barracuda,

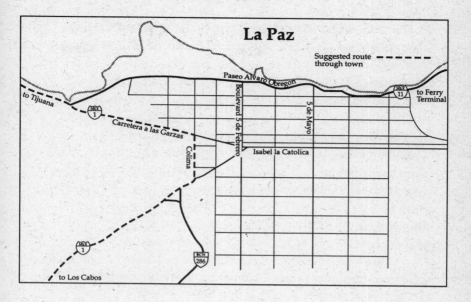

skipjack, snapper and grouper. South toward Isla Cerralvo, roosterfish and jack crevalle show up, as do marlin once in awhile.

The Mosquito Fleet use Super Pangas and charge $165 for three people to fish out of La Paz and $180 for two people to fish out of Las Arenas, about 45 miles south of La Paz. Contact them at the La Concha Beach Resort about three miles northeast of town on the road to Pichilingue, or call them in La Paz at 011-52-112-2-1674 or 2-4490. In the United States, write them at 2361 Veteran Avenue, Los Angeles, CA 90064; (310) 479-0234, fax (310) 444-9846.

The Dorado Velez Fleet can be reached at the Los Arcos Hotel, at Alvaro Obregón 498, facing La Paz Bay or at Apartado Postal 402, La Paz, Baja California Sur, México; phone 011-52-112-2-2744, extension 608; also try 1-5577 or 5-4794.

Diving and snorkeling

Baja Diving Service can be reached at Independencia 107-B, La Paz, Baja California Sur, México; 011-52-112-2-1826. The cost is $80 per person for a day trip to the famous El Bajo sea-mount, where huge manta rays and schools of scalloped hammerhead sharks may be seen at certain times of the year. A closer day trip to Los Islotes with the sea lion colony or the wreck of the Salvatierra, a sunken modern-day ferry, south of Isla Espiritu Santo is $70. They provide tanks, weight belts, lunch and sodas on all trips. Snorkeling trips cost $40 per person and include snorkeling gear, lunch and refreshments. Full diving gear rentals are $15 and lessons are offered. They have a recompression chamber at Pichilingue.

Boating

Trailer boats may be launched at several places. We prefer the ramp at Marina de La Paz at the foot of Legaspy, though the Palmira Marina on the east side of town is also good and closer to the Sea of Cortéz. Each charges about $4.

Cruising and camping by boat around Islas Espiritu Santo, Partida and other islands farther north is a great experience.

Sightseeing

You'll find plenty to see and do in La Paz. An often overlooked spot worth visiting is the Anthropological Museum at Altamirano and Cinco de Mayo. Strolling the Malecón along the waterfront in the evening is very pleasant, as is watching the sunset from the Los Pelicanos Bar in the Los Arcos Hotel on the Malecón at Rosales. The Municipal Market at Revolución and Degollado is a delight to browse through. It has attractive displays of fruits, vegetables, fresh fish, fresh meats, baked goods, clothing and hardware, sold from stalls with each vendor specializing in one type of item. If you don't camp at Playas Balandra or Tecolote, you should at least drive out to have a picnic and enjoy their beauty.

Shopping

La Paz is a free port and there are numerous shops in the downtown area with a wide selection of merchandise from all over the world at reasonable prices. There are also two large department stores where we tend to restock on clothing, Dorian's on 16 de Septiembre and 21 de Agosto and La Perla a block away on Martínez between Esquerro Mutualismo and Mijares.

The Weaver on Abasolo between Jalisco and Nyarít has handwoven rugs and native fabrics created by the owner.

Dining

There is a large selection of good restaurants. We like Bismark on Degollado and Altamirano, and El Moro east on the Malecón.

Nightlife

There is Scorpio's Nightclub on Boulevard Forjadores and Tabachines and El Taste Restaurant and Nightclub on the Malecón and Juarez Avenue, open from 10 p.m. to 3 a.m.

Ferries

Many people take the ferry to Topolobampo (Los Mochis) or Mazatlán from La Paz. See Travel Tips—Ferries, also Licenses and Permits, for details (see page 56).

East Cape area
(campgrounds 12-17, pages 244-248)

Aside from Cabo San Lucas, this has to be Baja's prime fishing area. Deep water comes into Bahía de Palmas bringing marlin and other migratory game fish close to shore. The Buena Vista fishing resorts have a fine reputation with anglers. It also bills itself as the windsurfing capitol of the world—perhaps a little grand, but reflective of the dependable occurrence of stout winter winds. While great for sail devices, it is less than great for boating. There are some great beaches for surfing between Los Frailes and San José del Cabo.

Fishing

Just about every type of fish in the Sea of Cortéz can be taken here—marlin (striped, blue and black), sailfish, roosterfish, wahoo, dorado, yellowfin tuna, amberjack, grouper, pargo, seabass, jack crevalle, pompano, snapper, sierra, lady-fish, giant needlefish and others. Deep, deep water comes close to shore in Bahía de Palmas, bringing in the big migratory game fish.

Boats can be launched across the beach in Los Barriles near Playa de Oro RV Park by hiring a four-wheel-drive, old Army truck with a boom on back for $20 to $25 each way, or at Martín Verdugo's RV Park (for guests) with a tractor or trucks owned by Verdugo.

Several hotels have their own fleets of sportfishing boats.

Hotel Playa del Sol in Los Barriles charges $110 to $150 for *pangas* and $220 to $250 for cruisers, depending on size. Tackle is included, but licenses are extra. Live bait costs $1.50 each and frozen flying fish cost $2. Contact the hotel at P.O. Box 9016, Calabasas, CA 91372; phone (800) 368-4334 or (818) 591-9463; fax (818) 591-1077.

Hotel Palmas de Cortéz in Los Barriles charges $115 to $150 for *pangas* and $215 to $250 for cruisers, depending on size. Tackle is $7.50 per day. Contact them at P.O. Box 9016, Calabasas, CA 91372; phone (800) 368-4334 or (818) 222-7144; fax (818) 591-1077.

Hotel Rancho Buena Vista charges $190 per day for three to four people in 24-foot cruisers, $205 per day for three or four people in 28-foot cruisers and $240 a day for faster 28-foot cruisers that can take up to four people. Tackle is included. They can be contacted at P.O. Box 1408, Santa Maria, CA 93456; phone (800) 258-8200 or (805) 928-1719; fax (805) 925-2990.

Cabo Pulmo Divers on the beach at Cabo Pulmo rents *pangas* for fishing at $25 per person for a half day.

Diving and snorkeling

Cabo Pulmo has super diving on what is considered to be the only coral reef in the Sea of Cortéz. At least one expert says there are others and coral does occur widely. Perhaps it all depends upon the definition of a reef, which seems to require a great expanse of corals and solid limestone from their consolidation.

Cabo Pulmo Divers has done well by us. They charge $45 for a one-tank dive with weight and guide, $60 for a two-tank dive and $30 for snorkeling. They also rent all necessary dive gear. Contact Mario Castro at Rozaura Zapata #955 e/Morelos y Victoria, Colonia Loma Linda, La Paz, Baja California Sur, México; phone 011-52-112-2-1631.

Sol Sports operates out of Hotel Buena Vista Beach Resort. They charge $75 for a two-tank boat dive and $40 for a beach night dive. They also offer courses. Quality gear (except wetsuits) and a guide are included for all dive trips. Lunch is included for daytime trips. All gear is available to rent, as are air fills. Contact Ronald and Marilyn Bastrom, Box 16, Buena Vista, Baja California Sur, México; fax 011-52-112-5-2333.

Windsurfing

This has become a mainstay of the local economy. The dependable winter winds bring windsurfers from all over the world. International tournaments are held with high attendance. During the height of the season, Bahía de Palmas is sprinkled with myriad colorful sails whipping back and forth at high speeds.

Sightseeing

The only zoo in Baja Sur is in Santiago, about 17 miles south of Los Barriles on Highway 1, then 1.5 miles north of the highway. To find the zoo, drive around the town square, go out the south side and continue for about one-half mile south, then one-half mile west and another half-mile south. Follow the enamel signs with an elephant and an arrow. There are several Mexican species, some domestic animals and a display of fossils from the area. It is worth a visit.

The town of Miraflores another eight miles south on Highway 1 specializes in leather goods. A tannery and shop with various leather articles is on the left as you enter town.

Pacific Coast area
(campgrounds 18-24, pages 248-253)

The vast beaches along the Pacific Coast south of Todos Santos were unknown by the great majority of Baja travelers until the rough dirt road was paved in 1984. Dedicated surfers had their favorite spots long before then—Playa San Pedro, Pescadero Beach and Playa Los Cerritos. Now campers taking the shortest route between La Paz and Cabo San Lucas have found those spots, too. The inevitable is now happening— fences have been erected blocking the way onto many beaches. However, the government has designated many others as public beaches to which access seems assured. Beach access signs say "SEDESOL—Acceso Playa Publica."

Todos Santos still remains a tranquil piece of colonial México, however, with wide shaded streets and restored old buildings. We spent a pleasant hour one afternoon listening to two boys just out of school playing guitars and singing in front of the church across from the town square.

Todos Santos sits on the Tropic of Cancer and is blessed with a dependable water supply. The fortuitous combination of climate and water led to development of a thriving sugar cane industry in the last century. The industry faded when the big spring which fed the crops failed in about 1950, then disappeared completely when the price of sugar fell in the mid-1960s. Ruins of several old sugar cane mills still exist. The local spring ultimately recovered and today sustains mango, papaya and palm trees in the lush arroyo below town.

Fishing

Pangas can be rented out of Punta Lobos (south of town with the lighthouse) from individual *pangeros.* The sandy access road is 1.5 miles south on Highway 19. At about 2 p.m., the *pangas* return from fishing and put their boats up on the beach. Check out the catch, which is mostly rockcod, but also some large sharks. Don't expect any frills, such as lifejackets, VHF radios, tackle, lunch or drinks when you go out with these fellows. It's up to you to be fully equipped.

Surfing

The beaches south of Todos Santos are popular with surfers. There are numerous points that create the right conditions for good runs.

Dining

Santa Fe Restaurant in Todos Santos on the south side of the town square is renowned. The restaurant at El Molino RV Park is also good.

Sightseeing

Walking around Todos Santos is interesting and there are a few nice shops. We enjoyed going through the Cultural Museum on Topete and Pilar streets.

For a unique experience, go to the beach at Punta Lobos to watch the *pangas* shoot the beach. The technique is to circle behind the breaker line until a big wave is spotted, then straighten out in line with it and give the motor full throttle, timing the approach so as to shoot out of the top of the wave as it breaks, continuing up the abrupt slope of the beach. If they don't make it to the top, a pickup hauls them up with a long rope.

There is a Botanical Garden three miles south of town on Highway 19 which will help you identify all the desert plants you have been wondering about.

Cape area
(campgrounds 25-30, pages 253-257)

San José del Cabo and Cabo San Lucas are rapidly joining together in one long strip of hotels and condominiums. Developers and others in the tourist business have coined the term "Los Cabos" to describe the strip, but it fails to capture the allure the towns have enjoyed since Ray Cannon first began enticing crowds of big game fishermen there with his Baja fishing stories in the early 1960s. The fishing was fantastic then and still is world-class.

Beaches that used to harbor campers through the winter months are now restricted to day use only. Camping must be done in RV parks. While camping opportunities are diminished, the Cape will always be very popular and on everyone's must-see list. Even when the last campground has been converted to something else, campers will commute from Todos Santos to experience the beaches—as some are doing now.

Fishing

Whatever the time of year, there are always game fish to seek—striped, blue and black marlin, sailfish, yellowfin tuna, dorado, wahoo, roosterfish and others. People with seaworthy boats can venture out on their own. The Cabo Island Marina ramp in town charges a stiff fee of $5 in and $5 out. Parking is available on nearby streets. The public ramp on the south side of the harbor is used to dress out the sportfish catch every afternoon. Parking is a problem around here. There is no fee, however. You can catch your own bait in the outer harbor, saving the $2 per piece that the local fishermen charge.

There are many sportfishing fleets—some better than others. Here are a few with good reputations according to people we know:

La Playa, just north of San José del Cabo on the coast road, is the place to hire panga captains who fish Gordo Banks for wahoo and dorado and whatever else may be around. They charge $150 for up to three people. Boats leave at 6 a.m. and return at noon, and also go out from 6 to 8 p.m. Reservations can be made on the beach from 11 a.m. to 6 p.m., or call Tomas Cantor at 011-52-114-2-1195. A tip: Discuss who gets the meat before departing. Captains and crews are accustomed to having it to eat or as additional income. We inadvertently upset them once by walking off with several big wahoo and dorado.

Reservation offices for Victor's Aquatics in San José del Cabo are located in the Hotel Stouffer Presidente (011-52-114-2-2250), Hotel Posada Real Cabo (011-52-114-2-1092 or 0155) and Hotel Fiesta Inn (011-52-114-2-0701). They charge $325 for up to four people on 24- to 26-foot cruisers and $395 for up to six people on a 28- to 32-foot cruiser for eight hours, leaving at 6:30 a.m. Tackle and fish cleaning is included. Contact Jig Stop Tours in Dana Point, California; phone (714) 496-3555; fax (714) 496-1384.

In Cabo San Lucas, the Gaviota Fleet charges $125 for three people in a panga, $285 for three people in a 26-foot cruiser, $315 for four people in a 28-foot cruiser, $360 for six people in a 31-foot cruiser, $395 for six people in a 33-foot cruiser and $450 for six people in a 36-foot cruiser. Contact Grupo Bahía, 404 Tennant Station, Suite B, Morgan Hill, CA 95037; phone (800) 932-5599 or (408) 776-1806; fax (408) 778-1513.

Pisces Fleet charges $335 for four people in a 28-foot cruiser and $425 for six people in a 31-foot cruiser for a full day. Included are 20 beers or sodas, 10-percent tax, licenses, tackle and fish cleaning. The office is located one block from the Giggling Marlin. Contact them at Apartado Postal 137, Cabo San Lucas, Baja California Sur, México; phone 011-52-114-3-1288; fax 011-52-114-3-0588.

Solmar Sportfishing Fleet is located across from the vendors' stands on the south side of the harbor. They charge $100 for a half day and $200 for a full day for four people in a panga, $235 for three people in a 26- to 27-foot cruiser, $280 for four people in a 28- to 29-foot cruiser, $300 to $350 for three or four people in a 31-foot cruiser, $315 to $335 for six people in a 33-

to 34-foot cruiser, $450 for six to ten people in a 38-foot cruiser, and $600 to $900 for 10 people in a 50- to 60-foot yacht. Included are tackle and licenses. Contact them at P.O. Box 383, Pacific Palisades, CA 90272; phone (800) 344-3349 or (310) 459-9861; fax (310) 454-1686.

Diving and snorkeling

You'll find sandfalls off the arches and several other interesting dive sites, a lot of dive shops and a state-of-the-art hyperbaric medical facility in Cabo San Lucas. We list those with which we and our friends are familiar.

Amigos del Mar is located across from the vendors' stands on the south side of the harbor in Cabo. They rent all gear by the piece, fill your tanks with a Certification Card and offer instruction. Fees are $35 for a one-tank dive (including tank, weights and refreshments), $66 for a two-tank dive and $25 for snorkeling. They also have a variety of boat cruises which don't involve diving or snorkeling. Contact them at Apartado Postal 43, Cabo San Lucas, Baja California Sur, México; phone 011-52-114-3-0505 or fax 011-52-114-3-0887 in Cabo. Phone (800) 447-8999 or fax (213) 545-1672 in the United States.

Club Acuadeportes is located at Chileno Beach at Kilometer 14 on Highway 1 and Hacienda Beach, in front of the Hacienda Hotel in Cabo. They rent dive gear by the piece, fill your tanks with a Certification Card and offer instruction. Fees are $35 for a one-tank dive (including tank and weights), $60 for a two-tank dive and $25 for a snorkeling trip. They also rent sunfish, catamarans, pedal boats, canoes, kayaks, wave-runners and other beach and water sports equipment, and offer boat cruises which don't involve diving. Contact them at Apartado Postal 136, Cabo San Lucas, Baja California Sur, México; phone (800) 347-6847 in the United States; phone and fax 011-52-114-3-0117 in Cabo.

Beach bumming

Heading for the beach for the day can cause a lot of wondering about just which one to hit. Here are the beaches between San José del Cabo and Cabo San Lucas. All are dedicated for day use only, allowing no camping:

- La Playa: just north of San José del Cabo, where the panga leave for fishing
- Playa Hotelera: in front of the hotels in San José del Cabo
- Playa Costa Azul: access off Highway 1 between Kilometers 28 and 29
- Playa Palmilla: at the Hotel Palmilla
- Playa Costa Brava: access off Highway 1 between Kilometers 18 and 19
- Playa El Tule: access off Highway 1 between Kilometers 16 and 17
- Playa Chileno: access off Highway 1 between Kilometers 14 and 15
- Bahía Santa María: access off Highway 1 between Kilometers 12 and 13
- Playa Médano: the big beach in Cabo between Las Cascadas and the Hotel Hacienda
- Playa del Amor: access by water taxi, heading toward the arch
- Playa Solmar: in front of the Hotel Solmar

Golf

Several highly-touted courses give golfers a lot to choose from. Starting from San José del Cabo and working west, the public Fonatur course in San José was the first in the Cabo area and is being expanded from nine to 18 holes.

Next to the west is the high-cost Palmilla housing complex with three nine-hole courses. Until it goes private, when all the lots and memberships are sold, the public can get in for $100 for 18 holes.

Continuing west, you'll find Cabo Real with 27 holes. Fees

will remain similar to those at Palmilla, until its membership is filled up.

Cabo del Sol is another exclusive housing development, but it is expected to cater to the public with its 18 holes. They had a few holes open already when we visited last fall.

Just east of Cabo is Cabo San Lucas Country Club which is aiming for two 18-hole private courses, though the public may get in for a while.

Other activities

There are all sorts of other things to do, including glass-bottom boat trips, catamaran cruises, para-sailing, horseback riding, all-terrain vehicles, scooters and whale watching. The Cape area is designed to keep visitors occupied.

Shopping

There are many enticing shops in town with good prices and wide selections for anything you might expect to find in México. On the south side of the harbor, there is an open-air vendor area, the Handicrafts Plaza, where launches from the cruise ships dock. Here the prices are higher, quality is questionable and it is a pressure-cooker environment because the cruise ship passengers have little time to compare, think and come to a reasoned decision. One that gets by the vendor is one lost forever.

The municipal market in San José del Cabo is special. It is on Mauricio Castro one block south of Doblada, the one-way street that gets you back to Highway 1 from Boulevard Mijares in the middle of town. Wandering around in here makes shopping for veggies, meat and fish enjoyable.

Dining

There are a lot of restaurants to choose from. At the simple end of the spectrum, a barbecue place near Bing's Ice Cream Parlor on the main street, Lázaro Cárdenas, across from the launch ramp has the best ribs and chicken you can hope to find anywhere. Eat it there or take it out.

At the other end (entrees up to $16), Da Giorgio's, on Highway 1 three miles north of Cabo, has such a spectacular view of Land's End and Cabo San Lucas in such a beautiful setting that lunch or dinner is a special treat. It is open air with a series of pools and waterfalls cascading down the cliff. Be there at sunset for the grandest view.

In the middle is the Faro Viejo Trailer Park Restaurant off Morelos near the Military Camp on the way out of town to Todos Santos. They serve twice as much as you can eat, so share a plate. It's hard to find, so call 3-1927 to get directions or take a cab.

Also in the middle is the improbable Señor Sushi's in Cabo, at Marina and Guerrero.

Nightlife

If you're looking for a night of carousing in Cabo and can't find satisfaction at the Giggling Marlin, Cabo Wabo, Studio 94 or Squid Roe, you aren't really trying. If you want a two-handed margarita and a block and tackle that hoists you into the air feet first, go for the Giggling Marlin. Gloria tried both and survived, but the second marg got her. All of the clubs have big crowds and loud music.

1.　　　　PLAYA BALANDRA

Reference: **Northeast of La Paz; map J, grid e7.**

Campsites, facilities: There is a small paved parking lot where about 12 vehicles can spend the night. Tents can be set up off to the side on packed desert soil. There are palapas on the beach, trash barrels and pit toilets. There is no water or security. Obtain supplies in La Paz.

Reservations, fees: All sites are first come, first served. There is no fee.

Who to contact: Drive in and park.

Location: It is on the paved road 4.2 miles east of Pichilingue, the La Paz ferry terminal north of town on the east side of Bahía de La Paz.

Comments: This is a protected cove that has a nice beach, great for swimming and lounging about on. However, it is sheltered from sea breezes by a ridge and can get hot. While overnighting is acceptable, it is not suitable for longer stays, nor for many rigs or tents. Local people use it for picnics and use can be heavy, especially on weekends. The beach had a much-photographed balancing rock, but it fell over some years ago. There has been talk of putting it back up somehow, but that hasn't happened yet. Winter is the best season to visit. For things to do in La Paz, please see page 222.

2.　　　　PLAYA TECOLOTE

Reference: **Northeast of La Paz; map J, grid e7.**

Campsites, facilities: There are two restaurant palapas. Note: The small one on the west end of this long beach is not always open. The larger restaurant has restrooms, but they are for diners only. There are trash barrels. There is no water or security. Obtain supplies in La Paz.

Reservations, fees: It is first come, first served. There is no fee.

Who to contact: Drive in and park.

Location: It is on a paved road 4.8 miles east of Pichilingue, the La Paz ferry terminal north of town on the east side of Bahía de La Paz. Go past the turnoff to Balandra.

Comments: The beach here is about 1.5 miles long, facing north to Isla Espiritu Santo across the four-mile wide Canal San Lorenzo. It is wide, soft sand backed with dunes and a wide level plain behind the dunes. It is exposed to north winds which make heavy surf; otherwise surf is minimal. Camp away from the restaurants in either direction behind the dunes in RVs or tents. The hill on the west end provides afternoon shade and an unobstructed view of Isla Espiritu Santo. The larger restaurant rents boats, jet skis and other watercraft and can arrange fishing trips. Winter is the preferred season, as summer is hot. For things to do in and around La Paz, please see page 222.

---

3.   CITY VIEW BEACH RV PARK (ejido)

Reference: **North of La Paz; map J, grid f5.**

Campsites, facilities: There are 55 pull-through campsites with concrete pads, 35 with full hookups and 20 with sewer only. There are flush toilets and hot showers. Don't drink the water. For security, there is a gate in the fence. The manager lives on the premises. Tent campers are welcome. Obtain supplies in La Paz.

Reservations, fees: Reservations are accepted. Fees are low—$9 per night with electricity and water and $6 without.

Who to contact: City View Beach RV Park, Kilometro 15 Carretera al Norte, El Centenario, La Paz, Baja California Sur, México; phone 011-52-112-5-7799 or 6302, extension 188 on both numbers.

Location: It is on Highway 1 as it meets Bahía de La Paz at Centenario, nine miles north of La Paz.

Comments: This is the best of the parks of this type in Baja and is operated by the owners of a small figurine factory (maquiladora) on the premises. This end of Bahía de La Paz is shallow and mud flats are exposed at low tide. It is also far from the city, which inhibits sightseeing, shopping, dining out and enjoying the ambience. Winter is the preferred season, as summer is hot. For things to do in La Paz, please see page 222.

---

4.   OASIS RV PARK

Reference: **North of La Paz; map J, grid f6.**

Campsites, facilities: There are 24 campsites with full hookups. There are clean restrooms with flush toilets and hot showers, laundry, a pool and a restaurant. Don't drink the water. For security there is a gate. Tent campers are welcome. Obtain supplies in La Paz.

Reservations, fees: Reservations are accepted. Fees are moderate—$11 per night for two people and $2 for each additional person.

Who to contact: Oasis RV Park, Kilometro 15 Carretera al Norte, El Centenario, La Paz, Baja California Sur, México; phone 011-52-112-5-6202, ext. 790.

Location: It is at Centenario, a bit south of City View Beach RV Park. (See Campground #3 for directions.)

Comments: This end of Bahía de La Paz is shallow and mud flats are exposed at low tide. It is also far from the city, which inhibits sightseeing, shopping, dining out and enjoying the ambience. Winter is the preferred season, as summer is hot. For things to do in La Paz, please see page 222.

---

5.   CASA BLANCA RV PARK

Reference: **In La Paz; map J, grid f6.**

Campsites, facilities: There are 43 campsites with full hookups. There are clean restrooms with flush toilets and hot showers, laundry, a pool, a tennis court and a store. Don't drink the water. For security, there is a gate in the walled compound and a guard. Obtain supplies in La Paz.

Reservations, fees: Reservations are accepted. Fees are high— $13 per night, $2 each for additional person. Long-term fees are $300 per month, $1,600 for six months and $2,900 per year.

Who to contact: Casa Blanca RV Park, Apartado Postal 681, La Paz, Baja California Sur, México; phone 011-52-112-2-0009; fax 011-52-112-5-1142.

Location: From Ciudad Constitución, drive 133 miles south on Highway 1 to La Paz. The park is in the west part of town near the Fidepaz development, at Avenida Delfines. The sign on the right is prominent.

Comments: This a newer, very nice park with young trees. It's near the Fidepaz development, which will consist of hotels, restaurants, a marina, a launch ramp—a complete tourist complex. The only problem is it ran out of money and there it sits. The park's high walls are white-painted concrete blocks and the reflected glare and heat struck us as too strong for comfort, however. Winter is the best season to visit, as summer is hot. For things to do in La Paz, please see page 222.

---

6.   EL CARDÓN TRAILER PARK

Reference: In La Paz; map J, grid f6.

Campsites, facilities: There are 80 campsites with full hookups, palapas and concrete pads for RVs, 36 of which are pull-throughs. There are 10 more sites for tents with palapas. There are several individual restrooms, each with a sink, flush toilet and hot shower. Other facilities include laundry and a pool. Don't drink the water at the campsites; it is brackish well water. There is one spigot near the pool behind space 51 with good city water. There is good security; the park is in a walled compound with a gate and a 24-hour guard. Obtain supplies in La Paz.

Reservations, fees: Reservations are accepted. Fees are moderate—$8 per night for tents and $10 for RVs for two people. Each additional person is $2. Guests staying one week get one day free. Fees are $7 per day per month. There is an extra charge for use of air conditioners.

Who to contact: El Cardón Trailer Park, Apartado Postal 104, La Paz, Baja California Sur, México; phone 011-52-112-2-

0078; fax 011-52-112-2-1261.

Location: From Ciudad Constitución, drive 133 miles south on Highway 1 to La Paz. The park is in the west part of town on the highway into La Paz. The sign on the right is prominent.

Comments: This is a family operation, the oldest park in La Paz and has served campers well for decades. Within the park, you'll find many old shade trees. Winter is the preferred season, as summer is hot. For things to do in La Paz, please see page 222.

---

7.   LA PAZ RV PARK

Reference: In La Paz; map J, grid f6.

Campsites, facilities: There are nine pull-through campsites and 86 others with full hookups and concrete pads. There are flush toilets, hot showers, laundry, satellite TV, a pool and a spa. The water is safe to drink. There is good security; the park is in a walled compound with a gate and guard. Obtain supplies in La Paz.

Reservations, fees: Reservations are accepted. Fees are high—$15 per night. Long-term rates are $90 per week, $300 per month, $1,700 for six months and $3,000 per year.

Who to contact: La Paz RV Park, Apartado Postal 482, La Paz, Baja California Sur, México; phone 011-52-112-2-8787 or 4480; fax 011-52-112-2-9938.

Location: From Ciudad Constitución, drive 133 miles south on Highway 1 to La Paz. Just past El Cardón, watch for a trailer park sign. Turn left toward the waterfront, then right on the last street to the park.

Comments: This is a clean park. There are palm trees, gravel driveways and concrete spaces, so there is no dust or dirt. They have beach facilities, though the park is set apart from the beachfront. Winter is the preferred season, as summer is hot. For things to do in La Paz, please see page 222.

8. AQUAMARINA RV PARK

Reference: **In La Paz; map J, grid f6.**

Campsites, facilities: There are 16 campsites with full hookups and concrete pads. There are clean restrooms with flush toilets and hot showers, laundry, a pool, a concrete launch ramp and berthing for boats. The water is safe to drink. There is good security; the park is in a walled compound with gates, a 24-hour guard and a dog. Obtain supplies in La Paz.

Reservations, fees: Reservations are accepted. Fees are high— $14.30 per night for two people and $2.20 for each additional person. Long-term rates are $84.70 per week and $11 per day for month-long stays.

Who to contact: Aquamarina RV Park, Apartado Postal 133, La Paz, Baja California Sur, La Paz, México; phone 011-52-112-2-3761; fax 011-52-112-5-6228.

Location: From Ciudad Constitución, drive 133 miles south on Highway 1 to La Paz. From El Cardón, drive east toward the center of La Paz three blocks past the CCC Supermarket to Nyarít. Turn left and continue to the waterfront.

Comments: Lush palms and flowering shrubs give this park a more tropical appearance than any other in Baja. Aquamarina has been a labor of love for owners and La Paz pioneers Richard and Maria Luisa Adcock. (Maria is México's first and only licensed woman ship's captain.) They also operate La Paz Diving Service for charter groups on the ship Marisla, which is docked in front of Aquamarina. The park is locked up at noon on weekends and holidays, but if you make a noise at one or both of the gates, the watchman will let you in. Winter is the preferred season, as summer is hot. For things to do in La Paz, please see page 222.

9. LA VENTANA CAMPGROUND

Reference: **Southeast of La Paz; map J, grid g8.**

Campsites, facilities: There are flush toilets and showers. Don't drink the water. There is no security. Tent camping is welcome. Obtain main supplies in La Paz, minor things in San Juan de Los Planes.

Reservations, fees: All sites are first come, first served. There are no fees.

Who to contact: Drive in and park.

Location: Take State Highway 286 off Highway 1 on the southern outskirts of La Paz for about 24 miles to a gravel road going north. Turn and head about four miles to La Ventana. The campground is on the north side of the village.

Comments: This campground is set in a cool palm grove, which can accommodate roughly 30 to 40 vehicles under the shade of the trees—a blessing in Baja. It is on a sheltered sand beach with a view of Isla Cerralvo 10 miles away across Canal de Cerralvo. Small, lightweight boats can be launched over the beach. Windsurfers frequent it during the winter, when the winds are strong and dependable. Nearby fishing is good. Large rigs can make it here, though the gravel road in may be rough. Winter is the preferred season, as summer is hot. For more on fishing in and around La Paz, please see page 222.

10. PUNTA ARENA DE LA VENTANA BEACH

Reference: **Southeast of La Paz; map J, grid h9.**

Campsites, facilities: There are no facilities or security. It is made for tent camping. Obtain main supplies in La Paz, minor things in San Juan de Los Planes.

Reservations, fees: All sites are first come, first served. There is no fee.

Who to contact: Drive in and park.

Location: Take State Highway 286 off Highway 1 on the southern outskirts of La Paz for about 29 miles to San Juan de Los Planes, then beyond onto the continuing washboard dirt road for 11.5 miles to the Punta Arena access road, which bears left. Follow it about four miles and you'll reach the beach. The lighthouse is in view to the east.

Comments: With Isla Cerralvo directly across the channel, this is a delightful spot for RVs or tents. As it is remote, you may feel more comfortable having others along for company. The beach extends about 10 miles north toward La Ventana and offers good fishing. At daybreak, schools of jack crevalle (toro) often work the surf in feeding frenzies. You may find roosterfish as well. Try casting into them for great sport. Fishermen put their pangas in here and can be helpful about fishing information. Sometimes they're even willing to hire themselves out as guides. Hike a couple miles to the west and you'll find a beached modern, rusty steel ship, named the Cedros, broadsided right at the surf line. It makes for a pleasant hike. Winter is the preferred season, as summer is hot. For other things to do in the La Paz area, please see page 222.

---

11.   BAHÍA DE LOS MUERTOS BEACH

Reference: **Southeast of La Paz; map J, grid h9.**

Campsites, facilities: There are no facilities or security. It is made for tent camping. Obtain main supplies in La Paz, minor things in San Juan de Los Planes.

Reservations, fees: All sites are first come, first served. There is no fee.

Who to contact: Drive in and park.

Location: Take State Highway 286 off Highway 1 on the southern outskirts of La Paz for about 29 miles to San Juan de Los Planes. Continue beyond Los Planes onto the continuing washboard dirt road for another 13.5 miles to the beach.

Comments: Tents and RVs may set up at the very north end of the bay. Fishing is good. You'll find a fishing camp here—the fishermen can tell you what is biting or hire out as guides. Some of the La Paz sportfishing operations drive their clients here for great fishing off Isla Cerralvo for pargo and roosterfish. Small boats can be launched across the firm beach. Winter is the preferred season to camp here, as summer is hot. For more on fishing in the La Paz area, please see page 222.

---

12.   LOS BARRILES BEACH

Reference: **North of Los Barriles; map K, grid c7.**

Campsites, facilities: There are no facilities or security. It is made for tent camping. Obtain supplies in Los Barriles.

Reservations, fees: All sites are first come, first served. There is no fee.

Who to contact: Drive in and park.

Location: Two miles upcoast from the center of Los Barriles, take a well-used set of wheel tracks one-quarter mile to the Sea of Cortéz, then go left for 200 yards along a nice beach with numerous campsites.

Comments: Free beachfront makes this a nice place to camp in tents or RVs. For small, maneuverable vehicles, there is a small campsite 2.1 more miles along the road to the east and a larger one two-tenths of a mile farther along; both are primitive and have no developed facilities. Several hotels in Los Barriles charter pangas and cruisers to fish the deep waters of the Sea of Cortéz. Winter is the favored season to camp here, as summer is hot. For information on the East Cape area, please see page 225.

---

13.   PLAYA DE ORO RV PARK

Reference: **In Los Barriles; map K, grid d7.**

Campsites, facilities: There are eight campsites with full hookups for overnighters. There are flush toilets, hot showers, laundry and a boat launch over the sand. The water is safe to drink. Security is good with a gate, a resident-owner and many people around. Obtain supplies in Los Barriles.

Reservations, fees: Reservations are accepted. Fees are moder ate—$10 per night. Long-term rates are $60 per week, $250 per month and $2,080 per year.

Who to contact: Playa de Oro RV Park, Apartado Postal 2, Los Barriles, Baja California Sur, México or 3106 Capa Drive, Hacienda Heights, CA 91745; phone (818) 336-7494.

Location: From La Paz, drive about 65 miles south on Highway 1 to Los Barriles. The park is on the north side of town.

Comments: This is a very shady park with lots of big trees. People with large trailers have found maneuvering difficult in the rather tight quarters among many permanent rigs. There is a nearby boat launch. If you don't have your own boat, several hotels in Los Barriles charter pangas and cruisers to fish the deep waters of the Sea of Cortéz. Winter is the favored season to camp here, as summer is hot. For information on the East Cape area, please see page 225.

---

14.   JUANITO'S GARDEN RV PARK

Reference: **In Los Barriles; map K, grid d7.**

Campsites, facilities: There are six pull-through campsites and 20 others with full hookups. Some have palapas. There are flush toilets, hot showers and laundry. The water is safe to drink. The park is secured with a guard. Obtain supplies in Los Barriles.

Reservations, fees: Reservations are accepted. Fees are moderate—$9 per night. Long-term rates are $55 per week, $200 per month and $2,400 per year ($3,000 with a palapa).

Who to contact: Juanito's Garden RV Park, Apartado Postal 50, Los Barriles, Baja California Sur, México; phone 011-52-114-1-0024; fax 011-52-114-1-0163.

Location: From La Paz, drive about 65 miles south on Highway 1 to Los Barriles. The park is on the north side of town, on the inland side of the road.

Comments: This park is on a slight slope and is not on the beach, but at a quarter mile away, it's within walking distance. In the park, dust is kept down by a layer of imported beach sand. The restrooms are clean, private and have locking doors; the coin-operated washing machine requires $1 and there is well-kept landscaping. Winter is the favored season, as summer is hot. For things to do in the East Cape area, please see page 225.

---

15.   MARTÍN VERDUGO'S RV PARK

Reference: **In Los Barriles; map K, grid d7.**

Campsites, facilities: There are 67 campsites with full hookups and 25 for tents, a few of which have electricity and water. Two are pull-throughs. There are clean restrooms with flush toilets and hot showers, laundry, a pool and boat launching over the sand on steel mats. The water is safe to drink. The park is secured with a guard. Obtain supplies in Los Barriles.

Reservations, fees: Reservations are accepted. Fees are moderate—$10 per night in front, $9 in back and $8 for tents. Long-term rates are $65 per week for an RV, $52 for tent camping; it is $225 per month in front, $210 in back and $125 per month for tents.

Who to contact: Martín Verdugo's RV Park, Apartado Postal 477, La Paz, Baja California Sur, México; phone 011-52-114-1-0054.

Location: From La Paz, drive about 65 miles south on Highway 1 to Los Barriles. The park is on the north side of town on the beach.

Comments: Martín is always busy around the park and works very hard to make sure everything is clean and kept up. There are nice rock and mortar walls which define the exterior boundaries of the property and contain grading within the park where there is a slight slope. This is a very popular place and long-term reservations for winter in front near the water must be made a year or more ahead. Winter is the favored season, as summer is hot. For things to do in the East Cape area, please see page 225.

16. LA CAPILLA RV PARK

Reference: **South of Los Barriles; map K, grid e8.**

Campsites, facilities: There are 20 campsites with full hookups and palapas. There are flush toilets and hot showers. The water is safe to drink. There is no security on the premises, but the owners live nearby. Tent campers are welcome. Obtain supplies in Los Barriles.

Reservations, fees: All sites are first come, first served. The fee is low—$7 per night.

Who to contact: Drive in and talk to the manager.

Location: Head 3.6 miles south of the road to Los Barriles on Highway 1. Turn left at the signed road to Rancho Leonero and continue 1.7 miles to the park (one-half mile beyond the sign indicating the turnoff to Rancho Leonero).

Comments: You'd say the facilities here are rustic, but this is a pretty nice place for tents—no asphalt or concrete to contend with, just desert soil to pound tent stakes in, on a beach, with an ocean view, open to cooling breezes and off by itself with no other developments around. The beach is clean white sand with a normally mild surf, enjoyable for strolling and shelling. It's also fine for putting in cartop boats and inflatables. Winter is the favored season, as summer is hot. For more information on things to do in the East Cape area, please see page 225.

17. CORRECAMINOS RV PARK

Reference: **In La Ribera; map K, grid e8.**

Campsites, facilities: There are 13 pull-through campsites with full hookups and some palapas. There are flush toilets, hot showers and laundry. The water is safe to drink. The park is secured with a gate. Tent campers are welcome. Obtain supplies in La Ribera.

Reservations, fees: Reservations are accepted. The fee is low—$6 per night.

Who to contact: Ed Baeza, La Ribera, Baja California Sur,

México; phone (503) 386-1557 or 386-7639.

Location: Turn off Highway 1 at Las Cuevas onto the paved road to La Ribera. Go about 6.5 miles, through La Ribera, then turn left at the sign for the park, continuing another half mile.

Comments: This park is well shaded by old orchard trees. There is camping for tents and pickup campers on the fenced-and-gated beach a quarter mile away. Ask to have the beach gate opened. Winter is the favored season, as summer is hot. For things to do in the East Cape area, please see page 225.

---

18.   EL MOLINO RV PARK

Reference: **In Todos Santos; map K, grid d1.**

Campsites, facilities: There are 20 campsites with full hookups. There are clean restrooms with flush toilets and hot showers, laundry, a pool and a restaurant. The water is safe to drink. The park is secured by a gate. Tent campers are welcome. Obtain supplies in Todos Santos.

Reservations, fees: Reservations are accepted. The fee is moderate—$10 per night.

Who to contact: El Molino RV Park, Todos Santos, Baja California Sur, México. There is no phone.

Location: From La Paz, drive 51 miles to Todos Santos, taking Highway 1 to Highway 19. The park is on the south side of town, behind the Pemex station.

Comments: Be sure to explore the remains of the sugar cane mill which are on the property at El Molino RV Park. The only drawback to staying here is the occasional noise from the adjoining Pemex at night. Winter is the best time to come, as summer is hot. For things to do in the Pacific Coast area, please see page 228.

19.   PLAYA SAN PEDRO

Reference: **South of Todos Santos; map K, grid d1.**

Campsites, facilities: There are no facilities or security. It is only suitable for tent camping. Obtain supplies in Todos Santos.

Reservations, fees: All sites are first come, first served. There is no fee.

Who to contact: Drive in and camp.

Location: The turnoff from Highway 19 is 4.4 miles south of the southern outskirts of Todos Santos, just before the signs and entrance road to San Pedrito RV Park. Go 1.5 miles in to the beach. Ignore the "Road Closed" portion of the sign, which also says "Entrance to Playa San Pedro."

Comments: A popular surfing spot, this is a beautiful sand beach about three-tenths of a mile long between two rocky points and backed by a large palm grove. It is perfect for tent camping out of small vehicles that float on sand. It is definitely not a place to take a trailer or large motor home, because of limitations in getting in and finding firm ground on which to camp. The road is sandy and suitable for one-way traffic only. Passing oncoming vehicles can be a problem. There are some rough spots where water has cut small banks. It is easy to get stuck in the soft sand in the palm grove. If you have any doubts about your vehicle's chances of clearing the road, you should park at the large abandoned home behind the palm grove and walk the rest of the way in to see if you are comfortable with proceeding ahead. Note: Many guide books and maps list this as Playa San Pedrito. We quizzed locals who stoutly maintained it was Playa San Pedro and the sign agreed. Winter is the best time to come, as summer is hot. For things to do in the Pacific Coast area, please see page 228.

---

20.   SAN PEDRITO RV PARK

Reference: **South of Todos Santos; map K, grid d1.**

Campsites, facilities: There are 72 pull-through campsites with full hookups. There are modest restrooms with flush toilets and hot showers, laundry, a pool, a restaurant and a bar. The water is safe to drink. For security, there is a gate. The owner lives on the premises. Tent campers are welcome in a designated area on the beach. Obtain supplies in Todos Santos.

Reservations, fees: Reservations are accepted. The fees are moderate—$12.50 per night, dry camping $3 per person, parking $2 per day. Long-term rates are $70 per week and $240 per month with hookups.

Who to contact: San Pedrito RV Park, Apartado Postal 15, Todos Santos, Baja California Sur, México. There is no phone.

Location: Take Highway 19 south of Todos Santos 4.5 miles. The turnoff to the park is marked by a large sign. Follow it two miles to the beach.

Comments: This spot is a longtime favorite among surfers. It's also one of our favorite camping spots and we spend a few nights here on every trip. Each site has a view of the ocean and a small palm tree. Other palms are scattered around. The beach in front of the RV spaces is treacherous, containing a huge pile of round boulders, which the ocean has chipped off of the rocky point to the north over the millennia. They are constantly rocking and rolling as waves bombard them, dangerous to bare feet out for a casual stroll. A safer sand beach begins a few hundred yards south. There is ample parking on firm ground behind the sand beach suitable for tents and self-contained RVs. Winter is the best time to come, as summer is hot. For things to do in the Pacific Coast area, please see page 228.

21.   LOS CERRITOS RV PARK (ejido)

Reference: **South of Todos Santos; map K, grid e1.**

Campsites, facilities: There are 50 pull-through campsites, all with sewer hookups but no electricity or water. There are flush toilets and cold showers. Don't drink the water. There is no security. Tent campers are welcome. Obtain supplies in Todos Santos.

Reservations, fees: All sites are first come, first served. The fee is low—$4 per night. Someone comes down from the ejido each day to collect.

Who to contact: Drive in and park.

Location: Take Highway 19 south of Todos Santos 7.2 miles. The turnoff for the park is marked. Follow the road two miles to the beach.

Comments: This campground is situated about a quarter mile from one of the most magnificent beaches in Baja and the full six-mile sweep of it is in view from the park. Surfers have come here for years and it's no wonder. Most people prefer to camp closer to the beach, particularly if they have self-contained RVs or tents. Drive around to the ocean side of the park to enter. Winter is the best time to come, as summer is hot. For things to do in the Pacific Coast area, please see page 228.

22.   PLAYA LOS CERRITOS

Reference: **South of Todos Santos; map K, grid e1.**

Campsites, facilities: There are no facilities or security, though the trash barrels and restrooms in the RV park can be used. Don't drink the water in the RV park. It is only suitable for tent camping. Obtain supplies in Todos Santos.

Reservations, fees: All sites are first come, first served. The fee is low—$3 per night.

Who to contact: Drive in and park. Someone will come to collect the camping fee.

Location: Take Highway 19 south of Todos Santos 7.2 miles.

Follow the marked turnoff for Los Cerritos RV Park two miles to the beach.

Comments: Here it is—one of the most spectacular beaches in all of Baja. Of course, surfers have known this for years. There is ample space to park or pitch tents in front of the RV park or to the north up against the rocky ridge. Winter is the best time to come, as summer is hot. For things to do in the Pacific Coast area, please see page 228.

---

23. PLAYA LAS CABRILLAS

Reference: **South of Todos Santos; map K, grid gØ.**

Campsites, facilities: There are no facilities or security. It is made for tent camping. Obtain supplies in Todos Santos.

Reservations, fees: All sites are first come, first served. There is no fee.

Who to contact: Drive in and park.

Location: Take Highway 19 south of Todos Santos 17.4 miles to the beach access sign (Kilometer 81).

Comments: This is a long, wide, steep beach with a strong undertow. While the camping area is limited, that means it's less crowded. The beach is very wide and is composed of fine, soft white sand which is perfect for lounging or strolling. You'll find hard-sand space for a few medium-sized rigs or tents just off the highway. Trailers could have a hard time maneuvering their way in. Winter is the best time to come, as summer is hot. For things to do in the Pacific Coast area, please see page 228.

---

24. MIGRIÑO BEACH

Reference: **North of Cabo San Lucas; map K, grid hØ.**

Campsites, facilities: There are no facilities or security. It is made for tent camping. Obtain supplies in Cabo San Lucas.

Reservations, fees: All sites are first come, first served. There is no fee.

Who to contact: Drive in and park.

Location: Go 27 miles south of Todos Santos or 16 miles north of Cabo San Lucas on Highway 19 to Kilometer 97 and the beach access sign.

Comments: The route in by dirt road is a little tricky, as there are other roads which might lead you astray. Make a sharp right turn at the sign, but not so far that you wind up on the spur heading north parallel to the highway. The road going off the highway at a 90-degree angle goes to ranch buildings. The correct road is the one between the other two—follow it and go left when confronted with a fork. After about a quarter mile, you'll come to a lagoon area behind the dunes. Bushes scrape on both sides. Some curves may be too tight for big motor homes and trailers. There is a lot of room for rigs and tents on hard-packed ground. Expect to see a lot of cattle. Due to its proximity to Cabo San Lucas, tourists with rented dune buggies often come up for the day. Winter is the best time to come, as summer is hot. For more information on things to do in the Pacific Coast area, please see page 228.

---

25. BRISA DEL MAR TRAILER PARK AND MOTEL

Reference: **West of San José del Cabo; map K, grid i4.**

Campsites, facilities: There are 80 pull-through campsites back from the beach with full hookups and 32 campsites on the beach with electricity and water only. There are flush toilets, hot showers, laundry, a pool, a seasonal bar and restaurant, ping pong and pool tables, a volleyball court and a horseshoe pit. Don't drink the water. There is no security. Tent campers are welcome. Obtain supplies in San José del Cabo.

Reservations, fees: Reservations are accepted. Fees are high—tenting is $9 per night on the beach, $11 with electricity and water and $15 with full hookups. Long-term rates are $90 per week (one day free) and $390 per month (four days free).

Who to contact: Brisa del Mar Trailer Park and Motel, Apartado Postal 45, San José del Cabo, Baja California Sur, México. There is no phone.

Location: Take Highway 1 about two miles west of San José del Cabo to Kilometer 28. Brisa del Mar is on the beach.

Comments: This park is very popular with snowbirds who come for the winter. It is on a lovely beach close to San José del Cabo and would seem to have a higher calling as a hotel or condo. Winter is the best time to come, as summer is hot. For things to do in the Cape area, please see page 230.

---

26. VILLA SERENA RV PARK

Reference: **East of Cabo San Lucas; map K, grid i2.**

Campsites, facilities: There are 54 campsites with full hookups. There are clean, tiled restrooms with flush toilets and hot showers, laundry, a pool, a restaurant, a bar, a gymnasium, an indoor handball court and a steam room. The water is safe to drink. The park is secured by a night watchman. Obtain supplies in Cabo San Lucas.

Reservations, fees: Reservations are accepted. Fees are high— $14 per night. Long-term rates are $87 per week, $326 per month and $900 for three months. Rigs can be stored for half price.

Who to contact: Villa Serena RV Park, Apartado Postal 111, Cabo San Lucas, Baja California Sur, México; phone 011-52-114-3-0509 in Cabo and (800) 932-5599 in the United States; fax 011-52-114-3-0497 in Cabo and (408) 778-1513 in the United States.

Location: Take Highway 1 six miles east of Cabo San Lucas. The park is on a ridge overlooking both the ocean and Land's End.

Comments: This is a popular spot and fills up in winter, mostly because it affords a fantastic view of Land's End. There is no beach, though a trail leads to the rocky shore. Winter is the best time to come, as summer is hot. For things to do in the Cape area, please see page 230.

27. EL ARCO RV PARK

Reference: **East of Cabo San Lucas; map K, grid i1.**

Campsites, facilities: There are 40 pull-through campsites and 24 campsites with full hookups, some with concrete pads. There are modest restrooms with flush toilets and hot showers, laundry, a pool and a restaurant. The water is safe to drink. The park is secured with a chain and by numerous people. Obtain supplies in Cabo San Lucas.

Reservations, fees: Reservations are accepted. Fees are moderate—$10 per night. Long-term rates are $250 per month and $2,484 per year.

Who to contact: El Arco RV Park, Apartado Postal 114, Cabo San Lucas, Baja California Sur, México; phone 011-52-114-3-1686.

Location: Go 3.3 miles east of Cabo San Lucas on Highway 1. The park is on a hill overlooking the ocean and Land's End.

Comments: The view of the harbor, the Arches and the rugged rocks of Land's End is stunning. The park is crowded, dedicated mainly to permanents, so it's rather unattractive for overnighters. Winter is the best time to come, as summer is hot. For things to do in the Cape area, please see page 230.

28. CABO CIELO RV PARK

Reference: **East of Cabo San Lucas; map K, grid i1.**

Campsites, facilities: There are 24 campsites with full hookups. There is a store and tiled restrooms with flush toilets and hot showers. The water is safe to drink. The park is secured with a chain and the manager lives on the premises. Tent campers are welcome. Obtain supplies in Cabo San Lucas.

Reservations, fees: All sites are first come, first served. Fees are moderate—$8 per night. Long-term rates are $210 per month.

Who to contact: Drive in and talk to the manager.

Location: Head 2.3 miles east of Cabo on Highway 1 to the park.

Comments: There is a palm at each site and a view of Land's End. The park is situated in an open field, which is not a very interesting place to camp. As the trees mature and improvements continue to be made, we trust it will become more attractive. Winter is the best time to come, as summer is hot. For things to do in the Cape area, please see page 230.

---

29.   CLUB CABO RV PARK

Reference: **East of Cabo San Lucas; map K, grid i1.**

Campsites, facilities: There are 18 campsites, of which 10 have full hookups. There are flush toilets and hot showers. The water is safe to drink. The park is secured with a chain and the owner lives on the premises. This park caters to tent campers. Obtain supplies in Cabo San Lucas.

Reservations, fees: Reservations are accepted. Fees are high— $14 per night with hookups, $5 per person per night tenting. The long-term rate is $275 per month.

Who to contact: Club Cabo RV Park, Lista de Correos, Cabo San Lucas, Baja California Sur, México; phone 011-52-114-3-3348.

Location: Drive east from Cabo to the (unmarked) street in the big arroyo going to Club Cascadas. Turn left on the sandy road to the east paralleling the beach and go past the back end of the Vagabundos del Mar RV Park. The park adjoins the Vagabundos Park on its east side.

Comments: The park is small, more like the yard of a house, is inconvenient to get to and has little to offer once in it. The turn in has too little swinging room for motor homes or trailers. It is suitable for pickups, vans and other small vehicles only. Winter is the best time to come, as summer is hot. For things to do in the Cape area, please see page 230.

30. VAGABUNDOS DEL MAR RV PARK

Reference: **East of Cabo San Lucas; map K, grid i1.**

Campsites, facilities: There are 49 pull-through campsites and 32 more campsites with full hookups. There are clean tiled restrooms with flush toilets and hot showers, laundry, a pool, a restaurant, a bar and a meeting palapa. The water is safe to drink. The park is secured with a gate and the manager lives on the premises. Obtain supplies in Cabo San Lucas.

Reservations, fees: Reservations are accepted. Fees are high— $13 per night for two people and $3 for each additional person. Long-term rates are $83 per week, $325 per month and $2,750 per year.

Who to contact: Vagabundos del Mar RV Park, Apartado Postal 197, Cabo San Lucas, Baja California Sur, México; phone 011-52-114-3-0290 in México or (800) 474-2252 in the United States; fax 011-52-114-3-0511 in México or (707) 374-6843 in the United States.

Location: Head one mile east of Cabo on Highway 1 to the park.

Comments: This one's a winner—one of the most attractive and best maintained parks in Baja. There are lots of trees and palms. If you're boating or fishing, an added bonus is that this is the closest park to the launch ramps in Cabo. Winter is the best time to come, as summer is hot. For more on things to do in the Cape area, please see page 230.

South Baja Sur's
10 BEST BEACHES

❀ ❀ ❀ ❀

---

1.   LOMA MARÍA TO TODOS SANTOS

Reference: **On the Pacific Ocean, south of the Bahía
Magdalena complex and north of Todos Santos; map J,
grid CØ to map K, grid c1.**

Location: A rough dirt road approaches the coast from about 17
miles south of Santa Rita on Highway 1 (about 51 miles
south of Ciudad Constitución) then runs alongside the coast
south to Todos Santos. The beaches extend for about 110
miles. Punta Conejo can be reached more directly by a 12-
mile fair dirt road leaving Highway 1 at Kilometer 80 (about
13 miles south of El Cien and about 68 miles south of Ciudad
Constitución). Other rough dirt roads leave Highway 1 for
coastal ranches 29, 40 and 41 miles south of El Cien.

Comments: This is as straight as a coastline can get, with very
few projections or points and no shelter for boats—just one
long beach. The beaches here are generally not frequented by
tourists. Punta Conejo is favored by surfers and boardsailers.
Four-wheel-drive vehicles in groups might find these pristine
beaches exciting to explore.

---

2.   PLAYA SAN PEDRO

Reference: **On the Pacific Ocean, south of Todos Santos;
map K, grid d1.** Please see the listing for Campground #19,
on page 249.

---

3. PESCADERO BEACH ☀

Reference: **On the Pacific Ocean, south of Todos Santos; map K, grid d1.**

Location: It extends about four miles between Punta San Pedro south to Punta Pescadero. San Pedrito RV Park (Campground #20, page 250) is at the north end.

Comments: We haven't found this one in other guide books or on maps. This beach is wide with soft sand and is a favorite of surfers. All but the northern part is remote, offering seclusion to those who wish to make the effort to attain it. The beach slope is rather steep, creating an undertow that can be dangerous to inexperienced swimmers. Winter is the best time to come, as summer is hot. For things to do in the Pacific Coast area, please see page 228.

---

4. PLAYA LOS CERRITOS ☀

Reference: **On the Pacific Ocean, south of Todos Santos; map K, grid d1.**

Location: This beach extends about five miles between Puntas Pescadero and Gaspareño.

Comments: This beach has a westward curve to it, exposing its unbroken five-mile sweep to clear view from Campgrounds #21, Los Cerritos RV Park, and #22, Los Cerritos Beach, at the north end. It is wide, soft white sand that is a joy to walk on.

---

5. BEACHES BETWEEN PUNTA GASPAREÑO AND LAND'S END ☀

Reference: **On the Pacific Ocean, south of Todos Santos and north of Cabo San Lucas; map K, grids f∅ - i∅.**

Location: Access is at Campground #23, Playa Las Cabrillas, and Campground #24, Migriño Beach, plus several four-wheel-drive roads off Highway 19.

Comments: This long, 33-mile stretch is essentially one immense unbroken beach, which is wide, backed by dunes, with soft white sand offering great opportunities for seclusion for those willing to hike. The slope is rather steep and the surf pounds, creating undertows which can be dangerous for inexperienced swimmers. Still, surfers like the points on this coastline. Development by private landowners along Highway 19 is forcing the closing of access roads.

6. SAN JUAN DE LA COSTA BEACHES ☀

Reference: **On the Sea of Cortéz, north of La Paz; map J, grids b6 - d4.**

Location: Access is by the 24-mile paved road to San Juan de La Costa, which leaves Highway 1 at Kilometer 17, about 10 miles north of La Paz, and the continuing dirt road going another 35 miles to El Mechudo.

Comments: There are a number of sand, pebble and mixed beaches along the western shore of Bahía de La Paz. The dirt road north of San Juan de La Costa has soft sandy stretches that can easily bog down larger vehicles, as is the case with side roads to the shore. Pickups, vans and four-wheel-drive vehicles do better. Trailers are difficult to manage here. Fishing for roosterfish, grouper, snapper, pargo, sierra and dorado improves the farther north you go.

7. LA PAZ BEACHES ☀

Reference: **On the Sea of Cortéz, northeast and east of La Paz; map J, grids e7 - h9.**

Location: These extend from Campground #1, Playa Balandra, and Campground #2, Playa Tecolote, around Punta Coyote south to Campground #11, Bahía de Los Muertos Beach. There are dirt roads east of Tecolote and a network of four-wheel-drive rough, sandy roads fans out from the southeast edge of La Paz to the northern area. Other dirt roads depart the pavement out of San Juan de Los Planes to the southern section. (See Campground #9, La Ventana Campground, to Campground #11, Bahía de Los Muertos Beach.)

Comments: Long beaches such as Tecolote, Cachimba, La Sorpresa and Arena de La Ventana are interspersed with sandy coves and rocky cliffs. This is a great area for exploring with groups of four-wheel-drive vehicles. The fishing here can be exceptional as well. For types of fish and names of companies leading sportfishing cruises out of La Paz, see page 222.

8. EAST CAPE BEACHES ☀

Reference: On the Sea of Cortéz, from north of Los Barriles to south of La Ribera; map K, grids c8 - e9.

Location: These beaches extend from four miles north of Los Barriles south to Punta Arena. Campgrounds #12 , Los Barriles Beach, to #17, Correcaminos RV Park, afford public access to this stretch of coast. A sandy road parallels the coast in both directions from Correcaminos and numerous four-wheel-drive roads lead off of it to the beaches.

Comments: These beaches are almost continuous for about 25 miles. They are soft white sand, becoming wider to the south. There is great opportunity for solitude, as many stretches are remote between public access points. The wide, sweeping beach at the southern end between Punta Colorada and Punta Arena invites long walks and is great for shelling. Private lands block many access points, but adventurous souls can find ways in. For the information on the numerous fishing, diving, snorkeling and windsurfing opportunities available in the East Cape area, see page 226.

9. PUNTA ARENA TO SAN JOSÉ DEL CABO BEACHES ☀

Reference: On the Sea of Cortéz, south of La Ribera and north of San José del Cabo; map K, grids f9 - h5.

Location: La Ribera is about seven miles east of Highway 1 on a paved road starting about 12 miles south of Los Barriles. Los Frailes is about 22 miles south of La Ribera. The beaches extend for about 33 miles south of Los Frailes. Below is a log of accessible beaches, with mile marks starting from Los Frailes:

Mile 8: Rancho El Tule—There is a wide arroyo to the beach. The people at the rancho seem somewhat hostile to travelers and have big speed bumps in front of the headquarters. They may not welcome campers—be nice.

Mile 10.9: access road to the beach

Mile 14.4: Rancho San Luis—on the beach

Mile 14.9: short access road to the beach

Mile 17.0: Rancho Boca de Las Palmas—wide arroyo accesses the beach

Mile 18.8: Rancho La Fortuna—wide arroyo accesses the beach

Mile 19.3: access road to the big beach

Mile 20.3: access road to the beach

Mile 20.8: Shipwreck Beach—good, short access road to this big beach, a favorite of surfers

Mile 22.6: big, sandy arroyo accesses the nearby beach

Mile 23.9: Playa Tortuga—access road to the beach

Mile 24.6: access road to the beach, between brush-covered dunes

Mile 25.5 to 25.7: several small parking areas off the coast road, just above the beach

Mile 32.0: access road to the big beach

Mile 33.4: La Playa—access road to the beach, just outside San José del Cabo

Comments: The main activity is surfing and there are plenty of places to go. However, only small, maneuverable vehicles can make it safely. Choice campsites on this long string of magnificent beaches are inaccessible to larger highway vehicles because of dangerous road conditions. Side roads to beaches are packed wheel tracks in sand. A paved road on a new alignment is being built south of La Ribera, which had extended five miles when we were last there. Ultimately, it is supposed to go down the coast to San José del Cabo. Coming into La Ribera from Highway 1, this road veers south before town. Obviously, whatever realignment the new paved road takes will alter the log given above, but at least you will have something to go by as this remote coast opens up.

---

10.   CAPE AREA DAY-USE BEACHES   ☀

Reference: **Between San José del Cabo and Cabo San Lucas; map K, grids i1 - i4.** Please refer to Campground #30—Vagabundos del Mar RV Park.

Comments: Spending the day on the beach soaking up sun and splashing around in the surf is the main activity. People camping in the Cape area find these beaches delightful to visit for a day's outing, though they can become quite congested. One by one, they are falling to development of one type or another, so you may find access to certain beaches restricted. Enjoy them while you can.

Lovely Playa Tecolote near La Paz faces Isla Espiritu Santo.

Index

A

B

ALL CAMPGROUND LISTINGS ARE IN CAPITAL LETTERS

C

ALL CAMPGROUND LISTINGS ARE IN CAPITAL LETTERS

ALL CAMPGROUND LISTINGS ARE IN CAPITAL LETTERS

ALL CAMPGROUND LISTINGS ARE IN CAPITAL LETTERS

F

ALL CAMPGROUND LISTINGS ARE IN CAPITAL LETTERS

ALL CAMPGROUND LISTINGS ARE IN CAPITAL LETTERS

M

ALL CAMPGROUND LISTINGS ARE IN CAPITAL LETTERS

N

O

P

ALL CAMPGROUND LISTINGS ARE IN CAPITAL LETTERS

ALL CAMPGROUND LISTINGS ARE IN CAPITAL LETTERS

ALL CAMPGROUND LISTINGS ARE IN CAPITAL LETTERS

R

S

ALL CAMPGROUND LISTINGS ARE IN CAPITAL LETTERS

ALL CAMPGROUND LISTINGS ARE IN CAPITAL LETTERS

T

APPENDICES

✺ ✺ ✺ ✺

Road Signs

When you first see these, you'll wonder what they mean. Since a few mean something that may be rather urgent, it is best to get acquainted with them before crossing the border:

SEDESOL

ACCESO A PLAYA

PLAYA MIGRIÑO

Acceso a playa—beach access

Ceda el paso—yield

Alto—stop

Circulación—traffic

Camino sinuoso—winding road

Concida cambio de luces— dim your lights

Conserve su derecha—
keep to the right

Desviación—detour

Cruce ferrocarril—
railroad crossing

Doble circulación—two way

Curva peligrosa—
dangerous curve

Escuela—school

Despacio—slow

Estacionamiento—parking

Estacionamiento para casas rodantes—trailer park

Hombres trabajando— men working

Ganado—livestock

Inspección—inspection

Gasolinera—gas station

Maxima—speed limit in kilometers per hour

Grava suelta—loose gravel

No estacionarse—no parking

No hay paso—road closed

Peligro—danger

No rebase—no passing

Pendiente peligrosa—
dangerous downgrade

No tire basura—no littering

Puente angosto—
narrow bridge

Peatones—pedestrians

Precaución—precaution

Restaurante—restaurant

Telephono—telephone

Sanitarios—toilets

Tope—speed bump

Semaforo—stop light

Vado—dip

Solo izq (izquierdo)—
left turn only

Zona de derrumbes—
falling rock

(When you say this with proper rolling of the double "r," it sounds like rocks tumbling down a hill.)

Metric System

❋ ❋ ❋ ❋

Length

Kilometer	0.62 mile	multiply by 0.6 to find miles
Meter	39.37 inches	multiply by 1.1 to find yards
Centimeter	0.39 inch	multiply by 0.4 to find inches
Millimeter	0.04 inch	multiply by 0.04 to find inches

Area

Hectare	2.47 acres	multiply by 2.5 to find acres

Weight

Kilogram	2.2046 pounds	multiply by 2.2 to find pounds
Gram	0.035 ounce	multiply by 0.035 to find ounces

Capacity

Liter	1.057 quarts	multiply by 0.26 to find gallons

Speed

Kilometers per hour	0.6 miles per hour
Miles per hour	1.6 kilometers per hour

Temperature

Celsius: $9/5, + 32 =$ Fahrenheit temperature

Fahrenheit: $- 32, 5/9 \times$ remainder $=$ Celsius temperature

Special Days in México

❁ ❁ ❁ ❁

January 6—*Día de Reyes.* Gifts are exchanged.

February 2—*Día de la Candelaria.*

February 5—*Día de la Constitución.*

Late February to early March, three days before Ash Wednesday—*Carnaval.* Ensenada and La Paz are worth seeing.

April, Palm Sunday to Easter Sunday—*Semana Santa.*

May 5—*Cinco de Mayo.*

November 1-2—*Día de los Muertos.* Cemeteries are visited and special bread is baked.

December 12—*Día de la Virgen de Guadalupe.*

December 24-25—*Día de la Navidad.*

December 31—*Fin de Año.*

INFORMATION SOURCES

❋ ❋ ❋ ❋

Tourism

United States

Mexican Office of Surface Tourism, 2707 North Loop West, Suite 450, Houston, TX 77008; (800) 446-8277.

Mexican Office of Tourism, 10100 Santa Monica Boulevard, Los Angeles, CA 90067; (310) 203-8191, fax (310) 203-8316.

Mexican Office of Tourism, 405 Park Avenue, Suite 1002, New York, NY 10022; (212) 838-2949, fax (212) 753-2874.

Mexican Office of Tourism, 70 East Lake Street, Suite 1413, Chicago, IL 60601; (312) 565-2786, fax (312) 606-9012.

Canada

Mexican Office of Tourism, 2 Bloor Street West, Suite 1801, Toronto, Ontario M4W 3E2; (416) 925-0704, fax (416) 925-6061.

Mexican Office of Tourism, One Place Villa Marie, Suite 1526, Montreal, Quebec H3B 3M9; (514) 871-1052, fax (514) 871-3825.

Fishing

Mexican Department of Fisheries, 2550 Fifth Avenue, Suite 101, San Diego, CA 92103; (619) 233-4324.

General Information

Vagabundos del Mar Boat and Travel Club, 33 North Second Street, Rio Vista, CA 94571; (800) 474-BAJA.

Mexican Consulates

United States

Consular Representative, 480 North Grand Avenue,
Nogales, AZ 85621; (602) 287-2521, fax (602) 287-3175.

Consular Representative, 1990 West Camelback Road #110,
Phoenix, AZ 85015; (602) 433-2294, fax (602) 242-2957.

Consular Representative, 553 South Stone Avenue,
Tucson, AZ 85701; (602) 882-5595.

Consulate, 382 Camacho Road, Calexico, CA 92231;
(619) 357-3863.

Consulate, 905 North Fulton, Fresno, CA 93728;
(209) 233-3065, fax (209) 233-5638.

Consulate, 2401 West Sixth Street, Los Angeles, CA 90057;
(213) 351-6800, fax (213) 389-9186.

Consulate, 201 East Fourth Street, Oxnard, CA 93030;
(805) 483-4684.

Consulate, 9812 Old Winery Place #10, Sacramento, CA 95827;
(916) 363-3885, fax (916) 363-0625.

Consular Representative, 588 Sixth Street, San Bernardino, CA
92401, (909) 888-3155, fax (909) 889-8285.

Consulate General, 1549 India Street, San Diego, CA 92101;
(619) 231-8414, fax (619) 231-4802.

Consulate General, 870 Market Street #528, San Francisco,
CA 94102; (415) 392-5554, fax (415) 392-3233.

Consulate, 380 North First Street #102, San Jose, CA 95112;
(408) 294-3414, fax (408) 294-4506.

Consulate, 828 North Broadway, Santa Ana, CA 92701;
(714) 835-3069.

Consular Representative, 707 Washington Street, Suite A,
Denver, CO 80203; (303) 830-0523, fax (303) 830-0704.

Consulate, 401 Fifth Street NorthWest #1710, Albuquerque, NM 87102; (505) 247-2139, fax (505) 842-9490.

Consular Representative, 458 East 200 South, Salt Lake City, UT 84111; (801) 521-8502, fax (801) 521-0534.

Consular Representative, 2132 Third Avenue, Seattle, WA 98121; (206) 448-3526.

Canada

Consular Representative, 1130 West Pender Street #810, Vancouver, British Columbia V6E 4A4; (604) 684-3547, fax (604) 684-2485.

The Surfrider Foundation

The Surfrider Foundation is a nonprofit environmental organization dedicated to the protection and enhancement of the world's waves and beaches through conservation, research and education. Surfrider believes that our treasured coasts should be valued and treated by the public as our most precious natural parks. Our mission is threefold: protection, preservation and participation.

The foundation was formed in August 1984, when a handful of Malibu surfers, concerned about the worsening conditions of our waves and beaches, met to discuss ways in which we could protect the coastal environment. Led by the visionary Malibu surfer and historian, Glenn Hening, the group decided to take action to address those concerns.

As we enter our 10th year, the Surfrider Foundation's diverse membership now includes surfers, divers, bodyboarders, sailors, sandcastle builders, beachcombers, lawyers, scientists, artists, musicians, teachers, businesspeople and students. Surfrider is represented by over 25,000 U.S. members, with 21 U.S. chapters, and affiliates in Australia, Japan, Brazil, England, Canada and France. Much of the Surfrider Foundation's environmental work is conducted on the U.S. east, gulf and west coasts and on Hawaii. Adapting Surfrider programs to their local beaches, chapter members act as coastal watchdogs within their local communities.

Thanks to our members and supporters, the Surfrider Foundation has tallied an impressive record of achievements in areas of coastal protection, water quality, beach access, wave preservation and community service. It is at the grassroots level that Surfrider has proven most effective. Surfrider Foundation members have served as powerful spokespeople for and caretakers of the ocean environment which they treasure.

The organization and its programs are funded entirely by personal and professional donations. Without these donations, Surfrider would not survive.

The foundation's recent achievements include:

- Winning the second largest Clean Water Act lawsuit in American history, brought against two pulp mills in Humboldt County that were charged with over 40,000 violations of the law;

- Winning the national "Renew America" Award in 1992, for our nationwide efforts to clean up the coasts;

- Convincing a major oil company to extend an outfall emissions pipe to two-thirds of a mile which had previously been dumping directly into the surf zone;

- Organizing events across the nation to publicize and educate citizens about the need for strengthening the Clean Water Act;

- Creating a net catch-system which, during rainy season, is dropped over flowing river channels to catch large debris and pollutants which otherwise would flow directly onto beaches;

- Working with city and county agencies nationwide on coastal water-quality data to improve permit monitoring compliance, as well as provide the public with vital information as to the state of their coastal waters;

- Creating a renowned water-quality lab in Santa Cruz, CA, which is run by volunteer support and interns from University of California, Santa Cruz;

- Developing a mitigation project for restoring a wetland in order to clean a dirty creek responsible for the closure of Doheny Beach, CA, thus setting a standard for restoring other wetlands and lagoons as nature's purifiers for coastal waters;

- Appealing to Congress on breakwater developments which would denigrate water quality and destroy miles of beach;

- Participating in Adopt-A-Beach campaigns nationwide;

- Educating hundreds of school children on beach safety, coastal pollution and beach ecology;

- Working with a national coalition of environmental groups striving to strengthen the Clean Water Act and enforce water quality standards;

- Creating a "hands-on" internship program for undergraduate and graduate level college students;

- Providing ocean environmental research materials for hundreds of students nationwide from elementary age to college graduate level.

OSCAR PADILLA MEXICAN INSURANCE
+
VAGABUNDOS DEL MAR TRAVEL CLUB

= Over 75 combined years of Mexican travel service
= California's oldest and largest Mexican insurance broker
= California's oldest and largest Mexican travel club

*It all adds up to the most qualified and experienced
Mexican travel service available!*

WHO IS OSCAR PADILLA MEXICAN INSURANCE?

In 1951 Oscar Padilla introduced Mexican insurance to California from his small office in Calexico, California. Since that time the agency has expanded into a network of nine border offices and nearly 200 California agents stretching from the Mexican border to Eureka. Over the years he has earned his reputation as the industry's innovative leader. In 1969 he revolutionized Mexican insurance by introducing the drive-thru concept to the United States insurance service process. *As its pioneer and innovative leader, Oscar Padilla is a name now synonymous with Mexican insurance.*

WHO IS VAGABUNDOS DEL MAR TRAVEL CLUB?

Vagabundos del Mar had its informal "birth" in 1966 as a few buddies venturing south into Mexico for some good fishing. After 30 years of uninterrupted member service, it is the oldest, largest and best Mexico travel group. In 1971 it was incorporated in the State of California as a non-profit, social club corporation, and has remained such so as to never sway from its primary reason for existing—friends, fun and family! That spirit has been maintained out of good times had by all at the numerous RVing and boating events held throughout each year, including an annual Fiesta Grande. FUN FOR ALL AND ALL FOR FUN! Sign up now! Only $45 for the first year.

NAME _____

ADDRESS _____

CITY _____ STATE _____ ZIP _____

VAGABUNDOS DEL MAR
190 Main St., Rio Vista, CA 94571
(800) 474-BAJA (474-2252) or (707) 374-5511
fax (707) 374-6943
Mon-Fri 8 a.m.–5 p.m.